MIRACLE OF DELIVERANCE

By the same author

Novels
A Necessary End
Live Till Tomorrow

Non-Fiction
Last Sunset

MIRACLE OF DELIVERANCE

The Case for the Bombing of Hiroshima and Nagasaki

Stephen Harper

STEIN AND DAY/*Publishers*/New York

To the memory of my brother
Flying Officer Douglas William Francis Harper
and all the others who did not survive

036919✓

18·95

First published in the United States of America in 1986
Copyright © 1985 by Stephen Harper
Maps by Rodney Paull
All rights reserved, Stein and Day, Incorporated
Printed in the United States of America
STEIN AND DAY/ *Publishers*
Scarborough House
Briarcliff Manor, N.Y. 10510

Library of Congress Cataloging-in-Publication Data

Harper, Stephen.
  Miracle of deliverance.

  Bibliography: p.
  Includes index.
  1. Hiroshima-shi (Japan)—History—Bombardment,
1945. 2. Nagasaki-shi (Japan)—History—Bombardment,
1945. 3. Atomic bomb—United States. 4. Deterrence
(Strategy) 5. World War, 1939–1945—Moral and ethical
aspects. 6. Nuclear warfare—Moral and ethical aspects.
I. Title.
D767.25.H6H34   1986   940.54'26   85-40966
ISBN 0-8128-3089-X

Contents

Acknowledgments

My thanks go to the editors of the *Spectator* and the Burma Star Association newsletter, *Dekho*, for putting me in touch with many veterans of the Zipper landings; to General Sir Ouvry Roberts, Brigadier J.M.K. Bradford, to Mr and Mrs Stanley Skinner (through whose kindness I'm able to use rare pictures of D-Day on Morib beach); to Lieut-Colonel Teddy Lock, Major George Mowat Slater, Major Roland Iliffe, Capt Jim Bowes, Capt Rex Wait, Capt Frederick Field, Mr A.G. Bradbury, Mr Bill Clarke, Mr R. Coleman, Mr Ronald Day, Mr Arthur Emmanuel, Mr Dick Everly, Mr Leonard Goddard, Dr John Gordon-Brown, Mr Frank Head, Mr John Hill, Mr Frank Humphris, Mr Frank Jenkin, Canon Pat Magee, Mr John Moore, Mr George Pearson, Mr E. Saunders, Mr Colin Sharman, Mr Thomas Taylor, Mr Clifford White; to Mr P.J.A. Mallaby and Mr Frank Rostron; to the staff of the Public Record Office at Kew, the Imperial War Museum, the British Library; the Kokuritsu Kobunshokan (National Archives of Japan); Gordon Martin and the Japanese section of the BBC; the Netherlands Central Bureau of Statistics; the editor of the Lake County Examiner, Oregon, USA; to Terry Fincher of Photographers International; to Tom Howard of the Associated Press picture library (an ex-Chindit who himself expected to be dropped into Singapore as a paratrooper but for the A-bombs); additional thanks to the Imperial War Museum for permission to quote passages from Dr Robert Hardie's diary of working on the Burma Railway, and to Quartet Books for permission to quote extensively from Wilfred Burchett's *At The Barricades*.

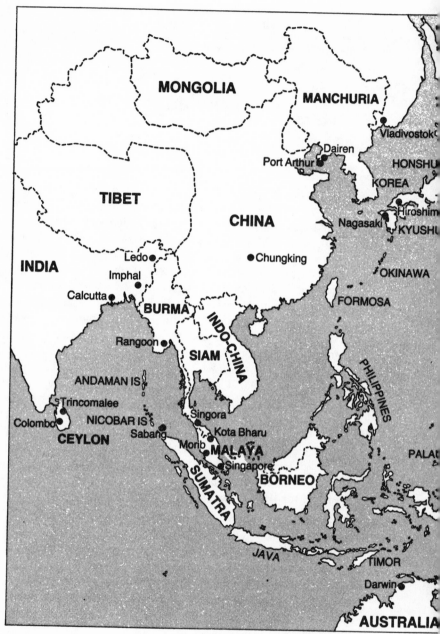

The Far East War Zone

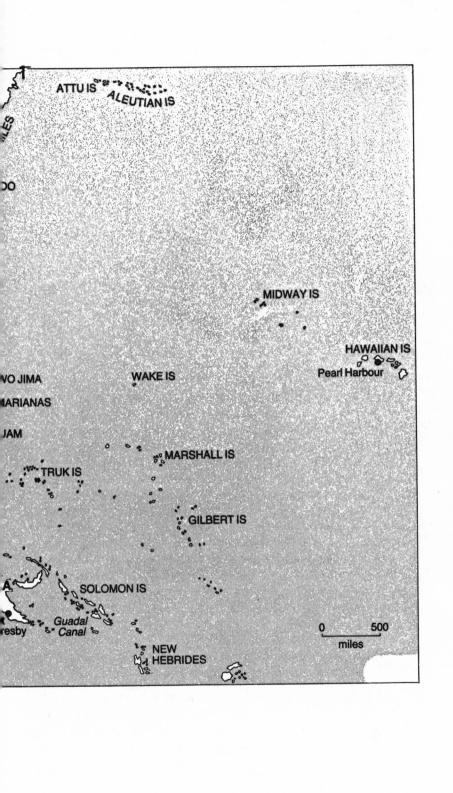

ATTU IS
ALEUTIAN IS

MIDWAY IS

HAWAIIAN IS
Pearl Harbour

VO JIMA

MARIANAS

JAM

WAKE IS

MARSHALL IS

TRUK IS

GILBERT IS

SOLOMON IS

Guadal
Canal

resby

NEW
HEBRIDES

0   500

miles

Preface

It is now forty years since the world entered the nuclear age and the horrific examples of Hiroshima and Nagasaki dictated the need for the great powers to hold back from resort to war. Six years earlier, as the Second World War began with forlorn Polish cavalry charges at the invading armoured Panzer columns of Hitler's awesome new *blitzkrieg*, the major nations put their scientists to work in a race to develop a weapon of such destructive power that an enemy would be terrorized into immediate submission. The scientists began with theoretical suppositions based on research by the British Nobel Prize-winning scientist, Ernest Rutherford, who had succeeded in splitting the atom in his laboratory at Manchester University a few years before. His researches indicated that an explosion of earthquake proportions might be achieved by atomic fission, and the priorities of war – victory whatever the cost – provided the immense financial resources to turn the theory into destructive reality.

Germany was thought to be well advanced with research when British commandos raided their heavy water plant in Norway early in the war. Happily for Britain, German scientists had not solved the atomic problem when their victory rockets, the V-1 and V-2, were produced in 1944, and the terror attacks on Britain, which they hoped would turn the tide of war back in their favour, were carried out with conventional high explosives. The Japanese announced their atomic research openly in the Tokyo parliament, the Diet, that same year, also seeing it as a possible saviour from defeat. Scientists in the Soviet Union, helped by information from spies and sympathetic scientists in the United States, were also working on atomic research. The race to develop a bomb was won by scientists from America, Britain and Canada, who successfully tested the first nuclear explosion in the New Mexico desert in July 1945.

Germany had followed Italy into defeat only two months before that test explosion, but the Third Enemy, Japan, had still to be crushed. Churchill had pledged Britain's role in the East in a House of Commons speech, 'The new phase of the war against Japan will command all our resources from the moment the German war is ended. We owe it to Australia and New

Zealand to help them remove for ever the Japanese menace to their homeland, as they have helped us on every front in the fight against Germany.'

Details of the test explosion, revealing that its blast was equivalent to 20,000 tons of conventional high explosive, reached the Allied leaders as they gathered for the last wartime summit conference at Potsdam on the outskirts of devastated Berlin. Churchill described his feeling at the news as 'a miracle of deliverance'. In *The Second World War* he wrote, 'We seemed suddenly to have become possessed of a merciful abridgement of the slaughter in the East . . . there was never a moment's discussion whether the atomic bomb should be used or not. To avert a vast, indefinite butchery, to bring the war to an end, to give peace to the world, to lay healing hands upon its tortured peoples by a manifestation of overwhelming power at the cost of a few explosions, seemed after all our toils and perils a miracle of deliverance.'

Churchill had gone to Potsdam conscious that many more casualty lists were likely to mar the euphoria in Britain over the end of the war in Europe. A great invasion force was already being mounted across the ocean from India and Ceylon to avenge the shame of Singapore's surrender three years before. The atomic bombs, exploded over Hiroshima and Nagasaki, came too late for the invasion to be called off – but Emperor Hirohito's command to his troops to lay down their arms came in time to prevent slaughter on the beaches.

The first waves of assault troops were quickly clear of the beaches, and into the cover of the plantations beyond. Trouble began when the first waves of landing craft with vehicles hit the beach. Lorries and jeeps and other motorized equipment sank deep in the mud that underlay the deceptive surface sand, and many were swamped by the incoming tide. Only the first wave of LSTs (Landing Ship Tanks) managed to get armour ashore before nightfall, twelve hours after the assault began. Had the Japanese still been fighting, men who were on the beach that day believed the landings would have been the bloodiest of the war.

The blunder was lost in the general jubilation over the end of the war, and hardly even noticed in the history books. The authors of the *Official War History* let it pass with telling understatement: 'Had the Japanese offered any resistance to the landings . . . the invasion force would have been roughly handled, and at least pinned down to the beaches for some time . . . in view of the chaos the troops landed at Morib might have had to be withdrawn. Although it was realized the information about the beaches might not be accurate, a risk was accepted that might have proved unjustifiable had the Japanese opposed the D-Day landings with even a few battalions.'

Those who landed on Malaya's Morib beaches in 'Operation Zipper' –

Admiral Mountbatten's own D-Day – had good reason to see the atomic bombs as the 'miracle of deliverance' Churchill had described. And it was seen as such by people throughout the Allied world who were awestruck by the miraculous way the war was being abruptly ended, and thankful for it. To those engaged in fighting Japan, and their families at home, the short-term view that the war was ending was the important thing. A long time passed before second thoughts brought moral reservations – from the comfortable long-term view.

The Americans, with recent experience in Okinawa of the heaviest casualties of their island-hopping advance towards Japan, were desperately anxious to force Japan to surrender before the following 1 November – D-Day for the invasion of Kyushu, the southernmost island of Japan. President Truman was horrified by the planning provision for facilities to handle 58,000 casualties in the first eight days, and numbed by estimates that half a million Americans would become casualties before the last Japanese resistance was overcome. The main Japanese island of Honshu was to be invaded in a second wave of landings the following March, and planning was going ahead on the assumption that organized resistance would continue until the middle of November 1946.

On their side, the Japanese were counting on inflicting a million casualties on the invaders, expecting that rather than continue to the end the Allies would offer better terms than the ignominious unconditional surrender which they had so far insisted on. After Hiroshima and Nagasaki, which they argued were less damaging than the big fire-bomb raids, the Japanese military were still calling for the sacrifice of ten million of their people in an 'honourable' defence of the homeland. Right to the last, the Japanese Cabinet remained split on whether to surrender or fight on, and Emperor Hirohito had to break the impasse and take the decision to surrender upon himself alone.

Deliverance – even at the horrendous price of Hiroshima and Nagasaki – was a close-run thing.

MIRACLE OF DELIVERANCE

PART ONE
The Third Enemy

1

When the Portuguese discovered Japan in 1542 they were regarded by the Japanese with disdain as 'unbathed, hairy-faced aliens with skins like plucked chickens', and fifty years later, when Jesuit missionaries had followed the trading ships, the Japanese military ruler, the Shogun, ordered all foreigners to be expelled from the country. Japan turned its back on the outside world for more than two centuries. Foreign ships were driven off, and the Japanese themselves faced death if they tried to travel overseas. With the coming of steamships in the last century, outsiders pressed their attentions more and more, refusing to leave Japan in feudal isolation. The Dutch, who made a point of not having missionaries, were eventually allowed to trade so long as their activities were confined to an island in Nagasaki harbour. Ships that approached the shore elsewhere were still fired on by shore batteries. In 1853, during an outcry over the imprisonment of the crew of a distressed whaling ship, the United States Congress took upon itself the unilateral decision to open Japan and Korea to trade. Captain Matthew C. Perry, of the US Navy, anchored in Tokyo Bay, and threatened to bombard the capital unless the Shogun agreed to accept an American consul-general.

The agreement gave extra-territorial rights, exempting Americans from trial in Japanese courts, making them answerable instead to consular courts under American law. This was an accepted Western agreement with primitive countries whose punishments and prison conditions were considered barbaric, and they prevailed in the Persian Gulf into the sixties. Other Western countries established consular offices in Tokyo under similar agreements.

The Japanese had their first taste of Western retribution a decade after Perry's mission when a joint force of British, American, Dutch and Russian warships bombarded the port of Kagoshima in southern Kyushu. This indiscriminate punishment was retaliation for the killing of a British representative by *samurai* warriors.

Foreign pressure brought internal stresses, and the military Shogunate was overthrown in a civil war in 1868. The hereditary spiritual leader,

Matsuhito, was restored to his family's ancient temporal power as Emperor Maiji, a name translated as Enlightened Ruler. The Japanese were worried that their country might share the fate of India, the Philippines and other Asian lands which were already under European imperial rule, and the new Emperor and his advisers decided that the only chance of national survival was to make Japan an equal of the European powers. In 1871 an elite group calling themselves The Great Embassy toured Europe and the United States to study the industrial and financial systems that nurtured the West's dominant power. They set out to do everything the West could do, confident in their superior ability to do even better. Their present success in the car and electronics industries is a part of that heritage.

The rigid segregation of classes – the nobility and priests, soldiers, peasants and artisans, merchants and outcast leather workers – was quickly phased out. It was made optional to wear swords or *samurai* hairstyles, and the *samurai*'s right to slaughter a commoner for an insult was ended.

The British built the ships and trained the officers of a new Imperial Japanese Navy, but the dominant group of military aristocrats looked to Prussia. Military conscription was introduced and Prussian officers trained a modern Japanese army. A Western-style parliament was modelled on the Prussian Diet, an assembly which rubber-stamped the edicts of the Junkers. Inside a generation, the Japanese were wearing European suits, and new factories were turning out copies of Western consumer goods.

Equality with the leading European nations meant that Japan had to make herself ruler of a colonial empire like theirs. Imperial ambitions had been nurtured since 1823 through the writings of the *samurai* scholar, Nobuhiro Sato, who had written in his *Secret Strategy of Expansion* that Japan was the foundation of the world, and should rule the rest of the world as overseas possessions. The Great Embassy was hardly back from its lengthy tour before Japan took the first step towards expansion with a military expedition to Formosa (Taiwan) in 1874. This led to a brief war with China in 1894, followed by a collision with Czarist Russian expansion in 1904 when Japan set the precedent for the surprise attack on Pearl Harbor thirty-seven years later. The new Japanese Navy launched a devastating attack on the Russian Far East Fleet as it lay in Port Arthur, and declared war two days later. The new Japanese army showed itself ready to accept massive casualties in frontal attacks, and overwhelmed the Russian defences to capture Port Arthur and the town of Mukden in Southern Manchuria.

Russian ignominy was compounded by the destruction of their Baltic Fleet after it had sailed 26,000 miles around the world in an attempt to restore Czarist fortunes. The peace treaty, mediated by American President Theodore Roosevelt, left Japan in possession of Port Arthur, the Southern half of Sakhalin Island and Korea.

This first defeat of a major white power by Asians marked the turn of unchallenged European rule over vast territories, which had been sustained by the deterrent threat of overwhelming punitive force behind the puny garrisons scattered over them. An Indian historian commented on the Japanese triumph over the Russians, 'It freed the minds of young men in India . . . from the spell of European invincibility.'

Japan became Britain's ally in 1902, and when war broke out in Europe Japan declared war on Germany, promptly occupying German enclaves on the China coast and the Marshall, Mariana and Caroline island colonies in the Pacific. She kept them as League of Nations mandated territories after the war.

But the postwar years brought bitter resentment of her British and American mentors. The European Powers had refused to agree to a declaration on racial equality which Japan wanted laid down in the Versailles Peace Treaty, and in 1924 Britain refused to renew the Anglo-Japanese Alliance. Britain claimed it contravened the new League of Nations covenant, but the real reason was American pressure for a common front against Japan's increasing naval power.

By the 1930s, rival military cliques were competing for influence over leading Japanese politicians, using assassination or the threat of it to channel policies towards more military expansion. The main factions were the Koda-Ha (Imperial Way), which advocated military rule under the Emperor; the Tsaei-Ha (Control Faction), comprising mainly middle-rank officers who wanted military rule and the conquest of China; and the Sakurai-Kai (Cherry Society) which vowed to purify national life under military control. Prime Minister Oasachi Hamaguchi, who had accepted naval parity with America and Britain at the London Disarmament Conference, was shot dead in 1930. A year later, Prime Minister Tsuyoshi Inukai, was murdered for sending an emissary to the Chinese leader, General Chiang Kai-Shek.

A bomb explosion aboard a Japanese-owned train in Manchuria in 1931 was used as a pretext to establish a protectorate under Japanese occupation. The League of Nations condemned Japan as an aggressor, and in 1933 Japan quit the League, abrogated the treaty limiting the size of her navy, and turned away from traditional friendship with the Anglo-Saxon powers. Japan then went on to sign the Anti-Comintern Pact with Hitler's Germany.

The long-feared military coup came in February 1936 when young officers of the Imperial Way tried to 'rescue the Emperor from advisors who favoured unmanly caution in pursuing the imperial goal'.

The rebels murdered politicians and generals who were considered moderate, and put out a manifesto under the heading 'The Great Purpose' which included this passage, 'It is clearer than light that our country is on the verge of war with Russia, China, Britain and America, who wish to crush our ancestral land. Unless we rise now and annihilate the unrighteous and disloyal creatures who surround the Imperial Throne and obstruct the course of true reform, the Imperial Prestige will fall to the ground . . . we are persuaded that it is our duty to remove the villains who surround the throne.'

In an unprecedented intervention in public affairs, Emperor Hirohito denounced the young officers' movement as mutiny, and General Tomoyuki Yamashita, of the Imperial Way, whose protégés led the revolt, ordered them to commit *seppuku* (ritual suicide) in front of their men. (General Yamashita later became known as the Tiger of Malaya for his conquest of Malaya and Singapore.) Only one did as his General ordered, another shot himself alone in a barrack room, and fifteen others were tried by court martial and shot. The scandal left General Hideko Tojo, a former head of the Kempei-Tai secret police in Manchuria, as the dominant force in Japanese politics.

Tojo and his fellow generals, influenced by the geopolitical thesis expounded by Germany's Karl Haushofer that empires based on the Euro-Asian land mass would replace seaborne empires like the British, made up their minds to conquer China. They provoked a skirmish with Chinese troops at the Marco Polo Bridge on the border of Japanese-occupied Manchuria in July 1937 as a pretext for a fullscale invasion. By November 1938, Japan had occupied all China's richest and most populous provinces and much of the coastline. General Chiang Kai-Shek's nationalists retreated to areas bordering Burma and Tibet and Mao-Tse-Tung's communists occupied northern areas adjoining Mongolia. The Japanese persisted in calling their operations 'the China incident', and it was never a serious drain on the more sophisticated resources needed in major campaigns against the Americans and British, even though two million Japanese and some seven million Chinese died in the eight years it lasted. Both Chinese factions were as concerned with countering each other's ambitions as with fighting the foreign invader. The Imperial Japanese Navy, which was expanding rapidly with new battleships and aircraft carriers, was chafing at its limited role as a mere beast of burden for the army. The China operations were a valuable battle school, particularly for bomber pilots who were later to score such staggering triumphs against the American and British fleets.

In December 1938, Japan followed ominously in Hitler's footsteps by declaring a 'New Order in East Asia', but in May 1939, with war in Europe clearly imminent, she cautiously pulled back from signing the Axis Pact with Hitler and Mussolini. Admiral Yonai, who had opposed Japan's accession to the Axis, became prime minister in January 1940, seeming to confirm Japan's neutrality in the war that had by then broken out in Europe.

Unfortunately, a week later the Royal Navy deeply affronted Japanese pride and aroused a storm of anti-British feeling. A British cruiser intercepted the Japanese steamer *Asama Maru* almost within sight of the Japanese coast, and took off twenty-one Germans of military age. The British ambassador, Sir Robert Craigie, pointed out that Japanese warships had carried out 191 searches of British ships off Hong Kong, but this comparison of Japan with a mere colony only stirred Japanese outrage further.

As in 1914, the Japanese were quick to take advantage of war between the European Powers. They began by demanding an embargo on war materials to China from Indo-China, Hong Kong and Burma; the removal of British troops from the international settlement in Shanghai, and a guarantee of oil and other vital supplies from the Dutch East Indies.

When France capitulated, the Japanese moved quickly to take control of French Indo-China. Japanese intrigues and pressures there included first engineering, then mediating, a border war between Siam (now Thailand) and the Vichy-French authorities in Saigon.

At the same time they put strong pressure on Britain, then hard-pressed to defend herself against invasion from across the English Channel. In response to this pressure Britain agreed to close the Burma Road, the main supply route into unoccupied China. Japanese demands for the withdrawal of British troops from Shanghai were also met.

Three months later, as the Battle of Britain reached its climax, a new Japanese government under Prince Konoye, believing that Britain faced imminent defeat, took Japan into the Tripartite Pact with Germany and Italy to become the third member of the Axis. Britain responded by reopening the Burma road.

Meanwhile Hitler was planning to extend the anti-Western alliance by bringing the Soviet Union into his camp, thus eliminating a back stab threat to both himself and Japan in operations against the Western powers. It would have been a follow-up to his immense diplomatic coup of August 1939, when Russia and Germany signed a pact for the partition of Poland. This had come at the very time Britain had a mission in Moscow seeking to strengthen an anti-Nazi line-up, and amounted to giving Hitler a licence to attack Poland. In the meantime Russia had occupied half of Poland, annexed the Baltic republics and fought a bloody war to obtain territory from tiny Finland.

Early in 1941 the Soviet Foreign Minister, Vyacheslav Molotov, was invited to Berlin and offered a share in the spoils from the dismemberment of the British Empire. The German Foreign Minister, Joachim von Ribbentrop, submitted a draft for a four-power alliance to replace the tripartite pact. Hitler's motive was to turn Russian influence away from the Balkans, and Ribbentrop defined the Soviet sphere of most advantageous access to warm seas as the Persian Gulf and the Indian Ocean. The Soviet reply made it clear that Stalin was not to be deflected from the Balkans. He agreed to accept the alliance providing that German troops were withdrawn from Finland; Soviet security in the Bosphorus was assured by a mutual security pact between Russia and Bulgaria under which Soviet forces would occupy leased bases within range of the Straits; that the area south of Batum and Baku (the oilfields of Iraq and Persia) were recognized as the centre of Soviet aspirations; and that Japan renounced coal and oil concessions in northern Sakhalin Island.

Hitler reacted angrily by ordering plans for an invasion of Russia to be ready by May 1941. He also ordered an all-out effort to bring Japan into the war in order to tie down British forces and divert American attention to the Pacific until he had defeated the Red Army.

During a visit to Berlin in March 1941 the Japanese Foreign Minister, Yosuke Matsuoka, was pressed to commit Japan to an attack on Singapore and other British possessions in the Far East. But Matsuoka demurred, saying Japan feared that Russia would take advantage and attack Japan in Manchuria. On his way home through Moscow in April he stopped off long enough to negotiate a five-year non-aggression pact between Japan and the Soviet Union.

When the German invasion of Russia came two months later Japan was at first in a quandary. However, the spectacular German advance to the edge of Moscow ensured that the Red Army would be kept too busy to intervene against them in the Far East anyway. Germany was also tying down the major part of the forces of the only European power not under their domination, the once mighty British. With its powerful fleet in Hawaii, only the United States stood in the way of Japan's imperial ambitions.

Island Japan was as vulnerable as Britain to any interference with her sea communications. Every drop of oil had to be carried across the sea from the southern resources area, mainly the Dutch East Indies. Japan had failed to browbeat the Dutch, whose homeland was occupied by Germany, into the kind of agreement that would have assured supplies, and she responded by stepping up the military threat. The more compliant Vichy-French agreed to Japanese use of the airfield at Saigon as a bomber base, and to Cam Ranh Bay as a fleet anchorage.

Churchill was deeply worried about Japanese intentions, fearing they would strike only at the interests of the European Powers, leaving America still on the sidelines. His main objective at talks with President Franklin D. Roosevelt off Iceland in August was to obtain a joint public declaration that would commit Britain and America to act together against Japanese aggression. Hitler's attack on Russia had lifted fears of imminent German invasion of Britain, but it was also seen to increase the likelihood of Japan's intervention on the side of the Axis. Churchill and Stalin were equally fearful of the calamitous consequences that could result while they were locked in the struggle with Germany.

But the most Roosevelt would commit himself to was a statement to be handed to the Japanese Mission which was in Washington seeking a general settlement. It merely said that the United States would protect its interests should Japan take further steps in pursuance of a policy of military domination.

However, the Americans took up another British suggestion at the Atlantic Meeting with immense enthusiasm. This was for a joint statement about the kind of world order envisaged for the future, intended by the British as a propaganda exercise, but taken up by the Americans as an eight-point statement of principles known as the Atlantic Charter. This document was to cause much embarrassment to Churchill when its implications for colonial territories were taken up.

Roosevelt was desperately anxious to avoid the war spreading to the Pacific, but his hopes of leaving Japan on ice until Germany was dealt with collapsed when Japan moved into Indo-China. He responded by announcing total trade sanctions against Japan until her troops were withdrawn from Indo-China and also from China.

This posed an immediate threat to the developing Japanese economy, and a longer-term threat to the great warships which would be immobilized without fuel oil. Stocks for industry and civilian use were sufficient for less than a year, though the military had built up sufficient oil stocks to keep warships and planes in action for two years. There was no way the Japanese could accept this sudden challenge.

A clear signal that Japan's response would be war came on 16 October when the leader of the Army's Control Faction, Lieut-General Hideki Tojo, was appointed prime minister. Three weeks later Emperor Hirohito presided at an Imperial Conference, the highest authority in Japan, when it was decided to go to war by the end of November unless the talks in Washington made progress towards recognition of Japan's rights in Asia. Military chiefs went straight from the palace to put Plan Z – the destruction of the American Fleet at Pearl Harbor – and other offensive operations in motion.

Messages from Tokyo to the Japanese embassy in Washington were being routinely intercepted and decoded, and the Americans knew as early as 20 November that the Japanese were preparing an ultimatum that was due to expire on 29 November. This may have stirred Roosevelt to send a personal message to the Japanese Government offering them free access to raw materials, free trade and commerce, financial cooperation and support and a new commercial treaty to replace one that had just expired. In return Japan was to withdraw from Indo-China and China and revoke the Axis Pact in favour of a non-aggression treaty with America, Britain, China, the Soviet Union and Thailand. The message reached Tokyo on 29 November, and was regarded as an ultimatum.

The Imperial Conference met on 1 December, and confirmed the decision to declare war on America and take over the colonial possessions of the European powers. The signal confirming Plan Z was sent to the Combined Fleet which was already four days out along the secret route to Pearl Harbor.

2

The plan for a devastating pre-emptive attack on Pearl Harbor was put forward by Admiral Isoruku Yamamato early in 1941. He argued that Japan's only chance of winning the gamble of war was to deal such crushing blows at the outset that the Western powers would agree an early peace that would recognize Japanese interests in Asia. If the war were prolonged, he warned, Japan was bound to lose against the strongest industrial powers in the world. His thesis was that the destruction of the American Pacific Fleet at Pearl Harbor would ensure the success of operations to secure the southern resources area. Admiral Yamamato had taken part as a twenty-one-year-old ensign in the destruction of the Russian Fleet at Port Arthur in 1904 when the precedent was set for starting war without warning. He had long regarded the aircraft carrier as the most powerful warship, and this belief had been confirmed by a visit to Taranto in southern Italy after twenty-one Swordfish biplanes from a single British carrier succeeded in torpedoing three Italian battleships in the harbour there in November 1940. In 1941 he was Commander-in-Chief of the Japanese Combined Fleet, which included six major carriers with more than 350 high-performance aircraft, armed with torpedoes far superior to any yet developed in the West, as well as new armour-piercing bombs. Most of his pilots already had combat experience in the war against China.

The naval general staff at first opposed the plan to attack Pearl Harbor, regarding it as a dangerous gamble. They favoured invasions of the Philippines and the Dutch East Indies, believing that these operations would draw out the American Fleet for destruction in a decisive sea battle with the more powerful ships Japan had developed in secret. But Admiral Yamamato's arguments prevailed, and preparations went ahead under an operational code (Plan Z) which was the same as for the attack on Port Arthur thirty-six years before. The provisional date was fixed for 8 December in Japan, 7 December across the international dateline in Pearl Harbor.

Because total surprise was vital, Japan's intentions were masked by continuing the negotiations which Admiral Kichisaburo Nomura had been engaged in in Washington and strengthening Japan's apparent interest in the talks by sending Saburo Kuruso, who as ambassador in Berlin had signed the Axis Pact, to lead it.

He arrived in Washington as a submarine force left Japan towing five midget submarines for operations against Pearl Harbor. A week later, on 26 November, a force of thirty-one ships sailed from Tankan Bay in the Kurile Islands, taking a route that skirted shipping lanes, with orders to sink on sight any ship that might put the secrecy of their passage at risk. On 6 December a signal confirmed the attack, and the Z-flag which had been flown during the victory over the Russian Fleet at Port Arthur was raised over the flagship *Akagi*.

A few hours before the attack planes were due to take off, news reached the Japanese fleet that the primary targets of the raid, four American aircraft carriers, were not in Pearl Harbor. But by that time the die was cast, and 353 planes were launched when the fleet was 200 miles from the unsuspecting target.

The Americans in Hawaii appeared to be oblivious to the mounting crisis. Those who were astir were beginning a relaxed Sunday, and washing was hung out to dry on the decks of the warships in harbour. Incredibly, no general alarm was raised even when an American destroyer reported sinking an unidentified submarine off the harbour entrance, and when approaching Japanese planes were picked up by radar, they were assumed to be a formation of American planes due to arrive that morning.

By early afternoon it was all over, and the Japanese fleet was steaming north, leaving eight American battleships either sunk or badly damaged and installations in flames. The Japanese lost all five midget submarines, nine fighter planes, fifteen dive bombers, five torpedo planes and fifty-five aircrew.

In America, outrage over the sheer treachery of the attack overlaid immediate concern at the lack of readiness that had ensured its devastating success. Later, eight investigating bodies were to fail to provide an adequate explanation for America's main fleet base being caught so incredibly off guard. Intelligence had warned of the likelihood of submarine and surface raider attacks against the British and American fleets, but had made no mention of a possible attack on the fleet base at Pearl Harbor. A routine intelligence report on the location of all major warships in the Pacific on 8 December put all the ships taking part in the attack in their home bases, Kure and Sasebo.

Some historians believe President Roosevelt put forward the demands which the Japanese interpreted as an ultimatum as a deliberate provocation. It is more likely he wanted to put on pressure to counter Japanese temptations to strike at the Soviet Union, then reeling under German attack. On 15 October, in one of his exchanges with Churchill about the

Japanese threat, Roosevelt told him that he thought the Japanese were headed north.

Churchill called the attack on America 'irrational', but it came as a great relief, ending worries that Japan might strike only at the colonial territories of European Powers.

President Roosevelt, who described the day of Pearl Harbor as 'a date that will live in infamy', broadcast to the American people when the full extent of the disaster was becoming clear: 'We may acknowledge that our enemies have performed a brilliant feat of deception, perfectly timed and executed with great skill. It was a thoroughly dishonourable deed, but we must face the fact that modern war as conducted in the Nazi manner is a dirty business. We don't like it. We didn't want to get in it. But we are in it, and we're going to fight it with everything we've got.'

In fact, the Japanese had intended to observe the diplomatic niceties and break off negotiations before the first bombs fell on Pearl Harbor. Their note, rejecting the latest American demands and breaking off the talks, was sent to the Japanese embassy in Washington on the evening of 6 December, a Saturday, and an appointment was made for it to be handed over in the State Department at one o'clock on Sunday afternoon. This would have given the United States little over half an hour to send out warnings to military units. But translation and insistence on meticulous typing of the 5000 words of the note took longer than expected, and when Kuruso and Nomura were finally ushered into the Secretary of State's office at 2.20 p.m., Pearl Harbor had been under attack for thirty-five minutes.

In any case, the Japanese war machine had been gathering momentum for a full month. Military staffs had been advised as early as 7 November that war would begin around 8 December, and operational orders went out to all formations that were to carry them out on 15 November. All naval forces were ordered to take up their zero-hour positions on 27 November. Confirmation of 8 December as the date for the wide-ranging surprise attacks was a formality when the Imperial Conference met on 1 December.

The American government had known of the Japanese intention to break off the Washington negotiations, a clear preliminary to war, for nearly twenty-four hours before the military authorities in Hawaii were taken by surprise at Pearl Harbor. Cables from Tokyo to the Japanese embassy had been decoded as they arrived in Washington on the Saturday, and copies sent to the Secretary of State and to the Secretaries of the Army and the Navy. President Roosevelt's immediate reaction when he was shown a copy at 9.30 that evening was to tell the Secretary of State for War, Henry Stimson, 'This means war'. He picked up the phone to alert the Navy chief, Admiral Harold Stark, but was unable to reach him because he was watching *The Student Prince* at the National Theatre. To avoid causing alarm by calling him out of the theatre Roosevelt left it till later. Even earlier American intelligence had reported that the staff of the Japanese embassy had destroyed one of their two coding machines and were busy burning papers. Military chiefs also recognized the significance of the time chosen for the delivery of the Japanese note – 1300 hours in Washington was sunrise in Hawaii. Urgent cables were sent off that evening to warn all military bases to be on full alert, but in Hawaii the warning was only passed to the commander-in-chief after the attack on Pearl Harbor had already begun.

The British, at least, were not taken by surprise when the Japanese invasion fleet arrived off northern Malaya. Way back in 1937, an army commander, General W.G.S. Dobbie, had warned against the accepted view that an attack on Singapore would come from the sea, arguing instead that the main danger would come from an attack in the north. In the autumn of 1941 they read the writing on the wall inscribed by the Japanese takeover of French Indo-China, and anticipated that the Japanese intended to land on the Kra Isthmus, fifty miles north of Malaya's border with Siam, a narrow neck of the peninsula that was also close to the borders of Burma. Planners in Singapore had drawn up a plan, codenamed Matador, which was aimed at forestalling Japanese plans by a pre-emptive British advance into Siam to secure the Kra Isthmus. However, political constraints caused by fears of being first to rape Siam emasculated Matador. As early as 8 August, Lieut-General Sir Henry Pownall, then vice-chief of the Imperial General Staff, noted, 'Japan is obviously going to have her next crack at Siam, although she is concentrating simultaneously in Manchuria and Korea so as to be ready to bite off the Russian maritime province . . . it is quite certain that America would not go to war for Siam and the last thing in the world we want to do is to have to take on Japan without America.'

In October, intelligence reports told of Japanese landing craft being built in Shanghai, of training in jungle warfare on Hainan island, the assembling of shipping and of new airfields being constructed in southern Indo-China.

By November, agents were reporting that landing craft had been embarked at Shanghai, that a convoy was being assembled at Hainan, and that shipping was being increased in Saigon and Cam Ranh Bay. The American consul in Hanoi also reported that the Japanese were expected to attack the Kra Isthmus and northern Malaya on 1 December.

On 6 December – more than twenty-four hours before the attack on Pearl Harbor – British agents reported that two Japanese troopship convoys had passed Cambodia Point in Indo-China and were heading west, one with twenty-five transports, six cruisers, ten destroyers, the other with ten transports, two cruisers and ten destroyers. This information was flashed to Washington in a triple-priority message.

In northern Malaya, British troops were put on six hours' notice to implement the Matador Plan, but further action was frozen while Japanese intentions were more fully ascertained. London had directed that Matador could only be carried out in the event of certainty of a Japanese landing in the Kra Isthmus – a crippling proviso for a pre-emptive operation. That same day the British ambassador in Bangkok, Sir Josiah Crosby, sent a message endorsed by his American diplomatic colleague, pleading that British troops should not occupy one inch of Siamese territory until the Japanese had struck the first blow. He said he had just had a meeting with the Siamese Foreign Minister and that Siam was with Britain against Japan, but it would be otherwise if Britain were first to violate Siamese territory.

Just the same British forces were in action several hours before the first bombs fell on Pearl Harbor. Shore batteries at Kota Bharu on the northeast coast of Malaya opened fire when Japanese ships approached late on 7 December, and soon after midnight the Japanese warships began bombarding beach defences. Landings began at 12.45 a.m. – one hour and ten minutes before the start of the attack on Pearl Harbor – from three transports anchored two miles offshore. Several landing craft capsized in the heavy swell, and the first wave suffered badly from artillery fire, and the determined resistance of the 3/7 Dogra Regiment of the Indian Army. Both sides suffered heavy losses, but after two hours the invaders had captured two strong points in the heart of the defences. The second and third waves, using the same landing craft, were hit by RAF bombing, and bombs hit all three transports, sinking one of them. According to Japanese documents the RAF inflicted 'staggering losses' on the landing forces despite heavy anti-aircraft guns which went ashore with the early assault.

But the Kota Bharu landings were a sideshow. The main Japanese forces began landing at Singora and Patani in the Kra Isthmus at 4 a.m. from twenty transport ships, with hardly even token resistance from the Siamese. But this was only reported to Singapore at 9.45 a.m. after a damaged RAF reconnaissance plane limped back to base. It was after 1 p.m. before orders were received from Singapore to cross the frontier into Siam, and 3 p.m. before the troops moved. Unexpected resistance by some 300 Siamese police was tackled with such kid-glove caution that advance troops were only three miles inside Siam when dusk fell.

Meanwhile, the Japanese 25th Army under General Tomoyuki Yamashita, totalling 35,000 battle-seasoned men backed by 150 tanks, 168 artillery pieces and 560 combat planes, were already beginning the long drive south after their walk-into capture of the Kra Isthmus with its port and airfields. They had advanced seventy-five miles, winning the race for the best positions, before meeting the British twenty-five miles inside Siam. Before the first battles were joined they had won the military intitiative at small cost, while Britain's political scruples about not being first to violate Siam's frontiers were wasted. A pro-Japanese government in Bangkok declared war on Britain and the United States, a declaration Britain accepted and America ignored believing it to have been made under duress.

The unsuspecting civil population of Singapore, 500 miles to the south, were awoken before dawn on 8 December by the sound of planes, bombs and gunfire as Japanese airmen raided two airfields. Alert radar crews had reported the approach of seventeen aircraft, and anti-aircraft batteries were at action stations, but no warning could be given to civilians because the Air Raid Precautions organization's headquarters was not manned. About 200 civilians were killed when bombs fell on an Asian district close to one of the airfields.

On 9 December the RAF main bomber force – six Blenheims – attacked the Japanese landing operations at Singora. Three of them were shot down by thirty Zero fighters and heavy anti-aircraft fire. Two more were destroyed soon afterwards while refuelling at Butterworth RAF station in an attack by Japanese planes. One succeeded in taking off as the raid began and bombed Singora again. Its pilot, Squadron-Leader A.S.K. Scarf, who died of wounds after crash landing back at Alor Star airfield, was awarded a posthumous VC.

This same day the Royal Navy, lynch-pin of British power in the east, sailed in an effort to intercept the Japanese invasion fleet. The battleship *Prince of Wales*, which had taken Churchill to his Atlantic Meeting with Roosevelt only a few months earlier, and the battlecruiser *Repulse* were attacked by eighty-four planes from bases 400 miles away in Indo-China. They were hit by torpedoes and skilful bombing and sunk with the loss of 600 lives. Escorting destroyers picked up 2000 of the crews. The Japanese lost only three planes.

Land-based RAF planes arrived at the scene too late. Churchill said he had never had a greater shock, but he was largely to blame. He had overruled Admiralty objections to the two capital ships going to Singapore without the aircraft carrier *Indomitable*, which was to have provided air cover for them. The *Indomitable* had run ashore in the West Indies, and had to be docked. No other carrier could be spared because of the more immediate threat to Atlantic convoys presented by the German raider, the battleship *Tirpitz*. Churchill had argued that the mere presence of these major warships in Singapore would be sufficient to deter the Japanese.

Thus within forty-eight hours the Japanese had eliminated the American and British fleets as a danger to their mobility across the eastern seas.

They had also won command of the skies over Malaya. Although the RAF had reacted quickly to the initial landings, bad dispersal arrangements like that at Butterworth caused early losses of many aircraft on the ground. In any case, air resources had been inadequate from the start, with only 200 planes of the 300 authorized establishment, and the main fighter, the Buffalo, was no match for the Japanese Zero. Fewer than 100 planes, most of them obsolete, survived the first days and these were withdrawn behind their 200 miles operating radius under a policy of conserving forces until reinforcements arrived.

On the ground in north Malaya the Argylls, the Leicestershires, and the 11th Indian Division were overwhelmed in stubborn fighting. The speed of Japanese movement, their skill in getting around obstacles and their bold use of tanks, took the British by surprise. The defending troops were ill trained, lacked tanks and had little air support and few anti-tank guns.

Meanwhile other Japanese task forces were assaulting strategic bases throughout the Pacific. Guam fell on 10 December, Wake Island three days later, Hong Kong on Christmas Day, and the Philippines capital, Manila, on 2 January. Later troop convoys into Singora brought troops to begin the push northwest into Burma.

Britain began movements of 300,000 men from other battlefronts to counter the new enemy in the east, and 50,000 reinforcements and new Hurricane squadrons were soon in Singapore. But the Japanese advanced relentlessly through the jungles and rubber plantations, outflanking British defences which were mainly on the roads. Other Japanese moved down the west coast in small boats captured as they advanced. They reached the Johore Straits, separating Singapore from the mainland, at the beginning of February to find the linking causeway to Singapore island only slightly breached. After using up almost all their available artillery shells in a three-day bombardment, 23,000 Japanese stormed across the straits and the causeway during the night of 8 February. In six days of sharp fighting they captured the city's water supply, and the commander-in-chief, Lieut-General Arthur Percival sent an emissary to General Yamashita. He was worried at the consequences of thirst and street fighting in a teeming tropical city, and in defiance of Churchill's urgent orders to fight on till the last redoubt, he surrendered Singapore's 130,000 defenders on St Valentine's Day, 1942. It was the biggest surrender in British military history, and a blow from which British prestige and power in the world was never to recover.

The Japanese had captured Singapore in seventy days – thirty days less than their timetable allowed, short of ammunition and supplies and against superior numbers. Lieut-General Sir Henry Pownall, who had arrived in the Far East only seven weeks before, wrote in his diary, 'I fear frankly we have been out-generalled, out-witted and out-fought . . . from the beginning to the end of this campaign we have been out-matched by better soldiers.'

For the second time this century the Japanese had humiliated a major

European power, exposing the myth of white invincibility as they had thirty-eight years before with their victory over Czarist Russia. They had won for themselves a reputation for invincibility that was to take Allied forces great efforts to kill.

Nine days after the fall of Singapore, Japanese command of the seas was completed with the annihilation of a hastily assembled force of Dutch, British, American and Australian warships, including five cruisers, in the Battle of the Java Sea – a forlorn engagement that might be compared with later Japanese suicide sallies. Japanese troop transports were then able to sail without challenge anywhere they chose throughout the Asian archipelago.

Meanwhile, Japanese armies pushing north through Burma captured Rangoon on 8 March, and remnants of the inadequate British forces straggled nearly a thousand miles into India. The Japanese advance paused on the River Chindwin with only 600 yards of water between them and India.

The extent of the peril was revealed by Churchill in a secret session of Parliament when he grimly reported that the Royal Navy had suffered loss, by sinking or crippling damage, of seven major warships, one third of its battleships and cruisers. To fill the breach the Navy overextended dangerously, and a new fleet was mustered under the command of Admiral James Somerville, who had won renown as a 'fighting admiral' in the Mediterranean. The new Eastern Fleet was based far back across the Indian Ocean from Japan's conquered domain, in the huge natural harbour of Trincomalee on the northeast coast of Ceylon, now Sri Lanka. Planners in the Admiralty suffered nightmare anxiety over the likely outcome if the new fleet was forced into battle with the Japanese carrier fleet, which since Pearl Harbor had made a devastating attack on the port of Darwin in northern Australia, the forward Allied base in the Pacific.

Early in April intelligence reports suggested that the entire carrier force had sailed into the Indian Ocean, and the harbours of Ceylon and India were hastily cleared of shipping. Colombo was heavily bombed on 5 April, Easter Sunday, but damage was much less than at Port Darwin because of the dispersal of shipping and the readiness of the defences. But that same afternoon the Japanese had the good fortune to sight the cruisers *Dorsetshire* and *Cornwall*, on their way to join the main fleet which had sailed to intercept the enemy carriers, and both were sunk by dive bombing. Trincomalee was attacked four days later and carrier planes lined up on the tarmac were destroyed at China Bay naval airfield and an ammunition dump was blown up. Again the Japanese found the harbour empty, but again they had good luck in spotting some of the ships at sea, and sank the light carrier *Hermes*, a destroyer, a corvette and two tankers. Another Japanese surface force in the Bay of Bengal sank twenty-three merchant ships, and a submarine group on India's west coast sank another five cargo ships. These operations cost the Japanese only seventeen aircraft against the loss of nineteen planes of the small British air defences in the attack on Colombo alone. These included six lumbering Swordfish torpedo bombers which arrived to set up an anti-submarine patrol in the middle of the attacks.

The Eastern Fleet had failed to make contact with the Japanese fleet despite wide-ranging reconnaissance flights from its carriers. This was no doubt a matter of relief to experts in the Admiralty who believed the motley collection of ships with their inadequately trained crews would not have survived the contest.

Fortunately for Britain, the Japanese ships withdrew from the Indian Ocean to join the drive towards Australia. But because of the threat to Ceylon, Eastern Fleet headquarters were moved even further back across the Indian Ocean, to Kilindini on the Kenyan coast. American Pacific Fleet headquarters had similarly been pulled far back, to San Diego, California, on the furthest edge of the Pacific.

In barely six months Japan had won domination of one third of the earth's surface. They had secured the oil, raw materials and food supplies they needed to be self-sufficient within their new empire. They had also succeeded at last in isolating China, restricting supplies from the west to those flown over 'the hump' from India for the next several years.

In the hope of getting the cooperation of colonial peoples they claimed to have liberated from white domination, the Japanese announced the establishment of their new order under the semantic label: The Greater East Asia Co-Prosperity Sphere. Men who had fled from European colonial rule to Germany and Japan returned home from exile. Others were released from internal colonial jails. Indian army prisoners of war, captured in Malaya, were cajoled into joining an Indian National Army to help the Japanese drive the British out of India. Officials of the former colonial administrations joined the surrendered allied soldiers, sailors and airmen in prison camps. So did white planters and business managers, white women and children. Throughout the area nearly 200,000 European civilians were held behind Japanese barbed wire in frightful conditions.

Besides the oilfields to fuel their war economy as well as their fighting ships and planes, the Japanese had grabbed 88 per cent of the world's rubber, 54 per cent of its tin, 30 per cent of its rice and 20 per cent of its tungsten.

All this at the cost of about 15,000 Japanese casualties, 400 war planes, and twenty-three minor warships.

3

President Roosevelt made no mention of Germany or Italy in his message to Congress asking for a formal declaration of war with Japan on the evening of the attack on Pearl Harbor. He knew from intelligence intercepts of messages between the Axis partners that Hitler had promised to join Japan immediately if she went to war with the United States: Roosevelt preferred to let the initiative come from Germany. Churchill spent three anxious days worrying that the whole weight of American power might be concentrated on Japan before Germany and Italy declared war on the United States on 11 December. The Washington correspondent of *The Sunday Times*, Henry Brandon, believed that 'without Germany's declaration of war President Roosevelt would still not have been able to rally the American people to fight the aggressors in Europe'. Roosevelt's policy of 'all aid short of war' to enable Britain to hold out had been dogged by vociferous opposition at every stage. Even those who supported him wanted to go no further than respond to Churchill's appeal, 'Give us the tools, and we'll finish the job.'

Roosevelt and his military chiefs had been committed to helping Britain survive from the time Churchill had become prime minister after the German invasion of the Low Countries, and he had made it clear that Britain would never submit to the German masters of continental Europe.

Britain feared that the United States would concentrate its attention on the Pacific war, which Churchill described in Parliament as 'the lesser war, for such I must regard this fearful struggle with Japan'. In America the isolationist press was clamouring for America to deal with Japan and leave the fighting in Europe to the British and Russians.

The moment he heard the news of the Pearl Harbor attack on the BBC, Churchill telephoned Roosevelt and arranged to travel to Washington to coordinate plans as allies. He arrived with a large delegation on 23 December, intending to stay for a week. As he told a secret session of Parliament on his return, 'We prepared to argue that the defeat of Germany would leave the finishing off of Japan a matter of time and trouble. We were relieved to find that these simple but classical conceptions of war, although powerfully opposed by the vehement isolationist faction, were earnestly and spontaneously shared by the government and dominant forces in the United States.'

Much to British relief, at the first joint-strategy meeting, the Americans themselves laid down that the Atlantic and European area must be considered the decisive theatre; that Germany being the prime enemy, Hitler's defeat was the key to victory, and the collapse of Italy and the defeat of Japan would be sure to follow.

A Combined Chiefs of Staff was formed to take overall charge of war operations from Washington, and they decreed the forming of the first unified command for the ABDA area, where Americans, British, Dutch and Australians were desperately trying to prevent the Japanese conquest of the southern resources area. The unenviable appointment as first Allied Supreme Commander for an area already becoming untenable went to Britain's General Archibald Wavell, renowned for his dashing victories over the Italians in the Western Desert.

A Munitions Assignment Board was formed with the power to allocate war supplies to all the allies in all war theatres, and Roosevelt announced a Victory Programme of Production. His directive called for 45,000 planes, 45,000 tanks and vast amounts of weapons and munitions for 1942, and 100,000 planes, 75,000 tanks and greatly increased production of all other war materials for 1943. This was the beginning of a flow of supplies to all fronts which Stalin toasted at the Teheran conference at the end of 1943 with the tribute, 'without American production the war would have been lost.'

Since the attack on Pearl Harbor most of the Latin American states had rallied to America's support and declared war on the Axis, and the conference drew up a joint commitment from all the associated nations promising to free the occupied lands and establish enduring peace. Roosevelt pondered the final declaration, and at the last minute was inspired to change the name of the alliance from Associated to United Nations.

On New Year's Day 1942, representatives of twenty-six nations gathered with Roosevelt and Churchill in the White House to sign the declaration that founded the United Nations. The greatest military coalition in history was formed, and a new world body was born.

4

The crews of the triumphant carrier force were feted in Tokyo as the Japanese exulted in what they were later themselves to call 'victory disease'. A German engineer working in Japan at the time noted a new arrogance among ordinary people towards Europeans as a race. The military planners were so imbued with the poor fighting quality of American, British and Australian troops that they began to split their forces, breaking their own cardinal principle that forces should be concentrated.

This widespread overconfidence was not shared by the man who had led the devastating air attacks on Pearl Harbor, Darwin and Ceylon, Captain Mitsuo Fuchida. He argued that Pearl Harbor had given conclusive proof that the main combat strength of any modern navy was its carrier force, and he derided the Imperial Navy's main fleet of seven battleships, held in permanent reserve in the Inland Sea. He said they were contributing no more to operations than the wrecks of the American battleships in Pearl Harbor. He believed his own air formations had been wasted on secondary objectives in their attacks on Darwin and Ceylon. They should have been used to find and destroy the American carriers that had escaped the attack on Pearl Harbor. After the war, he wrote that the Japanese fleet lost the initiative to an enemy who was quicker to learn from defeat than the Japanese naval chiefs were to learn from victory.

The American carriers were already making their survival felt. Their planes raided the main base in Japan's outer defence screen, Rabaul in New Britain, and targets in the Marshall Islands, Wake Island, Marcus Island and eastern New Guinea. The attack on Marcus Island, little more than 500 miles from Tokyo, roused Japanese fears of a shaming attack on the seat of the Emperor, and air defences were strengthened around Tokyo.

The commanders of the Combined Fleet wanted to draw the American carriers into a decisive battle in which they expected to destroy them, and recommended an invasion of the American island of Midway as a sure way of luring them into battle. But the Imperial General Headquarters turned their plan down in favour of continuing the advance towards Australia, where a huge American build-up was beginning with great liners like the *Queen Elizabeth* shuttling large numbers of troops.

At this point the Japanese received the first shock to their confidence. Air-raid sirens sounded in Tokyo barely four months after Pearl Harbor when Lieut-Colonel James Doolittle led a formation of sixteen Mitchell bombers in a daring raid on Tokyo and seven other Japanese cities. The twin-engine Mitchell, adapted for launching from carriers, had longer range than normal carrier aircraft and caught the Japanese defences by surprise. Most managed to drop their one-ton bomb load and continue to bases in China, but the Japanese beheaded three of the eight airmen who baled out from planes shot down.

Soon after this severe blow to Japanese pride, the US Navy won a tactical triumph in the Coral Sea in the first naval battle fought entirely by carrier-borne aircraft. Each side lost a carrier, but the Japanese were also forced to withdraw their invasion fleet and abandon the assault on Port Moresby.

But it was the Doolittle raid that made the Japanese High Command change the strategy and move against Midway Island. However, instead of concentrating what could have been the most formidable naval force ever assembled, they decided to split their forces between a main assault on Midway and a diversionary move in the North Pacific. This was the invasion of the islands of Attu and Kiska in the Aleutians, a feint towards North America itself. However, the Americans had broken the Japanese naval code, and Admiral Chester Nimitz was able to defeat the superior Japanese force moving towards Midway, destroying five carriers and some 280 aircraft. Midway was saved. The strategic consequences of the victory at Midway put it on a par with Trafalgar and Lepanto. Had the Japanese succeeded in capturing it, and also destroying the American carriers missed at Pearl Harbor, they would have isolated Australia and been able to carry the war to the shores of California.

Instead they could only make futile gestures, dropping incendiaries on forests in Oregon from a submarine-launched seaplane and releasing balloon bombs. Some 9000 balloon bombs were sent, but only one inflicted casualties. In the week the war ended in Europe a woman and five youths were killed while on a Sunday school fishing outing near Lake View, Oregon.

Midway marked the turning point of the Pacific War. From then on the Japanese were always on the defensive as American power rapidly increased with her factories and shipyards turning out 'the tools of victory' in a burgeoning stream. Logistical problems of operating over vast ocean distances were resolved by organizing the ingenious provision of supplies and repair facilities in fleet trains that enabled American fighting ships to stay at sea for many months at a time.

Japanese expectations that America would be stunned into accepting the new Japanese empire as a *fait accompli*, nurse her wounded pride and make an early peace, were confounded. They realized they were now in for a long war – just what her most experienced leaders had feared. They had lost the gamble undertaken with the attack on Pearl Harbor. Now, as they saw it, their only hope of obtaining a negotiated settlement had to be making the price of war prohibitively costly in American blood. They pinned their hopes now on the Western philosophy that held life dear, and political leaders' preoccupation with minimizing their nation's casualties.

Imperial General Headquarters ordered the development of an 'Invulnerable Barrier' running in a great arc from Burma, down the Malay peninsula to western New Guinea, and up through the Carolinas and Marianas to the Kuriles. They designated the area behind it 'an absolute national defence sphere' to be held at all cost.

5

In the west, the Japanese pursuit of the retreating remnant of the British from Burma reached the broad River Chindwin, close to the Himalayan foothills on the border of India. Torrential monsoon rains turned the hill tracks into rushing streams and the river was swollen to 600 yards in width. Behind this barrier a new Imperial Army with British, Indian and African troops took the Phoenix as its emblem to signify its determination to rise from the ashes of defeat. But the new 14th Army was so low on the Allied priorities list that plans for its first offensive into North Burma in joint operations with the Chinese during the dry season from April 1942 had to be called off. They were short of weapons and ammunition, the very basics of infantry fighting.

Meanwhile, the Eastern Fleet, stretched as it was to try to meet the flexible choices available to the Japanese Navy, was called on to divert ships for operations in the Mediterranean as well. The American entry into the war brought no immediate relief for the overextended Royal Navy. American ships were transferred from the Atlantic to fill the yawning gap in the Pacific, and others were fully engaged against a U-boat offensive against ships silhouetted against the glare of resort lights on America's unblacked-out eastern seaboard. At this time, too, convoys to Malta through the Straits of Gibraltar were suffering such heavy losses from land-based aircraft that Churchill even suggested that the Eastern Fleet should fight a convoy through to Malta from Suez.

All supplies to the Middle East were having to go around the Cape, and there were fears that the Japanese might have their eyes on Madagascar, the huge Vichy-French controlled island off the coast of southeast Africa which straddled the shipping lanes. If the Vichy-French authorities submitted to Japanese pressure for facilities there as they had done with such dire results for Britain in Indo-China, the Japanese would dominate the whole of the Indian Ocean and cut the Cape shipping route to Suez. In May 1942 a British task force captured the Madagascan capital, Diego Suarez, after three days fighting, just in time. Two days later the flagship of the British force, the battleship *Ramilles*, was torpedoed by two Japanese midget submarines which penetrated the harbour. The Japanese submarine force sank twenty ships along the sea lanes in the next month before returning to their base in distant Penang, off the coast of Malaya.

Despite some political agitation and disturbances in the early months of the Far East war, India was developed as the main British base for a build-up of twenty army divisions, a hundred and fifty-four RAF squadrons and thirty Fleet Air Arm squadrons. It was also supporting American and Chinese forces as a transit area for supplies flown over the Himalayan 'hump'. After a year of patient build-up, General Wavell, who became commander-in-chief in India after the ABDA command territories were overrun, launched a limited offensive down the Arakan coast to try to take Akyab. It failed, and Churchill blamed Wavell's insistence on frontal attacks. Wavell was removed from direct military command gracefully by being appointed Viceroy of India.

A separate South-East Asia Command – SEAC – was created in August 1943 with Vice-Admiral Lord Louis Mountbatten as Supreme Allied Commander. It covered lands under Japanese occupation between southern China and the Dutch East Indies island of Java where General MacArthur's South-West Pacific Command began. Mountbatten was fresh from commanding Combined Operations, the joint services organization for raids on the coast of German-occupied Europe, and Churchill expected he would make maximum use of limited resources to make morale-raising strikes at the Japanese across the Indian Ocean. Churchill, aware that Britain could not match the mass armies of the continental powers, instinctively reverted to Britain's ancient fighting tradition of maritime strategies, the use of highly trained forces where the enemy was weak or exposed. Ironically, the retreat from Dunkirk had restored this strategic freedom which had been lost in the attrition of trench warfare in the First World War. Churchill's first directive to Mountbatten charged him with the task of liberating all the colonial territories lost by Britain, France and the Netherlands.

Mountbatten entered into his new command with impetuous enthusiasm, and quickly interested Churchill in a plan for an amphibious operation to capture the northern tip of Sumatra – Operation Culverin – which would have been a huge leap back towards Singapore. However, no amphibious craft could be spared from Europe, and Mountbatten substituted a less ambitious project for the recapture of the Andaman Islands, lying further to the north of the entrance to the Malacca Straits.

This won the support of Roosevelt because it was the kind of operation his Chinese protégé, General Chiang Kai-Shek, was demanding if his troops were to join in operations in northeast Burma aimed at reopening an overland supply route. The Americans planned to build a new road from Ledo in Assam to link with the upper Burma road to Kunming, but

British chiefs regarded this as a waste of effort and were pressing for resources to reopen the old Burma road from the railhead of the railway from Rangoon by an amphibious assault on the Burmese capital.

The Andamans plan – Operation Buccaneer – was put before the Allied Combined Chiefs of Staff just as tentative plans for a cross-Channel invasion of Europe in 1943 were being postponed because of British arguments that it could not be mounted before 1944 with any certainty of not being thrown back into the sea. The Americans, impatient to use landing craft and other war materials pouring from their shipyards and production lines, used this postponement to earmark more resources for use against the Japanese. The American Chief of Staff, General George Marshall, denied any intention to reverse the Germany-first policy, explaining that the operations in Guadalcanal in the Solomons had established a disturbing factor. The Japanese were making the military cliché about 'fighting to the last man and the last round' a reality. They were not susceptible to the mathematics of superior force which induced most troops to lay down their arms when the struggle became hopeless. They had held out in the Solomons for six months.

General Marshall said the American Chiefs of Staff were anxious to prevent the Japanese consolidating their gains while their enemies concentrated on operations in Europe. They feared that if China collapsed Japan would become impregnable. He promised that resources for the European theatre would still have top priority. However, the interpretation of priorities was made by the American Joint Chiefs and not the Allied Combined Chiefs, and there can be no doubt that greater resources were diverted to the Pacific than a strict policy of Germany-first ought to have allowed. This soon showed up the meagreness of the resources Britain was able to divert against Japan from the deadly struggle across the English Channel. At the end of 1943, when Britain still had more troops in fighting contact with the enemy than America, 1,878,000 Americans were poised against Japan compared with 1,810,000 against Germany. America had 7857 warplanes deployed against Japan compared with 8807 against Germany, and 713 warships in the Pacific compared with 515 in the Atlantic and the European theatre.

The Allied leaders gathered for a summit meeting in Teheran in November 1943. When Stalin heard about Operation Buccaneer he complained bitterly at the diversion of landing craft from operations in Europe, where he was demanding the opening of a Second Front to take pressure off his armies. He scathingly dismissed operations in South-East Asia as a sideshow, and Churchill, who was arguing for operations in the Balkans, tamely accepted Stalin's arguments.

Roosevelt's reluctance to let down Mountbatten and Chiang Kai-Shek was overcome, and landing craft which were to have taken part in the assault on the Andamans were returned to the Mediterranean, where they later took part in the superfluous landings in Southern France, which Churchill and Field Marshal Montgomery were later to list as one of the four major mistakes of allied strategy. Redeploying these troops weakened the Allied advance in Italy which might otherwise have continued without pause to Trieste and Vienna.

Churchill anticipated a furious reaction from Mountbatten and moved to pre-empt it by rebuking him for overstating his requirements. 'Everyone has been unpleasantly affected by your request to use 50,000 British and Imperial troops . . . against an Andamans garrison of 5000 Japanese,' he wrote. 'I was astounded to hear of such a requirement, and cannot feel sure you are getting the right military advice. While such standards as you have accepted for the Andamans prevail there is not much hope of making any form of amphibious war.'

Mountbatten, who still nursed dark thoughts over the disaster of the Dieppe raid when half of the 5000 troops who had landed, mostly Canadians, were killed or captured, later described Churchill's rebuke as the greatest put-down of his career, attributing it to purely political motives. He told his unofficial biographer, Richard Hough, 'The Americans, with all their experience and terrific resources in the Pacific, were using a 6 to 1 superiority when air cover was from carriers.' Churchill had ignored the fact that only 34,000 were frontline troops, a ratio of barely 7 to 1 which was considered prudent to achieve success in a theatre that had suffered defeat for two years and badly needed a success to boost morale.

The Americans were all for a more limited plan – Operation Bullfrog – for the capture of Akyab, the main port of the Arakan coast, nearly half-way to Rangoon. They thought it would take pressure off MacArthur and Admiral Chester Nimitz, Supreme Commander of the island-hopping advance across the Pacific, and help placate Chiang Kai-Shek. But the British Chiefs of Staff scuppered it by claiming some of SEAC's tiny landing craft resources for operations in the Mediterranean. An even smaller amphibious operation – Pigstick – against the Mayu peninsula with a follow-through to take Akyab had to be cancelled when even more landing craft were ordered back to the Mediterranean. In order to placate Stalin and take some pressure off his armies a substitute had been found for the year's postponement of the Normandy landings – Operation Torch, the Anglo-American landings in French North Africa.

So while successive amphibious assaults were carrying the Americans island hopping towards Japan, it was clear that no major British amphibious operations could be carried into Japanese-occupied territories until resources could be transferred from Europe after Germany was beaten.

Churchill had been keen to bypass Burma, likening going into the Burma jungles to fight the Japanese to going into water to fight sharks, but because of lack of resources the British had no option other than to pursue the war against Japan through the Burma jungles.

That suited the Americans. Their only interest in Burma was in opening an overland supply route to China. With supplies limited to the air lift over the 16,000-foot Himalayan 'hump' from India, they were pressing for North Burma to be cleared so that they could build the new road from Ledo to link with the upper Burma road.

Mountbatten had to make do for a while with the exploits of Major-General Orde Wingate's Chindits, the special units (named after a Burmese mythical beast) which landed far behind the Japanese lines by glider. The fatality rate was one in three, and Wingate himself was killed. The Chindit columns were supplied by air drop, a technique which played a major supply role in the later triumphant advance through Burma.

While Mountbatten's amphibious projects were being considered and rejected, a build-up of British forces on the western bank of the Chindwin had been going on steadily. By the end of 1943, the armies that had been looking at each other warily across the broad river for over a year were both ready to launch major offensives. But Mountbatten was still arguing for a seaborne assault against Rangoon rather than the favoured American plan – Capital – for a land offensive aimed at capturing North Burma.

These strategic arguments were settled by the Japanese, who struck in what turned out to be a diversionary offensive in the Arakan in February 1944. The British routed the Japanese advance, but only after the commander of the 14th Army, General William Slim, had thrown in his entire reserves.

The Japanese put in their major thrust – the so-called March on Delhi – across the Chindwin river a month later, and quickly surrounded the major British bases of Imphal and Kohima. The Japanese were held after a big air lift of troops from the Arakan, but bitter fighting continued for three months. Key features in the Shenam Saddle sector changed hands several times, and casualties on both sides were heavier than in any other action of comparable size in the Second World War. By June, a British counter-offensive lifted the siege of Imphal, and put the Japanese in full retreat back across the Chindwin, leaving 53,000 dead and almost all their equipment behind. Most of the remainder of the Japanese force of 100,000 died of starvation in the jungle before reaching safety.

The Japanese Foreign Office official, Kase Toshikazu, described the battle in his 1951 book, *The Eclipse of the Rising Sun*, as the 'worst disaster yet chronicled in war'.

The memorial to the 13,000 British and Indian dead at Kohima bears these words:

> When you go home
> Tell them of us and say
> For your tomorrow
> We gave our today

Success in smashing the diversionary offensive in the Arakan marked the turn of the tide of British defeat in Asia, as Midway had marked it for the Americans. The subsequent near-run victory at Imphal-Kohima was the decisive battle of the war in South-East Asia. It ended the myth of Japanese invincibility, and gave the British the initiative in the major land campaign against the Japanese. By pushing their forces across the Chindwin, the Japanese had played into the hands of General Slim. It allowed him to smash the bulk of the Japanese armies on the western side of the river rather than having to meet them in strength in the Burmese jungle.

The Japanese were in such disarray afterwards that the pursuing 14th Army met little concerted resistance till their advance reached the parallel Irriwady river valley deep inside northern Burma. Beyond that, the 14th Army had to fight doggedly forwards for another year, supplied mainly by air drop, before a Japanese counter-offensive gave them the opportunity to deliver a knock-out blow. This came at Meiktila in March 1945, and cost the British 2307 killed, 8107 wounded and almost as many again sick from jungle ailments. The Japanese lost a third of their forces before the survivors fled into the Shan hills where Karen tribesmen, loyal to Britain, cut down many more before they could reach Thailand. Mandalay, in central Burma, fell within days, and the advance continued towards distant Rangoon.

The land forces were given close naval support as they moved down the Arakan coast. Destroyers sailed into river estuaries to bombard Japanese strongpoints, and a series of amphibious hooks began what was called the Chaung War. Landings at Akyab in January 1945 were unopposed, but a week later the Japanese reacted strongly to landings on the Myebon Peninsula, inflicting many casualties with mortars and 75-mm and 105-mm guns so skilfully entrenched in the jungle that they were impossible to silence despite heavy RAF bombing. In February, a beachhead at Ru-Ywa was made almost untenable by accurate Japanese artillery fire, and follow-up troops were diverted to a new beachhead better screened from enemy observers.

In September 1943, Admiral Somerville had moved Eastern Fleet headquarters back to Ceylon, but his forces remained too weak to undertake offensive operations that would have taken naval pressure off the Americans and Australians in the Solomons. However, reinforcements came when the Japanese Imperial Navy moved its main base to Singapore in February 1944, arousing fears that they might make another powerful sally into the Indian Ocean.

These reinforcements included the battleships *Queen Elizabeth* and *Valiant*, the battlecruiser *Renown*, the Fighting French battleship *Richelieu*, and the aircraft carrier *Illustrious*. Plans to send the battleship *King George V* and the carrier *Victorious* as well were cancelled because they were needed to counter the threat to Russian convoys posed by the German battleship *Tirpitz*, which maintained its threat from a Norwegian fjord until first crippled by Midget submarines and finally sunk at its moorings by RAF bombings. The very existence of *Tirpitz*, poised to attack at any time, was threatening. The US Navy obligingly filled the gap by sending the carrier *Saratoga* for a spell of duty with the Eastern Fleet.

Churchill, who had been carping about the ships of the Eastern Fleet being kept in idleness, immediately pressed his 'fighting admiral' to live up to his reputation, and in April 1944 the Eastern Fleet sailed on its first offensive operation. Planes from the *Illustrious* and *Saratoga* hit the Japanese base at Sabang, an island off the northern tip of Sumatra covering the entrance to the Malacca Straits seaway to Singapore. Admiral Somerville was delighted, and the two carriers carried out a second raid together, this time on the Japanese naval base at Sourabaya in eastern Java, before the *Saratoga* returned to the Pacific. Planes from the *Illustrious* bombed Sabang again in June as well as Port Blair in the Andamans. In July, planes from the *Illustrious* and the newly joined *Victorious* strafed Sabang's three airfields, the battleships *Queen Elizabeth*, *Valiant*, *Richelieu* and *Renown*, five cruisers and five destroyers, bombarded the harbour area, and the Dutch cruiser *Tromp*, two Australian and one British destroyer sailed boldly into the harbour to blast away at ships, wharves and workshops at point-blank range.

In operations intended to take naval pressure away from American assaults in the Pacific, the carriers *Victorious* and *Indomitable* attacked Sigli in northern Sumatra in September, and in October the main fleet carried out a series of raids and bombardments in the Nicobar Islands.

Much as Churchill was concerned to regain Britain's lost imperial possessions, and see Dutch and French authority restored to theirs, he was equally determined that British forces should play a role in the final conquest of the Japanese homeland. He insisted on forming a British Pacific Fleet to fight in Japanese waters under American supreme command despite robust objections from the American naval chief, Admiral Ernie King, who along with other American chiefs had come to regard operations against the Japanese home islands as a private American war. But Roosevelt promptly accepted Churchill's offer of a fleet, and the Chiefs of Staff were forced to give way.

So it was that the newly formidable Eastern Fleet was split in two, the most modern ships going to the British Pacific Fleet, the remainder staying in SEAC as the East Indies Fleet.

Before its departure from SEAC, the British Pacific Fleet carried out the biggest air attacks the Royal Navy had so far launched. Their raids hit oil installations and Japanese bases in Sumatra, culminating, in January 1945, in a devastating attack on the oil refineries near Palembang on the east coast of Sumatra, the enemy's biggest source of refined fuel outside Japan. Ninety-five planes from the carriers flew 150 miles over jungle-clad mountains to hit the oil installations and three nearby airfields. Five days later they returned to pound them again. In the two operations forty-six planes were lost – sixteen in combat, eleven by ditching, fourteen from deck crashes, a loss rate of one plane for every ten sorties, higher even than the loss rate of Bomber Command in Europe. Production at the refinery was impaired for the rest of the war, and sixty-eight Japanese aircraft were destroyed, thirty in combat, thirty-eight on the ground. (Nine of the missing Allied aircrews were captured and taken to Singapore for interrogation by the Kempei Tei secret police. Some eight months later, shortly after the Emperor's order to his troops to surrender, they were beheaded, and three Japanese officers who admitted responsibility committed suicide.)

By the end of 1944, the Special Operations Executive, under the code name Force 136, were making numerous landings in Japanese territory. Most of the early landing operations were carried in Dutch Navy submarines specially designed for the low depths of the Malaysian archipelago. Parties were put ashore in the Andamans and Sumatra, some were unobserved, a few were discovered and wiped out.

The British submarine *Tally-ho* sank the German U-boat *UIT21* during one operation, but had to let the Japanese seaplane carrier *Kamikawa Maru* sail safely past although within torpedo range because of the risk of drawing attention to a party the *Tally-ho* was putting ashore that night.

Sabotage operations included two raids on shipping in Singapore harbour led by Lieut-Colonel Ivan Lyon, of the Gordon Highlanders, one of the escapees from the fall of Singapore. He sailed from a base in Exmouth Gulf on the northwest coast of Australia in September 1943 and sank or incapacitated seven Japanese ships in the harbour with limpet mines. He was captured during a raid a year later and executed 'with honour' just over a month before the war ended.

6

In the Pacific, the Americans were able to begin the counter-offensive only ten months after Pearl Harbor. The first objective was the strategic island of Guadalcanal in the British Solomon Islands, dominating the Coral Sea approaches to New Guinea and Australia. Most of the Japanese on the island were construction workers completing a new airfield, and they fled when the preliminary bombardment opened. The assault force of 11,000 marines quickly overran the airfield, but the Japanese poured in reinforcements and the fighting went on for seven months. The Japanese lost 25,000 dead, the Americans 1592 – a pattern of total resistance that was to be repeated again and again in the island-hopping advance towards Japan and a ratio that shows the care American commanders took to minimize their own casualties.

While the struggle for Guadalcanal was at its height, the Japanese suffered their first defeat on land in Papua, New Guinea. Australians, with American support, pushed them back over the Owen Stanley mountains from their furthest southerly advance to within thirty miles of Port Moresby, and captured the key town of Buna on the northeast coast. The little-known, bitterly fought action cost Australia 5700 killed and Japan 12,000, and lifted the threat to Australia.

Australian and American land-based bombers also scored a brilliant success in three days of bombing known as the Battle of the Bismarck Sea. They sank four Japanese destroyers and all eight of the troopships they were escorting. The troopships carried a whole army division.

Naval forces supporting the land battles clashed in the Eastern Solomons and off the Santa Cruz Islands. The Japanese lost two battleships, a carrier, a cruiser and six destroyers; the Americans two carriers, three cruisers and eight destroyers. These heavy losses, with other ships put out of action by damage, left the Americans so short of carriers that they appealed to the Royal Navy for help, and the carrier, HMS *Victorious*, joined the American Third Fleet to cover landings in New Georgia which completed the reconquest of the Solomons. For a time, the *Victorious* and the *Saratoga* were the only carriers available on the Allied side, but by the end of 1943 American factories were supplying an abundance of ships, planes and weapons of every kind. Nine new fast carriers joined the Pacific Fleet in the first six months of 1943, tipping the carrier balance decisively in America's favour. They were escorted by new battleships bristling with anti-aircraft guns. Their new planes included the Hellcat, the first carrier fighter that was a match for the Japanese Zero. By the middle of 1943, the Americans had 18,000 Navy planes, by the end of 1944 the total was around 30,000.

As American power increased remorselessly, Japanese power was declining. Their losses in ships and planes were outstripping any hope of replacement, and their experienced air crews were starkly depleted by casualties. Replacements were not coming anything like fast enough from flying schools.

The Supreme Commander in the Pacific, Admiral Chester Nimitz, was ready to deploy amphibious forces far across the sea. But first he decided to eliminate the small Japanese foothold in the Aleutians, which as part of offshore North America rankled as deeply as the German occupation of the Channel Islands had with Britain. Although it had no strategic importance, 2350 Japanese on Attu Island fought to the death, only twenty-eight were captured alive. Their sacrifice caused the deaths of 552 Americans of the 11,000 assault forces – a poor balance of losses in Japan's strategy of attrition.

In November 1943, Nimitz captured the Gilbert Islands where the tiny atoll of Tarawa became a notorious bloodbath with 4580 Japanese and 1009 Americans killed in three days of furious fighting. Small Japanese garrisons in the Marshall Islands were quickly overwhelmed in February, 1944, leading in June to bitterly contested battles for islands in the Marianas with airfields from which long-range bombers could reach Japan.

It took two months to capture Saipan, held by 32,000 Japanese with tanks and artillery brought from Singapore, and cost 16,525 American casualties, including 3426 dead. On the Japanese side 30,000 soldiers and 22,000 civilians died, some of them, including women, choosing to jump from clifftops rather than surrender. The Japanese commander, Admiral Nagumo, who had commanded the attack on Pearl Harbor, was among the suicides. Within artillery range of Saipan was the island of Tinian, from which the atomic bomb raids were to be launched fourteen months after its capture. Half its garrison of 9000 were killed by shelling before the marines stormed ashore, and the rest were killed fighting to the last.

Next came Guam, a United States possession, where most of the 19,000 Japanese fought to the death, though a few hid in caves, the last one surrendering in 1960. The arithmetic of comparative casualties (1463 Americans died and 5646 were wounded) was falling far short of Japanese hopes. The sheer weight of American fire-power had turned the kill factor dramatically against the defenders.

The armada of 500 ships supporting these invasions tempted the Imperial Japanese Navy to make its last serious challenge to the United States Navy. They mustered nine carriers, five battleships, thirteen cruisers, twenty-eight destroyers and 473 aircraft in a Mobile Fleet. Poised against them were fifteen carriers, seven battleships, twenty-one cruisers, sixty-nine destroyers and 956 planes.

These ships fought the biggest naval action involving aircraft carriers in history on 19 June 1944 in the Battle of the Philippine Sea. Americans who fought in it called it the 'Great Marianas Turkey Shoot' because more than 300 Japanese planes were shot down. Two Japanese carriers were sunk by American submarines and a third was sunk by bombing. The surviving Japanese carriers, some damaged, sailed home with almost empty aircraft hangars.

This victory marked the end of Japanese air power, and gave the American Navy access to the South China Sea, which had been a no-go area for Allied surface warships for more than two years. The capture of the Marianas provided heavy bomber bases within 1500 miles of Tokyo and other industrial targets in Japan.

The speed of Nimitz's amphibious advance across the vast distances of the Pacific persuaded the planners in Washington to change the basic strategy of the war against Japan. They scrapped plans for General MacArthur's armies to advance through the southerly archipelago to Formosa and the Chinese mainland, subsequently using China as the base for battering Japan into submission. Instead they took up the ocean policy Churchill and the American Navy chiefs had always advocated.

But MacArthur, who was already preparing to leave the Australians to mop up in New Guinea and New Britain, insisted on turning aside from the direct approach to recapture the Philippines, and got his way. He had been ordered to leave his troops there to surrender in 1942, and had vowed 'I shall return'.

The American conquest of the Marianas was a critical breach of the inner defence ring, the so-called 'Impregnable Barrier' the Japanese had hoped to hold until the Western powers found their losses unacceptably high and agreed to a negotiated settlement. It forced an even more agonized rethinking of strategy at Japanese Imperial General Headquarters. Their answer was the Sho (meaning Victory) Plan which called for all available resources to be concentrated to prevent the enemy from capturing his next objective. It was activated in October 1944 when it became clear that an American invasion of the Philippines was imminent.

Vice-Admiral Takijiro Ohnishi was sent to take charge of the First Air Fleet in Manila with authority to use a desperate new tactic. He intended to make maximum use of the First Air Fleet's depleted aircraft in carrying through his task of putting American aircraft carriers out of action for a critical period while the Second Japanese Fleet sailed without air cover to intercept the invasion troopships.

Ohnishi found the First Air Fleet in a worse state than he had feared. It was reduced to a mere thirty aircraft, and plans to transfer the Second Air Fleet from Formosa had been delayed by the attacks on their airfields. His only prospect of success lay in putting into operation a tactic that had been in his mind for some time. There was no chance at all that he could carry out his instructions to neutralize enemy carriers by using his thirty planes in conventional bombing attacks.

At Mabalacat Field, Ohnishi told the senior officers of the 201st Air Group that there was only one way they could use their meagre aircraft strength with maximum effectiveness. That was to organise suicide attack units composed of planes, armed with 250-kilo bombs, whose mission would be to make sure of hitting their targets by crash diving into enemy carriers.

The officers looked grimly thoughtful. Tai-stari (body crashing) had been known to happen in the heat of dog-fights, and pilots of crippled bomber planes had sometimes deliberately crashed into enemy ships rather than take a slim chance of survival in the ocean. Pilots knew the chances of returning from raids on the American Fleet were becoming markedly slimmer as their own numbers dwindled and the enemy's increased. It made good sense to die at maximum cost to the enemy – tens of thousands of soldiers had already done so in Banzai (human bullet) charges rather than surrender.

It was an accepted part of the military code, based on Bushido, but to make suicide a formal tactic, leaving not even a slender chance of returning to base, was something else. A long silence was broken by the executive officer, Commander Tamai, who demurred at accepting responsibility in the absence in hospital of the group commander. Vice-Admiral Ohnishi told him curtly that he had already put it to the group commander on the telephone, and he had left it to his officers. Commander Tamai, an avuncular figure, asked to leave the room to think it over. He returned after consulting one of his lieutenants on the likely attitude of the pilots, and agreed to the new tactic.

Twenty-four pilots volunteered immediately for the first unit which took the name of Shimpu Special Attack Corps. It was divided into four formations, each taking its name from part of the poem: 'The Japanese spirit is like mountain cherry blossom, radiant on the morning sun'. Their badge was a white silk scarf tied around the forehead.

Hardly were these arrangements completed when first sighting reports came of the American Fleet's approach, and on 21 October the first Special Attack flight took off from Mabalacat on what was thought to be a one-way flight to certain death. Led by Lieutenant Yukio Seki, their task was to crash into the decks of enemy carriers before they could launch their planes. But search as they would they were unable to find the enemy ships and returned alive and disappointed to base. Another suicide formation took off from Mabalacat that evening, but was forced to turn back by torrential rain.

Allied records say that the first suicide attack took place soon after dawn that same day. Presumably it was a 'freelance' attack, unknown and unmentioned in Japanese records. The plane crashed into the bridge of the cruiser, HMAS *Australia*, off Leyte, killing twenty of her crew, including the captain, and wounding fifty-four others. The ship managed to limp back to base.

For three days of the biggest naval battle ever fought, the suicide pilots of Mabalacat were frantic with frustration, holding themselves responsible for the mortal wounds American carrier planes were inflicting on the Imperial Navy. Vice-Admiral Takeo Kurit, commanding the First Striking Force, was complaining bitterly over the radio at the lack of air support.

Four days and four futile sorties after their first take-off on a suicidal mission, a formation of five planes led by Lieutenant Seki was at last able to press home the first special attacks. On 25 October they sighted the elusive American carriers as returning planes were landing on them. Lieutenant Seki crash dived through the flight deck of the carrier, *St Lo*, blowing up stored bombs and torpedoes and sinking the ship in minutes. Other planes severely damaged the light carriers *Kitkun Bay*, *White Plains* and *Kalinin Bay*.

Ohnishi's suicide tactics had come too late to influence the battle for the Philippines. They failed completely in the objective of putting American carriers out of action during sorties by two Japanese fleets against the American invasion transports. The American carriers were able to launch their planes to sink the heavy cruiser *Zuikaku*, the last of the Pearl Harbor raiders, two light carriers and a destroyer. They also damaged and slowed down other ships which were later finished off by surface gunfire. This was one of six actions over three days known as the Battle of Leyte Gulf, the biggest sea battle in history. It had opened disastrously for the Japanese when a coordinated attack by two US submarines sank their flagship, the cruiser *Atago*, and heavily damaged another. More than 280 ships and hundreds of planes took part, compared with 250 ships and five seaplanes engaged in the major sea battle of the First World War off Jutland. The Japanese lost four aircraft carriers, three battleships, two cruisers and nine destroyers. American losses were one light carrier, two escort carriers, three destroyers and seventy-nine planes.

It was the decisive victory of the Pacific War, comparable to Trafalgar. It eliminated any further challenge to the US Navy's domination of the Pacific, and ensured the reconquest of the Philippines. Most damaging of all to Japan, it cut sea communications with the vital 'southern resources area' for which she had gone to war.

By the end of 1944, Leyte was firmly back under American control after 3593 Americans and 65,000 Japanese had died in bitter fighting. General MacArthur went on to invade the main island of Luzon in January 1945 – sending his troops back over the beaches the Japanese had used in their invasion three years before. The reconquest of Luzon was the biggest land campaign of the Pacific War, costing 11,000 further American dead. Of the original 200,000 Japanese defenders, some 50,000 were still holding out in the mountains when the Emperor ordered all Japanese forces to lay down their arms nine months after the landings.

Before their bases in Luzon were overrun by the American advance, 424 special attack sorties were flown from them. For the loss of 335 planes they sank two carriers, three destroyers, five transports and six other ships. They also damaged twenty-three carriers, five battleships, nine cruisers, twenty-three destroyers, five escorts, twelve transports and ten other ships.

Vice-Admiral Ohnishi's operations were adding a new dimension of terror for the Allied forces as they advanced towards the Japanese homeland over the bodies of men who fought to the last.

8

By the time the direct advance towards Japan was continued, the Japanese had used the respite to improve the fortifications at Iwo Jima, 700 miles from Japan, and American marines lost one third of their assault force when they landed in February 1945. The Japanese commander, Lieut-General Kuribayashi, sent out a final order: 'Each man will make it his duty to kill ten of the enemy before dying.' When resistance ended after three months, 21,900 Japanese bodies were counted, and 876 were captured. Total American casualties were 6812 killed, over 19,000 wounded. But the Americans were now established 4000 miles nearer Japan than their starting point at Guadalcanal.

There were only two suicide attacks during the Iwo Jima fighting, but the Japanese military were taking up the idea of Special Attack forces in a big way. The air force suicide pilots had become known as Kamikaze, meaning Divine Wind, a name taken from the legend of the Shinto God Ise who saved Japan in August 1281 by raising a typhoon which dispersed an invasion fleet of 3500 ships sent from China by Kublai Khan. Kamikazes had inspired the sacrificial yearnings of Japanese youth, and training schools for Kamikaze pilots were established in Formosa. They were instructed by surviving veterans of past battles who were being held back to take part in the final battle in defence of the homeland.

Recruits for the Special Attack formations were mostly straight from college, and their training concentrated on taking off and flying in formation. Proficiency in landing was considered unnecessary.

The naval air force was developing another kind of suicide mission, the Jinrai Butai (Divine Thunderbolt) Corps of human bombs. Its recruits needed little flying skill, and their equipment was economical. They flew in rocket-boosted wooden Okha gliders packed with 1800 kilos of explosives, slung under bombers and released at a height of 7000 feet outside the range of enemy gunfire to glide into enemy ships.

Other branches of the armed forces were also vying for a share of the glory. The submarine service, whose midget subs and manned torpedoes had always been little short of suicidal, developed a Kaiten (the Turn

Towards Heaven) Corps whose role was to stay with torpedoes to ensure they hit enemy ships. Eighty of them died in attacks on Allied shipping in waters around their homeland. The underwater service was also developing huge 3500-ton submarine aircraft carriers, each capable of carrying three torpedo bombers, intended for a suicidal attempt to destroy the Panama Canal in the autumn of 1945. The Navy was also forming squadrons of suicide motorboats – Shinyo Squadrons – for use against invasion ships.

In April 1945, the American advance reached Okinawa, only 340 miles from Japan, the first island regarded by the Japanese as a part of their country.

The Japanese were determined to make Okinawa an object lesson in the price the Americans would pay in blood if they dared to invade Japan. They decided to put the pride of the Imperial Japanese Navy, the super-battleship *Yamato*, at the head of a Special Attack Force. The 71,699-ton *Yamato* was the world's biggest battleship, first of seven secret superships ordered in 1934 to outmatch the US Navy, reckoned to be limited to ships of less than 63,000 tons in order to pass through the Panama Canal. The *Yamato*, commissioned ten days after the attacks on Pearl Harbor and the sinking of the *Prince of Wales* made battleships obsolete, had survived three years of war without firing her nine 18.1-inch guns in action, although she had suffered a torpedo hit and bomb hits on the fringes of the major naval battles. Her sister ship, *Musashi*, had been lost in the Battle of Leyte Gulf after being hit by twenty torpedoes and seventeen bombs. The third supership was converted into an aircraft carrier while still under construction, and was sunk on her maiden voyage by four torpedo hits from the US submarine *Anchorfish*. Orders for the remaining four superships were cancelled.

As the American invasion fleet of 1300 ships carrying 183,000 men assembled off Okinawa, the *Yamato* sailed with an escort of one cruiser and eight destroyers, intending to run ashore off the invasion beaches and blaze away with her massive guns until her last shell was fired. But long before the *Yamato* and the other ships in this suicide armada reached Okinawa they were caught up in what was to be the last naval action of the war, the Battle of the East China Sea.

As the *Yamato* raced towards Okinawa at twenty-seven knots, burning up the Japanese Navy's last fuel reserves – enough for only a one-way trip – she and her escorts were attacked by 380 American carrier planes. The *Yamato* was hit by at least eleven torpedoes and eight heavy bombs, and sunk. The cruiser and four destroyers were also sunk, leaving four destroyers to limp home with 269 survivors picked up from waters in which more than 4250 Japanese sailors died. The Americans lost ten planes and twelve men.

Despite the Kamikaze plane attacks American warships – unlike at the eighty-ship invasion of Guadalcanal – stayed off the landing beaches to give support throughout the battle. They were subjected to ten mass attacks by a total of 353 Kamikazes and Okhas in which sixteen ships were sunk and 185 damaged, including ten battleships and five cruisers. The American flagship *Bunker Hill* was hit by two Kamikazes in quick succession, killing 396 of her crew. Nearly 5000 sailors were killed and about the same number wounded.

Although hundreds of conventional air attacks were also made, 80 per cent of the damage was credited to suiciders. The Americans lost 763 planes.

All told the capture of Okinawa, last island in the chain leading to Japan, was the costliest of the Pacific War. The Americans lost 12,500 dead, including the commanding general, Simon Bruckner, and 36,500 wounded. More than 110,000 Japanese were killed, including 30,000 civilian home guards.

The British Pacific Fleet played a fringe role. Its two battleships, four carriers, six cruisers and fifteen destroyers operated as Task Force 57 with the American Third Fleet. Its task was to blast airfields in the Sakishima Islands and Formosa to prevent their use as staging posts for Japanese aircraft reinforcements transferred from China to Okinawa. The carriers flew 5335 sorties around the clock to drop 1000 tons of bombs, and battleships and cruisers went close inshore to bombard targets. British losses were eighty-five killed or missing, eighty-three wounded, 160 aircraft lost.

A Kamikaze crash dived into the flight deck of the *Indefatigable*, but the wreckage was cleared up and flying operations resumed after quick drying cement was used to level dents in the steel, crash-proof flight deck. The destroyer *Ulster* was hit and badly damaged. Another Kamikaze was shot to pieces by the *Illustrious*'s Bofors guns 300 yards away, throwing debris over the flight deck.

While Britain was celebrating VE-Day, the British ships were engaged in furious battle with Kamikazes. *Victorious* was hit by a Zeke carrying a 250-kilo bomb which holed the flight deck, and soon afterwards another Kamikaze scored a glancing blow after flying through withering fire to slither across the flight deck and over the side. A third Zeke was shot down in the sea. A fourth dived through heavy fire onto aircraft parked on *Formidable*'s flight deck, destroying nineteen of them. But the debris was cleared away and *Formidable* was taking on aircraft within an hour.

British carriers stood up to Kamikaze attacks better than American carriers because of their armoured flight decks. They also carried Japanese-speaking officers to give early warnings of attack by listening into radio orders from the Kamikaze command planes – known as Gestapo planes – which shepherded the inexperienced suicide pilots, assigned them their targets, and then went home to report.

9

The determination of the Japanese to fight to the death rather than be captured faced the fighting men of the Allied nations with a daunting prospect even before the development of Kamikaze tactics. As General Slim, commander of the 14th Army in Burma, remarked, 'Everyone talks of fighting to the last man and the last round, but only the Japanese actually do it.' This reputation gave the Japanese a psychological advantage over soldiers from other lands who clung to the hope that they would have the luck to survive even the heaviest actions. They saw the Japanese first as invincible jungle fighters, then as cruel demons, members of a race apart, disciples of the devilish Bushido creed. Yet this also forced Allied troops to develop a fanatical fighting spirit of their own out of the belief that they would be tortured or shot if they surrendered.

In fact, the feudal order of *samurai*, whose members practised the ancient Bushido code, had been officially abolished in Japan nearly seventy-five years before the war. However, its code of 'death before dishonour' had been preserved in the officer corps, soldiers chanted 'our highest hope is to die for the Emperor' until it became an obsession. At the start of the war with the West the Prime Minister, General Tojo, incorporated *samurai* ideals in a soldier's code called the Senjinkun. This laid down that it was shameful for a soldier to try to prolong his life by surrendering and becoming a prisoner-of-war. His duty was to fight on until he was killed or otherwise kill himself.

These attitudes were shared by politicians. Japan had declined to ratify the Geneva Convention on the treatment of prisoners-of-war, and Allied fighting men who fell into their hands were treated with contempt as creatures unworthy of consideration.

The military code gave officers the right to order suicidal Banzai (human bullet) charges, and allowed commanding officers to suggest suicide to subordinates to atone for failure, suggestions usually taken as an order. A written Japanese order, captured in Luzon, gave instructions for the wounded to stay at their positions and fight on, and for unit commanders to ensure that those unable to do so ended their own lives.

Members of the armed forces were indoctrinated with the belief that those who died for the Emperor, the descendent of Amaterasu Omikami, the Sun Goddess who founded Japan, would themselves join the Gods. Ceremonies were held every six months at the Yasakuni army shrine in Tokyo to deify the fallen whose names were placed in an ark. Many soldiers attended their own funeral rites before leaving for the battle zones as a public demonstration of their determination to die for the Emperor.

The life of a Japanese soldier was likened to the cherry blossom, regarded as a symbol of purity, loyalty and patriotism, but short-lived. It was assumed that all were equally brave, so no awards were made for gallantry or exceptional bravery. The only medals struck were for campaigns or long and distinguished service.

At the same time, the military authorities catered to the human frailties of their troops by supplying official groups of camp-following prostitutes, and officers sometimes turned a blind eye to rape. Japanese soldiers, individually, were men of flesh and blood with similar human emotions to those of their enemies. Their officers complained that they chattered on jungle patrols, and map-reading by officers and NCOs was said to be lamentable. It seems not all Japanese lived up to the legend of invincible jungle fighters. Coordination between artillery and infantry was often poor, but they achieved great accuracy with artillery, mortars and air bombing. Their readiness to take foolhardy risks often came off.

An Australian captured in Malaya, Kenneth Harrison, had this to say in his book *The Brave Japanese*: 'I have seen Japanese afraid on many an occasion, but of one thing I have no doubt – in a position where he is fighting for his country and his Emperor the Japanese would fight till he died. I was given the privilege of fighting against possibly the bravest soldiers of all time.'

Throughout the war, only 16,500 prisoners were taken by the Allies, and one third of these were Koreans or Formosans. Those who found themselves taken alive, often courted death. Forty-eight were killed in a riot at a prison camp in New Zealand, and at Cowra Camp in New South Wales 234 were shot when a thousand prisoners rioted.

One of the rare exceptions was a Japanese captain who was captured by British commandos at Ru-ywa, Burma. Before being flown to a prison camp in India he wrote a thank-you letter to his guards whose 'kindness, cheerfulness, philanthropy and love of peace' had made him change his mind about committing suicide at the first opportunity. He added, 'I believe that if all Japanese people knew your real intentions they would stop war without delay and with grace.'

The unique Japanese attitude to death was repeatedly demonstrated. Whole garrisons fought to the death on island redoubts across the Pacific and in the jungles of Burma. Doomed remnants committed mass suicide in hopeless Banzai charges, pilots of crippled planes rammed enemy fighters and sometimes crashed into enemy ships. Even today, capital punishment is not a public issue in Japan. Executions are carried out, as they always have been, in secret. Relatives are only notified afterwards, and no official records are made public.

So it was a logical step to formalize the Japanese attitude to death in large-scale premeditated suicide attacks to make maximum use of dwindling numbers of aircraft and inadequate pilot training facilities. One man in one plane, even an old plane hardly serviceable for normal combat, flown by a novice pilot had a good chance of sinking or gravely damaging an enemy ship and causing hundreds of casualties.

One of the few veteran pilots who dissented on grounds of conscience was the flying ace, Sakai Saburo, who had lost an eye over Guadalcanal in 1942. During the battle for Iwo Jima he was ordered to lead a formation of eight Kamikaze planes against targets in Saipan. Five of the formation were shot down by American Hellcat fighters fifty miles from Saipan, but he evaded pursuit and continued with the remaining two planes towards their targets, only to be thwarted by bad weather and forced to return to their base in Iwo Jima. There, Saburo told his commander of his objection to Kamikaze operations, and was posted back to Japan to spend the rest of the war as a flying instructor. Later he wrote about his reasons, 'I appreciated better than most the wisdom of relying upon my own strength and my own skill to escape death, which in a dog-fight was never more than a split second away . . . a *samurai* lives in such a way that he will always be prepared to die. . . . However, there is a great gulf between deliberately taking one's life and entering battle with a willingness to accept all risks.'

Vice-Admiral C.R. Brown of the US Navy believed that Kamikaze tactics were conceived too late to stay the inevitable defeat of Japan. He described his own hypnotic fascination watching attacks by Kamikazes, 'with the detached horror of a terrible spectacle rather than as an intended victim.' He viewed the suicide pilots with a strange mixture of respect and pity.

The difference in heroism on the opposing sides was fundamental – the Japanese Kamikaze was given no hope of escape, Allied fighting men always had hope, if sometimes only a slim one, of survival.

The attitude of Kamikazes themselves was often poetic, as though they thought of themselves, in the words of Admiral Ohnishi, as 'Gods without earthly desires'. Ohnishi was himself a poet and wrote this poem about life:

> In blossom today, then scattered
> Life is so like a delicate flower.
> How can one expect fragrance to last for ever?

One Kamikaze pilot wrote to his father before his last take-off, 'During my final plunge, though you will not hear it, you may be sure I shall be saying 'chichiue' [revered father] to you and thinking of all you have done for me.'

Another wrote, 'The world in which I lived was full of discord. As a community of rational beings it should have been better composed. Lacking a single great conductor, everyone let loose with his own sound, creating dissonance where there should have been melody and harmony.'

They were among the best educated of Japan's youth, hastily trained and posted to Kamikaze units. One wrote home before leaving for Okinawa, 'I was selected quite unexpectedly to be a special attack pilot. Once the order was given for my one-way mission it became my sincere wish to achieve success in fulfilling this last duty.' Another wrote to his parents before taking off on his last flight, 'I wish I could be born seven times, each time to smite the enemy.'

Rarely before had men been sent to certain death in such an organized, premeditated way, trained in a tactic that left them no chance of survival. The Kamikaze motto was 'We die for the great cause of our country.' Few questioned their orders. Their greatest concern was to be sure of hitting their target and taking many of the enemy with them in their funeral pyre.

The military chiefs in Tokyo, who sent these college boys to die, were themselves ready to die rather than surrender. Many were to do so. They blamed Germany's unconditional surrender at the height of the battle for Okinawa on lack of a Bushido spirit. As the war swept inexorably closer to the Home Islands they began calling for 100 million Japanese to die defiantly in a final mass banzai.

PART TWO
Operation Zipper

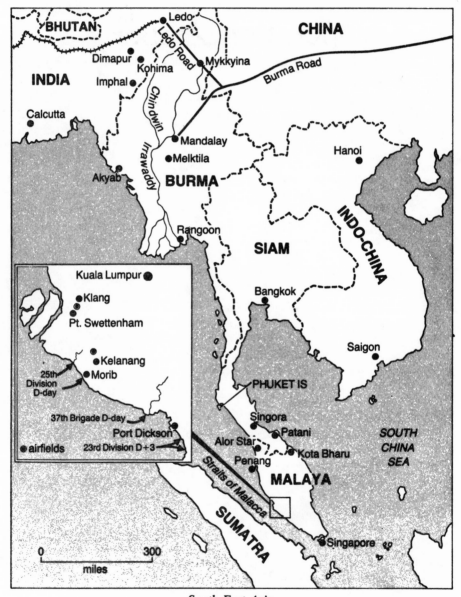

South-East Asia

1

Allied hopes of finishing the war in Europe by the end of 1944 were thwarted in September by the failure of the Arnhem airborne attempt to open a way for an armoured push into the North German plain. Allied forces were further bogged down by flooded rivers and an early onset of winter – although these conditions failed to deter the Germans from their damaging offensive in the Ardennes in December. These setbacks delayed the transfer of men and equipment to the Far East.

Soon after the Normandy landings the Chiefs of Staff decided to keep intact six of the nine Beach Groups used in them for operations in the east, but when Mountbatten asked for two experienced Beach Groups to be earmarked for operations in SEAC early in 1945 he was told they could not be made available until after Germany's defeat. Beach Groups comprised about 2500 men from all three services, and each was able to move about 1000 tons of stores a day over an invasion beach. Instead Mountbatten merged five small Beach Groups in India, capable of moving 500 tons a day, into two Beach Groups with 1000-ton capability.

Further delays in mustering a SEAC amphibious force came when disaster hit one of the first substantial transfers of landing craft after hasty modifications for tropical conditions. Merchant ships, towing a landing craft on each beam, left the Clyde on Friday, 13 October 1944 despite gale warnings. Threequarters of the landing craft were lost in the Bay of Biscay along with many crew members.

Later landing craft were made more seaworthy and were ordered to wait for fine weather before heading for Gibraltar and the east. Most were carried in landing ships. They were of many types, carrying from twenty-five to 250 men and every type of equipment. Some were capable of firing 1000 rockets at a time.

It was the spring of 1945 before SEAC was able at last to build up a substantial amphibious capability. By this time the Japanese had been driven out of northern Burma, and Mountbatten had moved his headquarters from landlocked Delhi to the island of Ceylon, signifying his release from the slogging overland strategy forced on him by limited resources. He took over the summer residence of the colonial governor in the cool hills of Peredynia, near Kandy, and in this tropical paradise assembled a staff of around 7000. His large glittering court included scores of pretty women in uniform. It was a world apart from the grim jungle battles and ships at action stations.

The Supreme Commander was forty-three years old, a comparative youthfulness that had barred his promotion to the rank of full admiral which would normally have gone with the job. His acting rank was on the insistence of the chairman of the Chiefs of Staff, Admiral Sir Dudley Pound, who argued that the average age of the army, navy and air commanders-in-chief under him was fifty-seven.

Even so the naval commander-in-chief, Admiral Somerville, showed his resentment at Mountbatten's preferment by barring the Supreme Commander from visiting his ships, and, when eventually Mountbatten's good-natured tolerance wore thin, they had a blazing row. Soon afterwards the crusty old Admiral was posted to a liaison job in Washington, where his bluff quarter-deck manner went down well with Admiral King and his senior officers.

Another High Command personality problem, which Mountbatten tackled with what the historian Ronald Lewin described as 'imperious and self-confident authority', arose from an insensitive gaffe by the Allied Land Forces Commander, General Oliver Leese. He decided to 'rest' the popular General Slim from command of his victorious 14th Army for the new phase of large-scale amphibious operations. Leese replaced Slim with General Sir Philip Christison, chosen because he had the advantage of experience in amphibious operations. Leese was apparently unaware that Slim had won a prize for a paper on amphibious operations years before. When Mountbatten intervened, Slim stayed with the 14th Army until taking over Leese's job as Allied Land Forces Commander a few months later, and Christison took command of the new 12th Army to complete mopping up Japanese remnants in southern Burma.

When victory was assured in Europe, Churchill became increasingly impatient for British forces to play a more spectacular role in the war against Japan. He believed the only prize that would restore British standing in the Far East would be the recapture of Singapore, and he told the Americans that 'a grievous and shameful blow to British prestige must be avenged in battle'. Despite the fact that more Japanese were killed in Burma than in any other campaign, the achievements of the 14th Army had been overshadowed by the culminating events in Europe and the speed with which the Americans had carried the war to Japan. The 14th Army was known as the Forgotten Army, a name first coined by the *News Chronicle* correspondent Stuart Emery in an article about its low rating for supplies, and a postwar book about the British naval effort against Japan carried the title *The Forgotten Fleet*.

As more ships and fighting units arrived in SEAC's bases in India and Ceylon, Churchill was impatient to get them into action, and he put forward his long-cherished plan for an amphibious assault on northern Sumatra once more. But with the promise of adequate resources at last, Mountbatten and his SEAC planners were not to be diverted from a bolder concept – a full-scale landing directly on the Malay peninsula as a prelude to an assault before the end of the year on Singapore itself, still the core of Japanese power outside Japan. In February 1945, the Combined Chiefs of Staff gave the go-ahead with a formal order to Mountbatten to complete the liberation of Burma as soon as possible, and then proceed to liberate Malaya and open up the Straits of Malacca.

The SEAC planners drew up a blueprint for a three-stage operation. The first stage was to be the capture of Phuket Island on the western side of the narrow Isthmus of Kra, where the frontiers of Thailand, Malaya and Burma converge. It was needed as a forward base for small ships and for airfields from which fighter planes could give cover for the main invasion across beaches half way down Malaya's west coast. This operation was to be carried out in late April or early May before the onset of Monsoon rains.

The main landing by nearly 200,000 men was to take place in October on beaches in the Port Swettenham–Port Dickson area, 200 miles north of Singapore. These forces would drive south to the Johore Straits to begin the third stage in December, the assault on Singapore.

The operations against Singapore were expected to last till March 1946, and would require reinforcements of men and weaponry from Europe, where at that time German resistance was expected to end by July.

On 15 May, exactly a week after the German surrender, the SEAC staff produced a study as a basis for the allocation of resources and a guide to detailed planning. This said that the beaches at Port Dickson and Port Swettenham were the only ones on the west coast of Malaya thought to be suitable for the quick discharge of vehicles, and they would also provide for a more speedy advance on the Johore Strait than bridgeheads even nearer Singapore.

The best beaches for an assault and for the continued maintenance of a large force stretched for some four and a half miles between Cape Rachado and Port Dickson, and another stretch of some five miles between Morib and Kg Bagan Island. Of the two, the beaches nearer Port Dickson were better, having firm sand and good exits. The Port Swettenham beaches seemed to have mud mixed with sand and generally unsatisfactory exits.

They suggested two alternatives. The first was simultaneous landings by one division over the Morib beaches to secure the air strips at Kelanang and Port Swettenham, and by another division over the Port Dickson beaches to secure Seremban. Both these forces were to be supported by armour. A third division would follow over either beach to secure Kuala Lumpur, the Malay capital.

The second was a two-division assault on Morib beach, supported by armour, to secure the two airfields and Kuala Lumpur with a follow-up division crossing the same beaches to secure Port Dickson and Serembang.

The planning staff favoured the second suggestion on strategic and tactical grounds but expressed doubt about the suitability of the Morib beaches for landings and subsequent maintenance of three divisions. They said that unless these doubts about the Morib beaches could be allayed it would be preferable to use the more suitable beaches at Port Dickson.

They thought that naval opposition would be negligible and that the Japanese had only about 150 serviceable warplanes in the area. They estimated Japanese army strength in Malaya at three divisions with nine battalions on Singapore island. Opposition to the D-Day landings might be as little as one battalion if surprise was achieved. They recommended an early advance from the bridgehead along main inland and coastal roads.

The American Chiefs of Staff had baulked at approving the plans when they considered them on 6 April, fearing that allocations of shipping might interfere with the 'main operations' against Japan. But after studying the detailed recommendations on 16 May, they approved them with the proviso that the release of resources must not hazard the timetable for the invasion of the southern Japanese island of Kyushu in November.

The first practical setback came from overanxiety that the onset of the next monsoon might bog down the 14th Army short of the key supply port of Rangoon. Until its capture the advance depended on 7000 air drops a day, and these had been maintained on critical margins since the withdrawal of seventy-five Dakota transports to the China air lift on the eve of the Battle of Mandalay. The remaining air crews, mostly Americans (the Hollywood actor Jackie Coogan among them), were having to fly beyond the danger point for men and machines to do so.

The army's overland advance had been accompanied down the Arakan coastal mangrove swamps by a series of small amphibious assaults – known as the Chaung War – in a motley collection of small naval craft, augmented by 500 makeshift boats the army made for themselves by felling teak trees.

Mountbatten decided to make sure of Rangoon's capture by mounting an amphibious assault codenamed Modified Dracula, a smaller version of the operation he had wanted to carry out a year earlier in preference to the overland slog. It was carried out by the most powerful amphibious force yet assembled in SEAC, two battleships, four cruisers, two aircraft carriers, five destroyers. Paratroops were dropped, shore defences were bombarded from the sea, and assault troops went in only to find that the

Japanese had already left. They had fled to avoid being cut off by the rapid advance of the 14th Army, which had covered 300 miles in twenty-six days. The pilot of a RAF Mosquito had already landed to check on a signal saying 'Extract Digit' which British internees had put on the roof of their prison. By then it was too late to call off the assault.

It meant that the ships and landing craft, for what turned out to be an unnecessary operation, could not be ready for the attack on Phuket Island at the time required, and Mountbatten was faced with putting off the Malaya assaults for six weeks.

He had also been rebuffed in a new argument for support from carriers of the British Pacific Fleet. He asked the Chiefs of Staff to arrange for them to sail into the Gulf of Siam to provide additional air cover from the opposite side of the Kra Isthmus during the ten days it was likely to take to capture and operate the airfields ashore. He was told curtly that there was no justification for diverting any part of the British Pacific Fleet from the main operations against Japan.

Meanwhile, the fall of Rangoon had been almost completely overshadowed by the German collapse in Europe. But with resources from Europe now assured, Mountbatten's planners recommended two major changes in the Malayan operations. The first was for the main invasion, Operation Zipper, to go ahead without the preliminary capture of Phuket Island, and the other was for D-Day to be brought forward from October to August.

The earlier date accorded with Mountbatten's wish to maintain the initiative and give the Japanese no time to recover from their defeat in Burma, so he readily accepted the additional hazards involved in making the landings without an advanced naval and air base. This meant that landing ships would have to sail to the assault beaches directly from India, and the initial assault would have no land-based fighter support. Mountbatten also decided to go ahead with the forces already at his disposal without waiting for reinforcements from Europe, provided he could be assured of the shipping, landing craft and carrier-borne air cover.

Mountbatten's decision to accept these risks was based on his understanding that four light carriers, released from the Atlantic war, would be joining the East Indies Fleet in time for Zipper. Once again his command's low priority was to be bitterly rubbed in. The commander of the British Pacific Fleet had asked for these four carriers to fill the gap while the *Indefatigable*, *Formidable*, *Victorious* and *Illustrious* were having the damage inflicted by Kamikaze attacks repaired. Then he made a case for holding on to them to strengthen his air cover for operations in Japanese waters.

Mountbatten fought hard to get them back, but he argued in vain that the success of the Zipper landings depended on the air cover the four carriers would provide. Instead he was told to make do with an additional escort carrier, giving him a total of nine. These were slower and less effective than light fleet carriers; some of them were converted banana boats fitted with a flight deck. Two general purpose escort carriers were also offered for use as ferries to take Spitfires from Ceylon to operate from captured airfields. These were already en route to the Pacific.

On 18 May Mountbatten swallowed his rage, and agreed to undertake Zipper with these forces. But he warned the Chiefs of Staff that the withdrawal of the original carriers would seriously reduce his ability to neutralize enemy air bases before the assault, adding that he would 'be grateful for any further help' that could be furnished.

To add to his anxieties, it also became clear that there would be no time before the monsoon to establish adequate all-weather bomber bases in southern Burma to support the Zipper landings. Instead he might have to rely on bombing support from newly established air bases in the Cocos Islands, two small atolls in the Indian Ocean 1000 miles southwest of Singapore. Throughout their domination of the area, the Japanese had seemed unaware of the small British garrison discreetly maintained there, and Cocos had been developed as a staging airfield between Ceylon and Australia. Two squadrons of heavy bombers were to be operational there in time for the Zipper landings, augmented by two more in time for the assault on Singapore.

By this time, Australian forces had invaded Borneo, and RAAF squadrons, equipped with Liberators, Mitchells, Beaufighters and Mosquitoes, were to join the bombardment of Japanese positions defending Singapore from airfields captured there.

Meanwhile, preparations were well in hand to use Rangoon as an advanced supply base for Zipper. In the first week after its fall, stores were landed at a rate of 1200 tons a day, and this had reached 2000 tons daily by the end of May when five deep-water berths and lightering pontoons had been put back into service. Priority was given to stockpiling sufficient stores to supply seven army divisions and an RAF group for forty-five days. The port also handled 50,000 tons of civilian relief supplies, and stores for the 12th Army, which was engaged in bitter fighting throughout June as the last Japanese army tried to break out towards Thailand.

Commanders for the various forces to take part in Zipper were appointed, and ordered to have a detailed joint plan for landings in the second half of August. They were General O.D. Roberts, commanding 34 Corps, Rear-Admiral B.C.S. Martin, Flag Officer of Force 'W', the assault ships and landings craft, and Air Vice-Marshal Earl Bandon, commanding 224 Group, RAF.

Mountbatten called them together in Delhi on 30 May to decide on a firm date for D-Day. Admiral Martin reported that tides would be suitable on only two dates, 27 August and 9 September. The Navy preferred 27

August because a landing on 9 September would have to be made before dawn to gain most advantage from the tide. Lord Bandon said the RAF could be ready for 27 August, and the Directorate of Shipping Transport in India said that shipping could be ready. But General Roberts argued for the later date, 9 September. He said some army units had to be re-formed because of demobilization, troops of the 5th Division being withdrawn from the Burma fighting would need more respite, and the 50th Tank Brigade had to come from the Middle East.

They decided that D-Day for Operation Zipper would be 9 September. General Roberts' 34 Corps was to be in control of both Zipper landings and the assault on Singapore, codenamed Mailfist. Three divisions of 15 Corps would begin to move through the bridgehead on D50 to reinforce the assault on Singapore, bringing the strength of the 14th Army in Malaya to two corps, totalling seven divisions and three armoured brigades.

The Chiefs of Staff approved the D-Day date, adding that they attached the utmost importance to the earliest recapture of Singapore. They also said that the shipping being made available was the absolute maximum and could not be augmented, and warned that any delay in launching Zipper would conflict with preparations for the first landing in Japan and probably lead to a reduction.

2

Shortly after Mountbatten had reluctantly accepted the army's need to put off the Zipper D-Day to 9 September, a stunning new problem arose that threatened a much longer postponement. It began with a statement in the House of Commons, whose members were soon to face the electorate for the first time since before the war. The resignation of the Labour leader, Clement Attlee, from the coalition government had resulted in a general election being called for 26 July, and until then Churchill was presiding over a Conservative caretaker government. This was yet another indication of how national unity fell apart after VE-Day.

On the eve of a debate on welfare, leave and 'Python' – the scheme for returning men to civilian life – the Secretary for War, Sir James Grigg, decided to court popularity for the government by announcing a speed-up in demobilization. Grigg gave Mountbatten barely forty-eight hours advance warning of this vote-catching move, which threatened to hamstring the combat effectiveness of many key formations in the Zipper order of battle.

The period of service qualifying for repatriation and demobilization had already been reduced from five years to three years and eight months, and this was being further reduced to three years and four months. One third of the men in SEAC came into this new category, including many of the most experienced troops and a high proportion of NCOs.

It meant that they were entitled to be released from fighting units and sent home as soon as transport became available, without awaiting replacements. 'Repat and demob' was already a delicate issue in SEAC, where many soldiers had served four or five years without the home leave enjoyed by men on most other fronts. They read of unfaithfulness by service wives, and saw pictures in their months' old newspapers of English girls with Italian POWs. Letters were late and irregular, making strangers of their own families and girlfriends. Demob was such an obsession that men identified themselves by length of service as in 'I'm a three and ten man', meaning he had served three years and ten months. Their *élan* began to fade as their turn for demob approached.

Grigg apologized to Mountbatten for the short notice, which he excused on the grounds that the debate in Parliament had been hurriedly called, as he said, 'no doubt for electioneering purposes'. He said he accepted that it would be necessary in individual cases, particularly of officers and specialists, to retain some men until replacements arrived, but he hoped these exceptions would not be very frequent. He added the pious hope that the effects would be 'no more than inconvenient'.

Mountbatten described this development as 'military insanity', and signalled London that far from causing some inconvenience it made it likely that Zipper and Mailfist would have to be postponed yet again. He asked for India Command and SEAC to be allowed to make the releases gradually to fit operational necessity.

The change was to make 33,000 men immediately eligible to join the already crowded transit camps in India, where men who had already served much longer were still waiting for a place in crowded troopships home. A further 60,000 would become eligible by the end of the year.

However, Python did not affect the volunteer soldiers of the Indian Army on whom the imperial Britain relied so heavily as a source of manpower. Between the outbreak of war in Europe and the Japanese aggressions, India had vastly increased its army and launched an immense programme of war production. The official history, *War Against Japan*, acknowledges this in a succinct tribute: 'Without these great efforts the British Commonwealth would have been hard put to survive the Japanese onslaught.' The Indian Army expanded from 180,000 men in 1939 to 2½ million in 1945, and despite conflicting loyalties with an Indian National Army of former POWs fighting irresolutely on the Japanese side, the British Indian Army won twenty of the twenty-seven VCs awarded during the Burma campaign.

The commander-in-chief in India, General Sir Claude Auchinleck, warned Grigg that the new releases would mean the number of men awaiting repatriation would far exceed the transport capacity available. He added that Parliament should be told the truth so that complaints could be avoided.

The SEAC land forces commander, General Leese, warned Grigg that wholesale use of the operational necessity clause, excluding the release of men with special skills, would have to be made if Zipper was not to be postponed for several months. The RAF also protested that their contribution to Zipper and Mailfist would be seriously affected.

Mountbatten told the Chiefs of Staff that any extensive use of the operational necessity clause or any other qualifications of the promise Grigg was making would have a disastrous effect on morale. He added bitterly, 'I regret it is beyond our power to exploit our recent victories, if, so far from receiving reinforcements now that the war in Europe is finished, we are instructed to return without relief . . . one third of the British officers and other ranks in this command and in India command, including the most experienced of these, before Zipper has started.'

Units in Burma would have to be milked so heavily to make up Zipper formations that operations there would be hampered and the build-up of the Rangoon stockpile slowed down. There would be no time to train replacements and units would have to go into battle with untried troops. The most serious shortage would be in medium artillery, but engineers, signals and landing craft units would also be drastically reduced.

Even so, the men withdrawn from units would still not get home, but would have to wait in transit camps in India for months, with 'dangers of highly dangerous developments from frustration', meaning mutiny.

Mountbatten signalled the Chiefs of Staff that it was absolutely essential for a public announcement in London accepting responsibility for exemptions from Python for men whose services had to be retained for pending operations. But Grigg still refused to make a statement himself, though he agreed to a joint statement by Mountbatten and Auchinleck warning of delays in transport home and the need to keep some key men in fighting units. They told the forces frankly, 'Either we can continue aggressive operations that will hasten the end of the war against Japan or we can devote the whole of our transportation facilities to sending you home immediately your three years, four months service is completed. Unfortunately, it is not possible to do both.'

Mountbatten also informed the Defence Committee in London that the balance of forces had deteriorated against him since the Zipper Plans had been drawn up. The Japanese had reinforced their numbers in Malaya while his forces had been reduced in numbers and efficiency because of demobilization requirements. The estimate of Japanese troops available to oppose the Zipper invasion had been raised from 52,000 to 86,000, and they had been told to hold Singapore at all costs. This meant that the invasion forces numerical superiority was now reduced to 8 to 5, and experience had shown that a superiority of 3 to 1 was necessary against fresh and full-strength Japanese formations.

He also made another plea for the return of the four light carriers he had lost to the British Pacific Fleet, mentioning his anxiety over Kamikaze attacks against the invasion convoys in the narrow confines of the Malacca Straits. But the Admiralty said there would be no time for them to support Zipper and be back with the Pacific Fleet for their role in the landings on Kyushu in November.

While this wrangling went on for many weeks, preparations continued to launch Zipper with a force reduced from seven divisions to six. The available divisions would also be weakened by the withdrawal of men due for repatriation before the end of the year.

3

At first the Japanese made some good guesses about British intentions. The commander of the Seventh Area Army, General K. Doihara, who was responsible for the Japanese forces in Malaya, the Andaman and Nicobar Islands, Sumatra, Java and Borneo, made his early dispositions in the expectation that the British offensive would open with an attempt to capture the Andaman and Nicobar Islands. At the end of 1944 this assessment was changed to face an amphibious attack against the Kra Isthmus. The assumed objective was the capture of airfields from which bombers could disrupt reinforcement routes from Thailand to Burma, particularly the railway extension built by prisoners of war. To meet this threat they reinforced their strength in Malaya and Singapore by withdrawing troops from what they called the North Australian Front and Indo-China.

After the fall of Rangoon this assessment was updated again. The new expectation was a bombing offensive against the Kra Isthmus and Malaya with the object of disrupting communications as a preliminary to amphibious landings on Phuket Island, off the Kra Isthmus, and the northern tip of Sumatra, thus obtaining command of both flanks of the entrance to the Malacca Straits. They calculated that the main assault would be a four- or five-division invasion in the Alor Star-Penang area of northern Malaya, but that it would not come before the monsoon ended in October.

They saw the objective of the landings in northern Malaya as the capture of airfields as a preliminary to further operations. These, they calculated, would include further large-scale landings by from three to six divisions between Port Swettenham and Port Dickson, followed by an advance towards the Johore Strait and an assault on Singapore.

By July 1945 they had revised the time scale, bringing the expected date for the initial invasion forward from November to September. They also now anticipated a simultaneous Australian assault from Borneo on the east coast of Malaya. To meet this threat they transferred a division to Malaya from Thailand, and transferred 5000 troops from Timor to Singapore. Anti-aircraft batteries and searchlight companies also moved to

Singapore from Sumatra. Other plans to withdraw troops from outlying garrisons to Malaya were thwarted by the sinking of two cruisers by the Royal Navy. Other measures included the regrouping of 1000 troops who had managed to escape from Burma, and surplus air force personnel and training instructors were drafted into new mechanized formations. A new tank battalion was also formed from men already in Malaya. Airfield defence units were also diverted to an ordinary infantry role, an indication of how much their air power had dwindled.

Six divisions were under orders to put up a resolute defence of the Andaman and Nicobar Islands, northern Sumatra and road and rail communications between Siam and Singapore. Resolute defence in Japanese parlance meant that every man was to fight to the death.

By the end of May 1945 the pressure which the British were putting on under the deception plan Operation Slippery had convinced the Japanese that the invasion would come in the Alor Star area in Malaya's most northerly state of Kedah. General Doihara ordered dispositions for the main defence to be prepared along a line through the Gurun Hills south of Alor Star. Fortifications were built, and three huge dumps were established to hold stocks of rice and ammunition sufficient for two years. He concentrated the bulk of Japanese forces outside Singapore – some 26,000 men – on this defence line 300 miles north of the Zipper beaches. To meet the Zipper invasion they would have to be moved along either a single main road or a railway, both winding through jungled hills where guerrilla forces directed by agents of Force 136 were expected to be able to block all movement for the vital days it would take to establish a secure bridgehead.

The British hoped to draw large numbers of the 77,000 fighting troops in the Singapore area northwards so that they could be cut off by amphibious leapfrog advances down the coast – tactics the Japanese had successfully employed three years before.

Unknown to British intelligence, working parties of prisoners-of-war from Changi had been transferred to work camps in Johore to excavate tunnel systems deep into hillsides and build other formidable fortifications. Other prisoners were at work on a new runway on Singapore island.

The Japanese were preparing to make their last stand in South-East Asia last a long time.

4

The Joint Force Commanders opted against using the most suitable beaches at Port Dickson for the D-Day assault. They believed that the Japanese would anticipate landings there because they were the best beaches on the entire west coast of Malaya. They decided to send the first assault waves into the Morib beaches, twenty miles higher up the coastline, although the little that was known about them had already caused doubts about their suitability. The firm beaches at Port Dickson would be used for a second assault three days after the first landings when the defenders would already be fully engaged by forces from the first beachhead. The Port Dickson beaches would then take over as the main landing area for the build-up.

In making their detailed plan to Mountbatten, the Joint Force Commanders said they had insufficient evidence to make an accurate appreciation of what the Japanese tactical reaction to the initial landings was likely to be. They thought serious opposition at that stage was unlikely so long as tactical surprise could be achieved. The chances of this were good because the assault was being made before the end of the monsoon, something which they believed the Japanese would never expect. They reckoned that at worst they would have three Japanese divisions to deal with in Malaya, not counting the garrison in Singapore.

The assault area, designated Area J, covered a seventy-five-mile stretch of coast between Kuala Selangor and Cape Rechado with a hinterland stretching to the Fraser Hills. The D-Day assault troops were to undergo the longest sea passage made by a British invasion force until the Falklands War of 1982. They were to embark at Bombay and sail 1600 miles to land on beaches far down the Malacca Straits with enemy-held coast on both flanks.

Troop transports would have to be off Morib at 3.30 a.m. on D-Day, ready for the first assault to hit the beaches at 6.45 a.m., shortly before dawn. The 25th Indian Division was to go across the northern beaches to take the airfields at Port Swettenham and Kelanang. The 37th Brigade of the 23rd Indian Division would be landing simultaneously at the southern end of the Morib beaches to secure the Sepang road bridge and exploit in the direction of Port Dickson. When these formations had moved clear of the beaches, the 5th division, sailing from Rangoon, would cross the same beaches to clear the road southwards and exploit towards Serembang and Kuala Lumpur.

Close air support would be provided entirely from seven carriers, each with twenty aircraft, but this support would begin to dwindle after the third day and cease altogether after ten days. The early capture of the airfields was essential so that land-based fighters could take over the air support role. Tactical bombing support would also come from heavy bombers flying from distant airfields in the Cocos Islands and southern Burma.

The assault on the northern Morib sector was to be supported by bombardment from a battleship, a cruiser, four destroyers, two sloops and thirteen landing craft. The southern assault would be supported by gunfire from a cruiser, two sloops and eleven landing craft. One battleship would be held in reserve.

The Force Commanders reported that it would also be essential to capture Port Swettenham within forty-eight hours so that the limited tonnages of vehicles and stores landed over the beaches could be rapidly augmented. The logistics were daunting – 182,000 men, 17,700 vehicles, 2250 pack mules and 225,000 tons of supplies and fuel had to arrive on successive dates according to an intricate pattern of requirements over a period of seven weeks. The build-up, mainly in India, occupied 800,000 men for several months. Stores amounted to 1,250,000 tons, keeping 6700 railway wagons in constant use for months. Indian railways were pressed into service, restricting travel for civilians and servicemen due for demobilization. The shuttle back and forth between the supply ports and the beaches involved 112 merchant ships. There were also fifty-eight warships, 366 landing ships and craft, and five hospital ships.

The D-Day assault units were assigned to ships sailing in seven convoys, six from India and Ceylon, one from Rangoon. Some were fast, some slow. All were to assemble with the main naval force at the top of the Malacca Straits and follow minesweepers to their anchorages off the beaches in the early hours of D-Day. The longest voyage by landing craft was to be thirteen days, the shortest, by troopship, nine days. Vehicles had to be put ashore in proper order, loaded with equipment ready for immediate use.

The only information on record about the D-Day beaches at Morib came from a 1928 survey which described them as 'more or less sandy'. Because of their unsuitability it was expected that they would be much less well fortified than the Port Dickson beaches. Efforts to establish more precise knowledge about the condition of the Morib beaches were circumscribed by the overwhelming need to keep the Japanese guessing about just where the landings would be made. No low-level aerial photographs were taken because there were not enough long-range reconnaissance planes available to fly decoy missions to many other beaches as well. High level photographs were taken in February and May. They were taken with infra-red cameras that were supposed to be able to determine the depth of the water.

The first photographs were taken on a reconnaissance of the whole west coast of Malaya on 17 February; they were sent to the Directorate of Military Survey at the War Office in London. Major C.A. Hart said the information was too nebulous and he would hesitate to give definite statements without 'more suitably taken photographs'. With that premise he thought that sand ridges shown in the pictures were not sufficient seriously to impede traffic, but there was a possibility of quicksands as well as silt and mud in standing water and vegetation. The back of the beach appeared firm.

More high level photographs were taken on 26 May, and these were interpreted by Professor J.D. Bernal, of London University, as follows: 'Beaches seem to be of sand. Ridge structures continuing below the water level shown on the photographs would make them very difficult, but passable by most forms of motor transport. It should be possible, however, to avoid them in most cases by following upstream lines, though a certain amount of silt and mud may be met with. The other hazard is the danger of grounding craft on offshore ridges and drowning vehicles.'

An attempt to reconnoitre the beaches, and make a thorough survey of surface conditions ended in disaster in June when two of three two-man specialist survey teams failed to return to the submarine that took them there. Apart from the loss of their reports, fear that they might have been captured and tortured caused immense concern that the all-important factor of security had been blown.

The surveyors were men of a Combined Operations Pilotage Party, one of the many secret specialist organizations. The COPPS teams had chartered the Normandy beach in great detail, helped by many thousands of holiday snaps, brought in by a radio appeal, that covered almost every feature of the European coastline. But in Malaya there were few holiday snaps to study, and the beach itself figured in sparse detail in the 1928 survey of the Morib area.

Only three months before the Morib survey, attempts to reconnoitre Phuket Island* – then planned as the initial phase of the invasion – had gone badly wrong. Survey teams to report on landing beaches and potential airstrips were landed from two submarines, the *Torbay* and

---

* After the war it was found that three of the Phuket Islands surveyors were shot dead in clashes, three survived after capture by Siamese forces, two captured by Japanese patrols were sent to Singapore and shot. The four missing from the Morib survey sought refuge with Chinese guerrillas until the invasion troops came ashore ten weeks later.

Thrasher, but all failed to rendezvous with the submarines which waited around for a week, and eight men were reported missing.

Because of that, the Morib surveyors were ordered to play things with maximum caution and not to venture as far as the top of the beaches. Despite that only one of the survey teams returned to report. The surviving team went back next night in the hope of finding the missing teams and to try to complete the survey. They failed to find their comrades, but brought back tests which showed that mud lay only eight inches below the surface sand, but this was passed over lightly by the naval officers making the intelligence appreciation of all the findings. They reported to the operational commanders that the texture of the beach was firm sand between high and low water marks, with firm bottom fifty yards below low water. However, they did add a cautious proviso. 'The general unsuitability of these beaches makes it desirable that they should be closed as soon as possible after D plus 22.'

The need for surprise was evident. There were about threequarters of a million Japanese in South-East Asia, 680,000 of them combatants. The garrison in Malaya was estimated at 72,000 fighting troops with a reserve of 25,000 available for deployment from Thailand. The Japanese had been nursing their remaining air strength for months because of shortages of replacement aircraft and spares. It was thought they had 415 aircraft in Malaya, and 121 in neighbouring Sumatra. These included about 250 non-combat planes and eighty training planes that could be used for Kamikaze attacks. All told it was reckoned that the invasion forces would have to deal with a hard core of 170 combat aircraft, probably used in massed assaults of 50 to 100 planes at a time.

Of Mountbatten's nine carriers, two were to be on constant convoy protection duty. The other seven carriers would have to operate in unswept waters on D-Day, launching 280 flying sorties, 90 of them in tactical support of the assault troops. All Allied planes would be painted with distinctive white bands around wings and fuselage. The carrier planes comprised three squadrons of Seafires, five squadrons of Hellcats, and one squadron of Wildcats of the 21st Assault Carrier Squadron. They would have numerical equality with the Japanese over the assault area, though the intelligence appreciation cautioned 'air equality over the assault area at all times could not be guaranteed, but fairly adequate protection could be provided.'

As airfields ashore were secured and repaired, the RAF's 224 Group would take over air support with three squadrons of Spitfires, three squadrons of Thunderbolts, three squadrons of supply-drop Dakotas and a half-squadron of Mosquito night fighters.

Because of security, no minesweeping could be done in the assault area until D-Day itself, when five flotillas of minesweepers would establish a swept channel for the passage of major warships and troopships.

Defences at Morib appeared to include an extensive trench system with fire points concealed in trees at the top of the beaches, with more prepared positions in the coconut plantations between the beach and the coast road. Jungle vegetation was also believed to conceal artillery positions. It was estimated that the enemy had only about 4500 troops in the landing areas, and counter-attacks might be expected as enemy reinforcements were thrown in piecemeal as they arrived. Among the troops in the area was a shipping engineering unit known to have experience in counter-landing operations. There were also 1200 trainees at an NCO school in Port Dickson.

Across the Straits in Sumatra, the Japanese 2nd Guards Division had been trained in amphibious warfare, and could pose a threat of a counter-attack against the landing beaches from the seaward side, supported by minelayers, motor torpedo boats and landing craft in a suicidal role. Troops would also have to watch out for suicide swimmers pushing rafts of explosives.

There was thought to be no risk of a serious naval challenge. The big guns of two cruisers, immobilized in the Johore Strait, would not have to be reckoned with until the assault on Singapore. The only other sizeable warships were three destroyers, which might try to mount a suicide sortie against the invasion beaches like the one that failed at Okinawa.

Since Britain, unlike America, was also at war with Siam, it was thought that six destroyers, three gunboats, three submarines and smaller craft of the Siamese Navy might be encountered.

In order to achieve surprise and establish a beachhead with minimum opposition, the deception operations (Operation Slippery) would endeavour to make the Japanese expect assaults against the Kra Isthmus, Northern Sumatra and the Sunda Straits, the seaway to Singapore between Java and Southern Sumatra, and even an airborne attack on Bangkok, the headquarters of the Japanese in South Asia. It was hoped the Japanese would not be able to make a firm guess of the landing being in Area J until the convoys had sailed south of Penang. By that time it would be too late to deploy major forces against the landings until the beachhead was firmly established. In the meantime, strategic air forces would be hammering the Singapore–Bangkok railway lines, destroying roads and bridges to hamper movement of troops into the area. Radar installations covering the approaches to the Malacca Straits were to be taken out, and a commando raid was to be made on One Fathom lighthouse, the Japanese forward lookout post.

Another combination of five fast and four slow convoys was to put the remainder of the 23rd Division and 3 Commando Brigade into the Port Dickson beaches on D3 to capture Port Dickson if it still remained in enemy hands. The RAF were to set up an airlift capability rising to 300 tons a day.

Five days later (D8) another group of five fast and four slow convoys would bring the build-up over the beaches to 97,500 men, 9200 vehicles, 1400 pack mules and 87,000 tons of stores and fuel. More build-up convoys would arrive off the beachhead on D23, D31, D44 and D53. With them would come the 26th Indian Division to bring the strength ashore to four divisions. Another two divisions and two tank brigades were scheduled to follow by the end of November for the assault on Singapore.

The drive south from the bridgehead was to begin twelve days after the first landings, and Singapore was to be invested as soon as possible to prevent the Japanese concentrating there. The assault across the Johore Strait, which varies in width from 1000 to 3000 yards, was to be made by two infantry divisions, 3 Royal Marine Commando Brigade, a tank brigade less one regiment, supported by 34 Amphibious Assault Regiment of the Royal Marines and an Assault Company of the RASC. The 6th Airborne Division was to drop by parachute.

Besides a devastating bombardment by a powerful naval force, the assault troops would be supported by the guns of two regiments of medium artillery and two regiments of self-propelled guns. Each of the army's guns was to fire 500 rounds, mounting a barrage totalling 3000 tons of high explosive.

This was the plan discussed at a conference of the C-in-Cs and Force Commanders under Mountbatten's chairmanship in Kandy on 8 July. The Navy representatives complained that the Morib beaches were flat and unsatisfactory for technical reasons. The army chiefs expressed concern over a shortage of headquarters ships, and a bare adequacy of troopships with none in reserve, and limitations on transport that meant some heavy vehicles could not be taken, a factor which they said would slow up the deployment ashore and exploitation towards Singapore. They all agreed that air support for the assault was meagre. Mountbatten himself was worried about delays in the arrival of LSTs. Only twenty-four of the sixty-four needed had arrived, but he had been assured that thirty were already on their way and sixteen more would be leaving Europe shortly.

The Force Commander also expressed doubts about early optimistic forecasts that Japanese opposition to the landings would be light. They believed the beach defences would be much stronger by September as intelligence reports indicated the Japanese were building up their forces, and were determined to make a stand at Singapore. These reports also indicated a concentration of suicidal aircraft ready to counter any assault. In case reinforcements (more bluntly, casualty replacements) were needed they asked for two more divisions to be available to them in November or December.

5

While Mountbatten's SEAC forces were preparing to move towards Singapore from the northwest, Australian forces under General Mac-Arthur's overall command were advancing towards it across the island archipelago from the east. They included the 6th and 7th Australian divisions which had been rushed back from the Middle East to stem the Japanese advance on Port Moresby, and had been pushing them back ever since. In April 1945 they reached Borneo, the last island before Singapore, separated from it by 200 miles of the South China Sea.

In a series of three amphibious landings they had taken Tarakan Island off the east coast, then Brunei in the northeast, finally putting 33,000 men ashore in the biggest Australian assault at Balikpan, the east coast oil centre, at the beginning of July. These landings were supported by the American Seventh Fleet and by American underwater demolition teams who cleared beach obstructions. The stiffest fighting was at Tarakan town, which held out for four days. The Australians suffered 225 killed, 669 wounded; the Japanese over 3000 dead with fewer than 200 captured.

The captured airfields were quickly made ready for operational use by Liberators, Mitchells, Beaufighters and Mosquitos of the RAAF in support of the Malayan invasion.

Radio contact had meanwhile been re-established with the leading agents of Force 136 in Malaya after a silence of ten months. John Davies and Richard Broome had been forced to retreat into deep jungle under increased Japanese pressure. They had been transmitting again for five days with a pedal-power generator before a woman radio operator in Ceylon picked up their faint signal. An attempt to land agents by Catalina, the only plane in SEAC with sufficient range, failed when the plane's noisy engines alerted the Japanese and they were all captured. When the long-range Liberator became available in SEAC, agents were dropped in after a twenty-hour flight from Ceylon.

Meanwhile British warships had established domination of the northern sea approaches to the Malacca Straits, the main seaway to Singapore. The Japanese Navy reappeared in the Indian Ocean a week after the fall of

Rangoon in an attempt to transfer troops from the garrisons in the Andaman and Nicobar Islands to Malaya. The heavy cruiser *Haguro* and the destroyer *Kamikaze* were spotted by a British submarine, and the East Indies Fleet raced from VE celebrations in Trincomalee to intercept them. Three Avenger bombers from the escort carrier *Emperor* damaged the *Haguro* with near misses, and destroyers went in under cover of a tropical rainstorm and sank her with torpedoes. The *Kamikaze* (Divine Wind), named before the development of suicide tactics, escaped yet again. Three weeks later the *Haguro*'s sister ship, *Ashigara*, was torpedoed in the Java Sea by the submarine, HMS *Trenchant*, and went down with 1200 troops she was ferrying to reinforce the Singapore garrison.

These losses reduced the once-powerful Imperial Navy's presence in Singapore to two heavy cruisers, *Miyoko* and *Takao*, both apparently damaged; the *Kamikaze*, which had belied the implications of her name and narrowly escaped several close encounters; and numerous auxiliary craft.

Agents carried by submarine from Australia landed in Johore at the foot of the Malayan peninsula to assess the possibilities of attacks on the warships. Their jungle hideout was found in January 1945, but some agents escaped the Japanese attack on it and were taken off a month later in the submarine *Thule* along with members of the crew of a B29 shot down in a raid on Singapore.

They reported that the Japanese cruisers might be a threat to the Zipper invasion convoys and ought to be eliminated. On the night of 30 July a Royal Navy frogman won the Victoria Cross for blowing up the *Takao* with a limpet mine, but an attempt on the *Miyoko* was aborted. Other frogmen cut underseas telegraph cables between Saigon and Hong Kong to add to Japanese communication problems.

The SEAC air forces were pressing attacks on strategic targets like the Bangkok–Singapore railway. In a typical week they flew 577 sorties, and Dakota transport planes flew 9428 sorties moving 9428 men and 7094 tons of stores. Among airmen lost in these operations was Wing Commander James Nicolson, who won the Battle of Britain's only VC. His Liberator was forced down in the Bay of Bengal with engine trouble. Mountbatten prohibited attacks on naval installations, harbour works and oil storage depots in Singapore, intending to capture a working base for further operations.

Force 136 officers and NCOs were being dropped into Malaya with increasing frequency to train the 5000 strong Malayan People's Anti-Japanese Army and restrain them from battle until the Zipper landings began. The guerillas were called the Hennessy Boys after the brandy advertisement because they wore three red stars on their khaki caps. Lieut-Colonel Jim Hannah of the Intelligence Corps planned to use them to mount round-the-clock ambushes on the main highway down which Japanese troops would have to move from the north to the Zipper beaches. He reckoned they could maintain a block for eight days before 50 per cent casualties made their effort ineffective. Other Force 136 agents were concentrating on locating POW camps and plans to save prisoners and internees from being massacred when the Japanese came under pressure from the British invasion.

Minesweeping operations began east of the Japanese-occupied Nicobar Islands on 5 July, and in the next five days 167 mines were blown up. The minesweepers were escorted by a strong naval force which included the battleship *Nelson*, the cruiser *Sussex*, two escort carriers and four destroyers. Planes from the carriers attacked Japanese airfields and installations in the Kra Isthmus, the Nicobars and Koto Raja airfield in northern Sumatra. Six planes were lost, but five pilots were rescued. The minesweepers went on to clear the approaches to Phuket Island, and one of them, the *Vestal*, was set ablaze and sunk by a Kamikaze plane which crashed onto her deck. Three other suicide planes were shot down by escorting warships. These operations also contributed to Operation Slippery.

Meanwhile the longest campaign of the Far East war was coming to an end in Burma, where the last Japanese army – the 28th – had been trying to break out across the Sittang River to Thailand. During July, the 14th Army killed 11,500 Japanese for the loss of ninety-six dead, and fewer than 6000 Japanese managed to escape before the battle ended on 4 August – just two days before the first atomic bomb enshrined Hiroshima in history. All told, the Japanese lost 128,000 killed in Burma.

Mountbatten marked the end by a message to the troops which said, 'You have fought a great campaign under hardships and difficulties that have probably never been equalled. You have beaten a stubborn enemy, a fanatical enemy from whose vocabulary the word "surrender" is officially deleted and replaced by the word "suicide" in the last resort.'

6

On 9 August, the day the second atomic bomb was dropped on Nagasaki, the Zipper land forces commander, General Ouvry Roberts, visited the South Wales Borderers in their embarkation camp in India. He was asked when the war against Japan might end, and replied, 'Might be two years, two months or three days.' He recalled many years later that the last possibility raised a huge roar of laughter from the soldiers. Such an early end, even with reports that a powerful new bomb had been dropped on Japan, seemed inconceivable. The 'miracle of deliverance' was still hidden in the weeks to come.

On 12 August General Roberts reported that his force was ready to sail, sufficiently complete to achieve its objectives, though its standard of training was considerably below par for the job it had to do. Junior officers in particular had had little experience in cooperation between various arms in an assault, and deficiencies were especially notable in signals units. Lackings in equipment and vehicles would be likely to slow down the advance from the bridgehead. He thought these overall weaknesses were bound to impair the efficiency of the force as a fighting unit, although a high proportion of the troops did have battle experience.

This guarded assessment reinforced the need to take the Japanese completely by surprise. The success of the deception plan in persuading the Japanese to make their anti-invasion dispositions far to the north was crucial, though this need for maximum security meant that reconnaissance of the landing beaches was so sketchy that the true nature of the beaches was not discovered until the landings took place.

Apart from the tanks, artillery and ammunition vehicles that would have to follow on the heels of the assault troops across the landing beaches, heavy construction equipment was to follow as soon as possible. It was anticipated that they would be needed to repair damage to the captured airfields from British bombardment and Japanese sabotage to make them operational. Since the assault would rely solely on seaborne air cover only for the first six days (after which it would peter out rapidly) there would be an urgent need for airfields ashore.

It was therefore crucial that the invasion should not be pinned down, or even delayed, on the beaches.

All the more remarkable that the landing beaches, blandly accepted as less satisfactory than others nearby, were not thoroughly examined, as were the Normandy beaches where secrecy was just as crucial. With forces reduced in numbers and efficiency and with barely enough air cover, this was only one of the risks Mountbatten accepted in launching his great invasion.

7

As detailed orders for Operation Zipper, under the title 'Exercise Button', were going out in the middle of July to all the units taking part, Mountbatten took the opportunity to visit General MacArthur at his Manila headquarters. Both men took to each other warmly at first meeting, and they quickly agreed to coordinate plans as their operational zones became closely linked by Allied advances. Mountbatten accepted MacArthur's suggestion that they should recommend to the Combined Chiefs of Staff a huge extension of SEAC boundaries. This meant bringing the whole of the Dutch East Indies, Timor, Borneo and French Indo-China under Mountbatten, leaving MacArthur free to concentrate his forces for the final operations against Japan.

Mountbatten was feeling buoyant at the prospect of commanding the next great Allied campaign, confident that the Malayan invasion would put his name in the pantheon of great British military commanders. After years as the 'cinderella' theatre of operations, SEAC was about to grab the spotlight as it wiped out three years of British shame over the surrender of Singapore. All the obstacles, the repeated denials of resources, seemed now to lie behind him. At last, only the Japanese enemy had to be overcome. Over their final dinner together MacArthur commiserated with Mountbatten over his supply problems. 'I am the best person in the world to judge how difficult it is to run a command when you are low on the priority scale,' he said. 'I have had a terrible time, while Ike [General Eisenhower, Supreme Commander in Europe] got everything he asked for. I also know you have had a worse time.'

After a brief return to his Kandy headquarters, Mountbatten decided to visit London to use the proposal for the extension of SEAC as an argument for reinforcements. But he was diverted to meet Churchill in Potsdam, where he was attending summit talks with the new American President, Harry Truman, and Stalin. When he went to dine with Churchill on the evening of his arrival, the prime minister checked doors and windows carefully before offering him a drink. He whispered as he told Mountbatten, 'You are going to have to revise your plans.' Mountbatten recalled thinking, Oh, no, not again – not more cuts – I've had enough. But Churchill went on, 'The war with Japan will be over in less than a month. We are going to use a new bomb, an atomic bomb, against the cities of Japan, and the Emperor will be forced to capitulate. You are not to mention this to a soul. You'll have to tell your people without explaining how or why. . .'

At his first meeting with the Combined Chiefs of Staff next day, Mountbatten was officially told that the war with Japan was now likely to end with capitulation about the middle of August, and he should make preparations for an early move into the territories they occupied within his command area. They also confirmed the extension of SEAC, and at Australian request their forces in Dutch New Guinea as well as those in Borneo were also included in Mountbatten's enlarged command. But the Americans insisted that General Chiang Kai-Shek's troops should occupy Indo-China north of the 16th parallel, while Mountbatten was responsible south of that line. Thus the Potsdam conference created the two Vietnams that were to bedevil the next three decades.

Despite the atomic bombs, the Combined Chiefs were still using 15 November 1946 as a provisional date for the end of organized resistance in Japan. Their directive to Mountbatten was that, subject to limits on resources imposed by operations against Japan, he was to liberate Malaya, capture key areas of Siam, and develop Singapore and other bases for further operations.

With Churchill's permission, Mountbatten sent a guarded telegram to his deputy, Lieut-General R.A. Wheeler of the US Army, and his chief–of–staff, General F.A.M..Browning, telling them only that there were strong reasons to believe that the Japanese might capitulate some time after mid-August. Accordingly, they were to begin contingency planning for a rapid reoccupation of Singapore, either through the Zipper invasion beachheads or directly into Singapore harbour as soon as Japan surrendered. He added that it seemed certain Japan would surrender before the end of the year.

Mountbatten himself had mixed feelings over Japan being blackmailed into surrender by the terror use of the atomic bomb. He believed they had to be demonstrably defeated in the field, that they must be made to lose face after the arrogant triumphs their treachery had won in the opening stages of the Far East war. He feared they would otherwise be able to claim, with much more justification than the Germans after 1918, that their armies had not been thoroughly defeated.

Despite the possibilities provided by the new bomb, the Combined Chiefs continued conventional planning for the final operations against Japan, and agreed that besides the role of the British Pacific Fleet, a British Commonwealth Land Force, with its own tactical air force. would take part in the invasion of the main island of Honshu, planned for the following March. In addition, ten squadrons of RAF long range bombers would join attacks on Japan from December 1945, increasing to twenty squadrons as more airfields became available. On the assumption that Singapore would be recaptured by Christmas 1945, SEAC was expected to provide two army divisions, and the East Indies Fleet would also take part.

The American Joint Chiefs would continue to control strategy, but they agreed to give the British Chiefs 'full and timely information of plans and intentions', with the proviso that in the event of disagreement the final decision rested with them. It was understood that if the British felt unable to commit their troops to operations proposed by the Americans, sufficient notice would be given for other arrangements to be made.

The French and Dutch, now liberated from German occupation, were also eager to make a contribution to final victory. The French offered an Army Corps of two infantry divisions with service and supporting units. The Dutch also offered troops. The American Chiefs of Staff, fearing a repetition of command frictions experienced in North Africa and Europe, merely accepted the offers 'in principle'.

The French and Dutch Governments were extremely anxious to take part in the liberation of their colonial territories, and both protested in Washington at the negative response to their offers of troops. The Dutch Government felt particularly aggrieved because they were even denied the use of Dutch ships in the Allied shipping pool.

Military experts in Washington were meanwhile arguing over strategy. Navy and Air Force experts asserted that an invasion of Japan was unnecessary because a tight sea blockade and devastating air attacks could bring Japan to defeat. But Army chiefs argued that experience against Germany had shown there was no justification in relying on air power or blockade, and troops had to go in on the ground.

So the decision was made to invade Japan. The first phase – codenamed Olympic – was to be an invasion of the southernmost Japanese island of Kyushu on 1 November by a force of 750,000 men. After preliminary capture of offshore islands as advance anchorages and for early warning of Kamikaze attacks, the assault was to go across two beaches on the western side of the most southerly peninsular, and another across beaches on the opposite side, 50 miles south of Nagasaki. Three assault divisions were to land on each beach supported by naval and air bombardments from a more powerful fleet and air force than supported Overlord in Europe.

Naval air cover was to be provided from fourteen fleet carriers (four of them British), six light carriers and thirty-six escort carriers. Land-based air cover was to come from 192 squadrons in Okinawa and Ie-Shima, and 12 squadrons on Iwo Jima. Heavy bombers – 80 B29 squadrons from the Marianas and 32 from Okinawa – were to concentrate on preventing reinforcements crossing the narrow channel separating Kyushu from the main island of Honshu, where the military headquarters for Kyushu were in the town of Hiroshima.

There was to be a diversionary feint towards Shikoko, smallest of the four main Japanese islands, and a fourth bridgehead was to be opened on the tip of Kyushu peninsula with another three division assault on D-Day plus 3.

In expectation of bitter resistance the planners allowed nearly four months for the Allied grip on Kyushu to be consolidated, and the main invasion – Coronet – was not to come until March, 1946. Then a force of nearly 1,800,000 men – spearheaded by nine army divisions, three marine divisions and two armoured divisions – from America and the British Commonwealth were to land on beaches north of Tokyo Bay and surge into the Tokyo Plain. They were to be reinforced by General Courtney Hodges' veteran First Army, comprising ten infantry divisions and one airborne division, as soon as it could be deployed from Europe. 200 air squadrons were to be deployed in support. All told some five million Allied fighting men were to have taken part in the battle to overwhelm last ditch Japanese resistance.

Already some of the sixty-seven American divisions which had fought in Europe were returning home, where men due for demobilization were replaced by newly trained youngsters, re-equipped where necessary and assigned to the Pacific. The logistics of moving thirty-eight divisions and far greater air strength than had ever been seen across such vast areas with no real base facilities nearer than Australia, provided American planners with their biggest challenge.

But most daunting of all about the coming Battle for Japan were the likely casualties the invading forces would suffer against fanatical defenders whose military leaders were ready to take ten million of their fellow countrymen into a suicidal last stand to atone for defeat. Looming in the background was the ominous threat of a vast armada of suicidal planes, for it was known that the Japanese had withdrawn their air force from combat to save them for a desperate last battle. Their capability of inflicting unacceptably high Allied casualties, mainly American, was the only card the rulers of Japan had left in their bid to win peace on terms that might prevent the shame of an Allied occupation.

President Truman's representative on the Joint Chiefs of Staff, Admiral William Leahy, impressed on his colleagues the president's injunction that planning 'must take into account economizing to the maximum extent possible, the loss of American lives'.

Truman had been appalled when he learned that planning provision had been made to handle 58,000 casualties in the first eight days after the Kyushu landings. The bitter experience of Okinawa, where 35 per cent of the troops engaged became casualties, weighed heavily, despite arguments that they were unlikely to be as heavy at Kyushu because the assault would go in from three sides simultaneously, giving more room to manoeuvre than there had been in the single-front assault at Okinawa. Truman told the military chiefs that he hoped there was a possibility of preventing 'an Okinawa from one end of Japan to the other'.

It was estimated that the Kyushu landings would be opposed by 350,000 regular troops, giving the invasion force less than the ideal 3 to 1 ratio established in the island-hopping campaign so far. The American commanders discussed the possibility of using the new atomic bomb, already in an advanced stage of development, as a tactical weapon to help the invasion forces. After the war, General George C. Marshall, the president's strategic adviser, told John P. Sutherland, of *US News* and *World Report*, that they had spoken of using nine atomic bombs – three in each of the two landing zones, and the other three against Japanese troop reserves. They thought nine would be necessary, said General Marshall, because they had no idea of the real power of atomic bombs. The question got no further than discussion, and receives no mention in planning documents.

Weighed against estimates of the Allied lives that might be lost in crushing the Japanese in a fight to the death, estimates of Japanese victims of the new atomic bombs seemed almost insignificant. President Truman revealed in his memoirs, *Year of Decisions*, that General Marshall had warned him that conquest of the Japanese home islands might cost as many as half a million American lives. The Secretary for War, Henry Stimson, was advised that the operations would involve American forces alone in a million casualties. The man who would have commanded the assault on Japan, General Douglas MacArthur, was predicting that guerrilla warfare might continue for ten years, and that there was virtually no ceiling on Allied losses.

8

Not all Japanese were ready to see their homeland and families perish in a fanatical last stand. A group of distinguished prewar leaders, who had tried to oppose the military gamble, began to exert their views again as the American advance came nearer. Japan's eventual defeat had become clear as early as the destruction of the once all-powerful carrier fleet, and was sealed by the fall of the Marianas and Okinawa. These disasters had brought the resignation of the main architect of the military policy, General Hideko Tojo, who blamed himself for losing the war, as early as June 1944.

After his resignation, sharp divisions over a new policy to end the war were resolved by the Emperor asking the Jushin, a council of elder statesmen, to select a new prime minister. They chose General Kunaiki Koiso, a retired officer, with Admiral Yonai, who had always opposed the war, as co-premier. The military showed their disdain by refusing the new prime minister full membership of Imperial General Headquarters, and they insisted on nominating the War Minister. Koiso responded by forming a Supreme Council for the Direction of the War with six members: himself, co-premier Yonai, who was also Navy Minister, Foreign Minister Mamoru Shigemitsu, who advocated giving the occupied territories immediate political freedom, the Army Minister, and the two Chiefs of Staff. Imperial General Headquarters provided the officers to staff the secretariat, thus ensuring it was fully informed on the council's deliberations.

Shigemitsu, a former ambassador in London, ordered a secret Foreign Office study to be made of the possibilities of ending the war. Its report recommended an approach to the Soviet Union to act as mediator. At the same time the Swedish ambassador in Tokyo, W. Bagge, was asked to arrange for his government to forward to London a proposal for a settlement in which Japan would relinquish all territories occupied since 1941, including, if necessary, Manchuria. This move was intended to probe whether the term unconditional surrender really meant what it said, and word came back that it meant exactly that. The Allied demand for unconditional surrender was first laid down at the Casablanca summit in

January 1943. It had been reiterated in December at a summit in Cairo, where it was also stated publicly that Japan would be stripped of all territories she had taken after 1895.

During this period other efforts to initiate peace moves were made by individual Japanese abroad, who could see how hopeless their country's position had become. They included the Japanese military attachés in Berlin and Berne who were in contact with American intelligence officials. They had not been seriously entertained because of the declared Allied policy of carrying on the war until all the enemy countries surrendered without any agreement on terms.

Contacts with Stockholm were kept open, and in March 1945 Ambassador Bagge led Shigemitsu to understand that the Emperor's position could be assured if Japan made peace proposals. He invited the Japanese government to ask formally for Sweden's good offices. This was overtaken by the fall of the Koiso government.

Koiso had been duped by officials of the puppet Manchurian regime into believing favourable peace terms might be got through the mediation of General Chiang Kai-Shek, and he was forced to resign when the moves proved to be spurious, having wasted nine whole months.

He was replaced by Admiral Kantaro Suzuki, a seventy-eight-year-old survivor of the 1936 military coup attempt. The new foreign minister was Shigenori Togo, who had opposed the military when he had been foreign minister before the war. The Supreme War Council now consisted of the Prime Minister and Foreign Minister; Navy Minister Yonai, who was no longer co-premier; Army Minister General Korechika Anami, and the Chiefs of Staff, General Yoshijiro Umezu and Admiral Soemu Toyoda. The secretariat provided by Imperial General Headquarters was replaced by four officers opposed to fighting to the bitter end. Yonai and Togo were for peace, Suzuki favoured seeking improved terms, and the remaining three military men were opposed to unconditional surrender whatever the consequences. Suzuki moved warily, ever afraid of assassination by military hotheads, and when Germany surrendered unconditionally he announced that the 'dire change in the war situation' would not make the slightest difference to Japan's determination to defend herself. He and others of the peace faction feared their opposition to the war had been too muted to save them from trial as war criminals, and this was inducement to hang on for terms short of unconditional surrender.

Togo's first decision at the Foreign Office was to do nothing about the peace feeler put out by Sweden, but to persist with approaches to the Soviet Union which had begun, at the express wish of the Emperor, the previous February, when the three Allied leaders were meeting in Yalta. The first approach had been made through the Soviet ambassador in Tokyo, and followed up by the Japanese ambassador in Moscow. The

Russians ignored both, and passed no word of them to their allies.

The Japanese were not to know that Stalin had promised to join the war against Japan as early as the Teheran Conference of November 1943. But he said he could not do so until after the war with Germany was over. In the meantime, to avoid provoking Japan before he was ready, Stalin refused an American request for base facilities in the eastern maritime provinces of the Soviet Union which they wanted for the air offensive against Japan. He even turned down an American suggestion that bombers they were sending him for the German front might be delivered to Soviet ports in the Far East and then flown across Siberia.

In October 1944, Stalin told his Western allies that the Red Army would be ready to launch an offensive against the Japanese three months after the defeat of Germany, so long as America provided adequate supplies and the Allies agreed to guarantee the return of territories Russia had lost to the Japanese in the 1904 war.

Stalin's shopping list for a three-month campaign was huge: 860,000 tons of dry cargo, 206,000 tons of liquid cargo, enough to supply 1½ million men; 3000 tanks, 75,000 vehicles and 5000 aircraft. His territorial claims were for the return of South Sakhalin and the Kurile Islands, lease of the ports of Port Arthur and Dairen and their hinterlands, and control of the Manchuria railways which had been built and operated by Russians in Czarist times.

President Roosevelt promised to do all he could. He was anxious for Russian soldiers to join in the last battles against Japan. He told his special envoy to Moscow, Averell Harriman, 'The defeat of Japan without Russian aid would be extremely difficult and costly.' At this time the Chiefs of Staff were expecting that the defeat of Japan would take eighteen months after Germany's surrender, and if German resistance was prolonged beyond the summer of 1945, landings might not be possible in Japan until well into 1946. Even before the heavy casualties of Okinawa, and the massive suicide attacks there, the likely casualties in an invasion of Japan itself were daunting. Apart from that consideration, Roosevelt was as relaxed over Soviet expansion in the Far East as he was trusting over Stalin's attitude to liberated Europe. His understanding of Russian desires to take back territories lost to a victorious Japan in 1904 was the reverse of his attitude to the motives of the European colonial powers in wanting the return of territories grabbed by Japan less than three years before.

Roosevelt told Stalin he saw no difficulty over South Sakhalin and the Kuriles, but he thought Dairen ought to be a free port under international control, the future he said he had in mind for the British colony of Hong Kong. His only sticking point was over the Manchurian railways, which he thought should be under joint Soviet-Chinese control.

At the very time Emperor Hirohito was ordering peace feelers to be put out through the Soviet Union's good offices, Stalin was signing a secret agreement with Roosevelt and Churchill at Yalta. This committed Russia to join the war against Japan three months after Germany's defeat, in return for the territorial guarantees he had asked for, and a bit more. The final agreement included several clauses that had not been discussed, slipped in by the Soviet drafters. One laid down that the 'pre-eminent interests of the Soviet Union shall be safe-guarded', another stipulated that 'the territorial claims of the Soviet Union shall unquestionably be fulfilled after Japan's defeat'. Averell Harriman raised objections to these insertions, but these were brushed aside by Roosevelt with the comment that he was not going to quarrel with Stalin 'over language'. The American copy of the agreement was locked away in a White House safe, and its contents were unknown even to the State Department until long afterwards. The reason for the secrecy was apparently Stalin's paranoid fear of attack on the Soviet Far East if word of it leaked out. Roosevelt died a few months later, and the other Western signatory, Churchill, was defeated in a general election nine months afterwards.

It had been Stalin's apparent scrupulous observance of the Neutrality Pact signed between Japan and the Soviet Union on the eve of Hitler's attack on Russia that trapped the Japanese into the futile bid for peace. The Pact had served both signatories well. It freed Japan to launch its conquest of the 'southern resources area'. It enabled Stalin to withdraw troops from the Far East at the height of his greatest peril from the German onslaught. But in the end it bogged down any chance Japan might have had of making peace before Hiroshima.

The Japanese even failed to see the writing on the wall when Stalin refused to renew the Neutrality Pact six weeks before Yalta and their first approaches for peace talks. With uncharacteristic guilelessness, they accepted Soviet assurances that their attitude would still be guided by the fact that the Pact remained in force till April 1946.

The first official Russian mention of Japanese peace feelers to the Western Allies came only in May 1945, almost casually from Stalin himself. He was talking with the American Special Envoy, Harry Hopkins, who had called to see him at the Kremlin about Soviet plans to implement the promise to enter the Far East war now that Germany was defeated. After telling him that Red Army troops deployed from Europe would be ready to launch an offensive by 8 August, Stalin went on to question the wisdom of sticking to the demand for unconditional surrender. He thought it would make the Japanese fight to the bitter end, whereas a modification of it might encourage them to yield. Once they surrendered, he added with frank cynicism, the Allies could impose their will and obtain the same results.

It was then that he casually mentioned peace feelers put out by 'certain elements' in Japan, but failed to make it clear that they had been official approaches.

In Japan, meanwhile, diehards were preparing to counter the gains of the Peace Party, and a critical clash between the two philosophies – for such had they become – came at a meeting of the Supreme War Council on 6 June, which had been called to formulate a policy for the future conduct of the war. The Navy Chief of Staff, Admiral Toyoda, told the council that it was believed that in the event of an early invasion half the enemy forces could be destroyed in the water. If the invasion was delayed and war production could be maintained enemy casualties would be even greater. His conclusion was that the Battle for Japan could be won, or at least sustained so long and hard that the enemy would offer acceptable terms rather than endure more losses and suffering. The only dissent from a decision to call for mass mobilization to offer all-out resistance to invasion came from the Foreign Minister, Togo. But the cabinet immediately endorsed the decision, and the next day it was accepted by the Imperial Conference. Even those of the Emperor's advisers who accepted inevitable defeat were still thinking that Japan might even lay down conditions for the withdrawal from conquered territories, namely that the peoples of the territories attained independence from European colonialism. An occupation of Japan by the victorious powers was not to be thought of.

Two weeks later, when the fall of Okinawa had dampened some of the euphoria over the stubborn resistance by the garrison, Emperor Hirohito commanded members of the Supreme War Council to disregard its call for all-out resistance and take all steps to end the war as soon as possible. This time, the only dissent came from General Umezu, the Army Chief of Staff.

They decided that Soviet mediation was imperative, and appointed a mission to go to Moscow to negotiate. It was to be headed by Prince Funimaro Konoye, who had resigned the premiership before Pearl Harbor after failing to restrain the military's commitment to war. It was to include the Emperor's senior adviser, Marquis Kido, Lord Keeper of the Privy Seal, and the former foreign minister, Shigemitsu. Prince Konoye was told privately by the Emperor that peace must be obtained at any price.

The Soviet Government was asked to receive the proposed mission on 13 July as Stalin was preparing to leave for the Potsdam conference. He decided to play for time, and replied that the proposal was too vague for him to take any action. However, Stalin did mention the approach at his first meeting with Churchill, and repeated his doubts about the wisdom of sticking to the demand for unconditional surrender. Discussing this with America's new president, Harry Truman, Churchill agreed with Stalin that the demand should be 'somewhat modified' to ease the way for the Japanese to accept it.

On 18 July Stalin gave Truman copies of two notes handed over in

Moscow by the Japanese ambassador, one from the Japanese Foreign Minister, and one from the Emperor saying it was his 'heart's desire to see the war ended'. Hirohito also said that he was sending Prince Konoye to negotiate terms for peace, for if the US and Britain insisted upon unconditional surrender he saw no alternative but to continue the war 'for the sake of survival and the honour of the homeland'. Truman told Stalin he had no respect for the good faith of the Japanese, and they agreed that Stalin should go on stalling the Japanese. Truman was already preoccupied with his own plans to bring the war to an abrupt end.

In any case the Japanese efforts to sue for peace were well known to the Americans from the start, despite the failure of their Russian allies to tell them about them. American intelligence had broken the Japanese code, allowing them to read every message passed between Tokyo and the Japanese embassy in Moscow. The American intelligence assessment was that the military would refuse to agree to surrender at this stage, even with assurances over the Emperor's position.

9

News that was to transform the history of the next few months and be at the root of international affairs for decades afterwards reached Potsdam in a cryptic message to the American Secretary for War, Henry Stimson. Its coded words 'Babies satisfactorily born' meant that the nuclear age had begun. The first test explosion of an atomic device at a remote desert site in New Mexico on 16 July had exceeded all expectations. Its blast had equalled the destructive power of 20,000 tons of high explosives, making it by far the most devastating weapon man's terrible ingenuity had yet fashioned.

The Americans, with a bit of help from their friends, had won the fearful race to be first in achieving an awesome power of mass destruction. Knowledge of the terrible potential of splitting the atom had been known to science for many years. The New Zealand-born scientist, Ernest Rutherford, was first to 'split the atom' during the First World War while carrying out experiments at Manchester University. He expressed the hope then that man would not learn to use atomic energy for practical purposes until the world was at peace. Ten months before the Second World War began the German physicist Dr Otto Hahn led a team which discovered that a self-sustained chain-reacting pile was a theoretical possibility, and scientists around the world warned their governments that this could lead to an unprecedented production of power and superexplosives.

The first known mention of an atomic bomb was made in a letter dated 2 August 1939 from the American scientist, Albert Einstein, to President Roosevelt. He told the President: 'In the course of the last four months it has been made probable – through the work of [Frederic] Joliot in France as well as [Enrico] Fermi and [Leo] Szilard in America – that it may become possible to set up a nuclear chain reaction in a large mass of uranium, by which vast amounts of power and large quantities of new radium-like elements would be generated. Now it appears almost certain that this could be achieved in the immediate future.

'This new phenomenon would also lead to the construction of bombs, and it is conceivable – though much less certain – that extremely powerful bombs of a new type may be constructed. A single bomb of this type, carried by boat and exploded in a port, might well destroy the whole port together with some of the surrounding territory. However, such bombs might well prove to be too heavy for transportation by air.'

With this warning of the shape of things to come, American scientists began to try to produce an atomic bomb just about the time Polish cavalry were vainly charging German Panzer columns, the seemingly invincible new weapon forged by Hitler's Nazis.

British scientists were also in the race with a project called Tube Alloys. In June 1942, Churchill and Roosevelt agreed to pool resources and concentrate the work in the United States and Canada.

Churchill wrote later in his book *The Hinge of Fate*: 'We knew what efforts the Germans were making to procure supplies of "heavy water" – a sinister term, eerie, unnatural, which began to creep into our secret papers. What if an enemy should get an atomic bomb before we did? However sceptical one might feel about the assertions of scientists, much disputed among themselves and expressed in jargon incomprehensible to laymen, we could not run the mortal risk of being outstripped in this awful sphere.'

Heavy water was known to be an exceptionally efficient moderator for slowing down neutrons in an atomic pile, enabling neutrons to split uranium 235 atoms and begin chain reactions. Heavy water, indistinguishable from other water, contains hydrogen atoms with both proton and neutron. Because America had little heavy water, they started a pile using uranium graphite as moderator, while another pile was built in Canada based on heavy water.

The new project, codenamed Manhattan District, was under the direction of General Leslie R. Groves, who later wrote of the frantic urgency under which work went on: 'Not until later was it recognized that chances would have to be taken that in ordinary times would have been thought reckless in the extreme . . . it became accepted practice to proceed vigorously on major phases of the work despite large gaps in knowledge.' One uranium reactor was established in a squash court at Chicago University in the heart of a residential district.

It was known that the Germans were already two years ahead in nuclear research and so haste was essential. Intelligence reports showed that they had increased demands for heavy water from the Norsk Hydro Hydrogen Electrolysis plant at Vermok in occupied Norway to 10,000 pounds a year, a sudden four-fold increase. Coupled with their embargo on the export of uranium from occupied Czechoslovakia it was clear that Germany was working on an atomic bomb, and the destruction of the heavy water plant became the highest priority if Germany's progress was to be slowed down and then overtaken.

A number of hazardous, near-suicide operations were planned and several were launched. In November 1942 two Horsa gliders towed by Halifax bombers crossed 400 miles of wintry North Sea carrying thirty-four commandos of the 1st Airborne Division. Both gliders crash landed far from the planned landing zone, and survivors were executed as 'spies and saboteurs'. One of the tow planes crashed into a mountainside soon after releasing its glider, and the four crew were killed. Only four of the forty-three people involved returned. Three months later, the heavy water factory was attacked by Norwegian commandos in British uniform, and they succeeded in entering the innermost sections of the plant and blowing up key apparatus. This was thought to have set heavy water production back two years, but the Germans succeeded in restoring partial production only four months later with an output of ten pounds a day. This was sent to Germany under such heavy guard that Allied scientists were grimly convinced that Germany was close to developing an atomic bomb. It was feared that the recently discovered V-weapons might carry nuclear warheads.

Another fullscale commando raid was considered, but because of the now almost foolproof German security the Combined Chiefs made the plant a first priority bombing objective instead. In November 1943, 460 Flying Fortresses and Liberators made a daylight raid on the factory and diversionary targets in Stavanger and Oslo. Over 700 500-pound bombs were dropped into the deep gorge in which the factory was sited. Four hit the factory, two on the key installations, but vital facilities which had been destroyed in the earlier commando raid were untouched. The Norwegian government in London, which had been given no prior notice of the raid, protested at the killing of twenty-two Norwegians in saturation bombing which they said 'seemed out of all proportion to the objective sought'.

The Germans subsequently sent unprocessed heavy water for refining in Germany. Some of this was contaminated by Norwegian workers, and in February 1944 a ferry boat carrying barrels of heavy water was blown up and sunk by resistance saboteurs. Twenty-six Norwegians, including women and children, went down with it.

One of the German nuclear scientists working on the bomb, Dr Kurt Diebner, said after the war: 'It was the elimination of heavy water production in Norway that was the main factor in our failure to achieve a self-sustaining atomic reactor before the end of the war. For the last experiments in 1945 there were only two and a half tons of heavy water available.'

The Soviet Union was far behind, and, despite obtaining detailed information about the Manhattan Project experiments from some disillusioned scientists, was not in a position to carry out a test explosion until

August 1949. Japan's own scientists, whose brilliance had given their country some important technological advantages in the early stages of the war, had also been trying to adapt known theories of atomic energy for military purposes. This was referred to publicly in the Upper House of the Japanese Diet on 7 February 1944 when Dr Aikitsu Tanakadade urged the Prime Minister to speed up the exploitation of uranium for military purposes. That was a full eighteen months before the first atomic bomb was dropped on Hiroshima.

In the spring of 1945, when the Manhattan Project scientists were confident that they would soon crack the final problems, Stimson appointed an interim committee of scientific, political and military experts headed by Dr Vannevar Bush to consider how to use the new weapon against Japan. The Manhattan Project's scientific director, Dr Robert Oppenheimer, advised them that the new weapon would achieve its maximum effects from blast and would need to be exploded above the ground. He suggested it was ideal for use against a concentration of troops or war plants and could be expected to kill about 20,000 people.

Early in June the interim committee compiled three recommendations: the atomic bomb should be used as soon as possible; it should be used against a military installation surrounded by houses or other buildings most susceptible to damage; and there should be no prior warning of the kind of bomb it was because there was a chance it might fail to explode.

These recommendations came at a time when appalling decisions had to be made involving vast numbers of lives. The world war in which hundreds of cities had already been destroyed and many millions had died was in its sixth year.

Even so, another group of scientists headed by Professor James Franck, sent a separate report to Stimson just a month before the first atomic device was ready for testing. They argued against the use of an atomic bomb because they said the military advantage, even if that meant saving many American lives, might be outweighed by a wave of horror and revulsion in the rest of the world.

The revulsion the scientists felt for the idea of an atomic explosion was because of its vast destructive blast and the furnace heat that would burn up a huge area. They seemed not to appreciate that the laboratory hazards of radioactivity would develop into the long-term agonies of radiation sickness.

With accurate prescience, Professor Franck's group pleaded, 'If the United States were to be the first to release this new means of indiscriminate destruction on mankind, she would sacrifice public support throughout the world, precipitate the race for armaments, and prejudice the possibility of reaching international agreement on the future control of such weapons.' Albert Einstein had earlier made an approach to President

Roosevelt to urge him against using atomic bombs because their use by America would set off a worldwide atomic arms race.

The atomic age began on 16 July 1945 when a ball of plutonium the size of a grapefruit was exploded atop a 100-foot tower at the desert air base of Alamogordo in New Mexico. A yellow fire ball reached a height of 2000 feet before turning vivid red and erupting into a distinctive mushroom cloud 40,000 feet high. The tremor shook houses 235 miles away in Gallup, and the flash was seen 450 miles away in Amarillo, Texas. At first the public were allowed to believe that an ammunition dump had exploded, and a security officer mused that trying to keep the secret would be like keeping the existence of the Mississippi River under wraps.

The immediate personal satisfaction the scientists felt at the success of their long research was quickly followed by wider, deeper doubts about the morality of using such a device against fellow human beings. Some felt it was too powerful even to contemplate using, while others still argued for it to be used to bring the war to an end and save Allied lives.

A petition signed by sixty-seven of the scientists who worked on the bomb urged President Truman not to permit its use against Japanese cities unless Japan was first given a convincing warning of the destructive force of the new weapon and then a chance to surrender. They also pressed for responsibility for its use to be shared by America's allies.

In Britain, the Danish physicist, Niels Bohr, persuaded the Home Secretary, Sir John Anderson, to ask the government to make a study to find the means to put atomic power under international control. Churchill, who had himself persuaded Roosevelt against sharing atomic secrets with Stalin, squashed the idea. His chief scientific adviser, Professor Lindemann (later Lord Cherwell), argued strongly for the atomic bomb to be used to shorten the war, and Churchill's formal agreement to its use was obtained by the Americans on 4 July. Churchill believed that Britain, having played a secondary role in the war against Japan and in the development of the bomb, ought to acquiesce in any decision the operational military commanders took.

President Truman and most of his advisers were committed to the use of the atomic bomb against Japan before news of the successful test reached them at Potsdam. They had already considered and rejected the idea of a demonstration explosion before the representatives of all nations, including the Japanese. Such a demonstration was thought to be impracticable, involving unacceptable delay in operations and also – and mainly – because a demonstration would not show the effectiveness of the bomb against a strategic target. Any idea of giving the Japanese advance warning was rejected on the grounds that it would enable the Japanese to move Allied prisoners-of-war into the threatened target area, and also because there was no certainty that the parachuted bomb would function properly.

Stimson had summed it up in these words: 'Nothing would be more damaging to our effort to obtain surrender than a warning or a demonstration followed by a dud – and that is a real possibility. Furthermore we have no bombs to waste, and it is vital that a sufficient effect be obtained quickly with the few we have.' Stimson believed there would be no genuine surrender unless the Emperor and his advisers were administered a tremendous shock which would carry convincing proof of America's power to destroy Japan. 'Such an effective shock,' he declared, 'would save many times the number of lives, both American and Japanese, that it would cost.'

That last argument was the overriding consideration.

One of the few who argued against using the bomb until the eve of the Potsdam conference was the American Chief of Staff, Admiral William Leahy, who had earlier protested to Roosevelt against a proposal to use bacteriological weapons. He described the idea of using the bomb as 'a professor's dream', and argued that its use would put America on a par with the barbarians in the Dark Ages. 'I was not taught to make war in that fashion,' he said. 'Wars cannot be won by destroying women and children.'

Recalling the deliberations at Potsdam, Churchill wrote in *The Second World War*: 'There never was a moment's discussion as to whether the atomic bomb should be used or not. To avert a vast, indefinite butchery, to bring the war to an end, to give peace to the world, to lay healing hands upon its tortured peoples by a manifestation of overwhelming power at a cost of a few explosions, seemed, after all our toils and perils, a miracle of deliverance.'

10

The success of the test atomic explosion was all that President Truman needed to start moves which he felt confident would end the war in the Far East before the dreaded invasion of Japan was due to begin in four months' time. That it was to come in the nick of time to save the lives of countless British and Indian fighting men in the imminent invasion of Malaya appears to have been fortuitous. He had what amounted to an ultimatum ready drafted when he arrived at Potsdam. It was in the form of a joint declaration from the three main contenders in the war against Japan – America, Britain and China. The Soviet Union, still being neutral in the Far East war, was not asked to join in what was to become known as the Potsdam Declaration. Neither was it thought to include a warning of imminent Soviet intervention, a factor that must have added massively to Japan's already dire situation.

The code name 'Terminal' for the Potsdam Conference was descriptively and ironically accurate. It was, indeed, the last get-together of the victors in Europe. One of the original triumvirate, Roosevelt, had died a few months before. Churchill, who had chosen the code name 'Terminal', was accompanied by his wartime deputy, the Labour leader Clement Attlee, just in case he had most votes in the general election they had both just fought at the British hustings. The count was delayed for the forces ballot around the world. Of the original Big Three, only Stalin remained in undisputed leadership.

Twelve of the thirteen sessions at the Cecilienhof Palace – on the edge of devastated Berlin – were taken up with bickering over the future of Europe, half of it occupied by the Red Army: quarrels soon to escalate into the Cold War that still divides East and West. That left only one session for the question that loomed largest in the minds of the Western leaders, how to achieve an early surrender of their Third Enemy, Japan.

This had been dominating discussions in Washington for several months. Some officials had become doubtful as to whether Russian help was needed, regardless of the atomic bomb. But in a report to Churchill and Truman on 24 July, the Combined Chiefs of Staff urged them to press

Stalin to keep his promise to join the war against Japan three months after Germany's defeat. When Truman asked Stalin to join the battle as soon as possible, Stalin told him the Red Army would be ready in the Far East in the middle of August.

During a break in the formal session, Truman walked over to Stalin to tell him that the Americans had a trump card he was sure would force the Japanese to throw in their hand. As he wrote in his memoirs, 'I casually mentioned to Stalin that we had a new weapon of unusual destructive force. The Russian premier showed no special interest. All he said was that he was glad to hear it and hoped we would make good use of it against the Japanese.'

The idea of a final warning to Japan of the consequences of continued resistance had been debated in Washington for many months. The State Department had never been too happy with Roosevelt's policy of seeking unconditional surrender, which they, like Stalin, saw as encouragement to the Japanese to fight on as long as possible. Presidential advisers had urged a declaration defining unconditional surrender in its application to Japan since the end of the Okinawa campaign in June. Joseph P. Grew, an under-secretary of state who had been ambassador in Japan for the ten years before Pearl Harbor, had long been arguing that an assurance about the Emperor was vital to obtain a Japanese surrender. Unless they were able to save some face by continuing to revere the Emperor, he believed most Japanese would fight on fanatically until overwhelmed. He had succeeded in persuading the American military chiefs that the Emperor was the key to a general surrender. They feared the Japanese might fight on for years in the occupied territories, even after the fall of the homeland, unless they received orders to lay down their arms from the Emperor himself. Indeed, some units and individual Japanese who failed to hear the Emperor's call to surrender were to do just that.

War Secretary Stimson put the Chiefs of Staff case in a memo to President Truman, recommending that a declaration should be made to Japan warning of what was to come, to give them an opportunity to surrender and 'permit' the military occupation of their country in order to ensure its complete demilitarization.

Stimson himself also thought that the Japanese should be assured that they would not be extirpated as a race or destroyed as a nation; that they would be allowed to have industries to sustain peacetime living standards; that the occupation would end when Japan had a peacefully inclined government, truly representative of the people; and that a constitutional monarchy under the present dynasty was not excluded. He gave his backing to a draft declaration drawn up by Grew which said that 'a peacefully inclined government could include a responsible monarchy under the present dynasty if the peace-loving nations can be convinced of the genuine determination of such a government to follow policies of peace which will render impossible any further development of aggressive militarism in Japan.' Stimson proposed that the warning should be carefully timed in view of the extremely sensitive national pride of the Japanese. He thought it should be made public before the invasion began, while the prospect of destruction was clear but had not yet brought about a general feeling of fanatical despair.

The State Department was divided over how the reference to the future of the Emperor should be made. The Secretary of State, James Byrnes, thought it smacked of appeasement the way it was presented in Grew's draft. Some of his leading officials argued that the cult of Emperor worship had been used by the war party in Japan to control the whole population, and the Emperor himself had encouraged the military in its aggressive pursuit of what he had called 'the national goal'.

They feared the Imperial Institution would endanger the future if it was allowed to survive. They also argued that it was unjust and illogical to eliminate and punish other elements responsible for Japan's aggressive expansion and spare the Emperor. Byrnes had his way, and it was decided it should be left to the Japanese people themselves to decide on the future of the Emperor and his House.

So it was that the draft declaration President Truman recommended to Churchill at Potsdam omitted the references to the Emperor which Stimson and Grew argued were vital to any chance of its acceptance. Instead it said that the occupying forces of the Allies would be withdrawn from Japan as soon as their objectives had been accomplished, and there had been established 'in accordance with the freely expressed will of the Japanese people a peacefully inclined and responsible government'. It also neglected to give any specific warning of the horror to come, only a hint in the words 'destructive power immeasurably greater' than before.

Churchill agreed to it on 23 July, and the final text was sent to Generalissimo Chiang Kai-Shek, requesting his agreement before the Declaration was made public. A copy was sent to the Soviet delegation, and when Molotov saw it he asked for its publication to be postponed for two or three days. Byrnes told him it had already been released to the press, explaining that the Soviet delegation had not been consulted about its substance because they were not at war with Japan, and the American and British Governments had not wanted to cause embarrassment.

Molotov then suggested that the American and British Governments should address a formal request to the Soviet Union to enter the war against Japan, basing it on the presumed Japanese rejection of the Potsdam Declaration and the wish to shorten the war and save lives.

The Americans prevaricated. They had no wish to be under any permanent obligation to the Soviet Union in a Far East settlement. They used diplomatic scruples as an excuse, saying they could not be a party to Russia's breach of its Neutrality Pact with Japan which still had eight months to run. In the end the three powers agreed on a bland formula based on the new United Nations Charter which required member states to take joint action on behalf of the community of nations to maintain peace and security.

Meanwhile publication of the Potsdam Declaration had been held up for President Truman's own considerations. He wanted to be sure that the warning that the alternative to acceptance, Japan's 'prompt and utter destruction', could be fulfilled.

Word reached him on 25 July that the new bomb had been safely delivered to the operational base of the special air force group that was to drop it.

The Potsdam Declaration was broadcast on the next day.

11

The Potsdam Conference was adjourned for the British leaders to return to London for the results of the general election in which Clement Attlee replaced Winston Churchill as prime minister. The Japanese foreign minister wanted to take advantage of the recess and he sent urgent instructions to his ambassador in Moscow to press the Russians further over the Konoye Mission.

The ambassador, Naotake Sato, was to emphasize that the Mission was being sent at the Emperor's express command, and to try to get a positive answer. He was authorized to make it clear to the Soviet leaders that Japan was ready to 'recognize the wishes of the Soviet Union in the Far East'. He was also to make it known that 'for Japan it is impossible to accept unconditional surrender under any circumstances . . . but we have no objection to a peace based on the Atlantic Charter'. The ambassador's brief went on, 'Should the United States and Great Britain remain insistent on formality [i.e. unconditional surrender] there is no solution to this situation other than for us to hold out until complete collapse on this point alone. It is necessary to have them understand that we are trying to end hostilities by asking for reasonable terms in order to secure and maintain our nation's existence and honour.'

These urgent instructions took three days to reach the Japanese embassy in Moscow, and another twenty-four hours passed before Ambassador Sato was able to obtain an interview with the deputy Soviet foreign minister, Solomon Lozovsky. They met late on the night of 25 July, the eve of the Potsdam Declaration's public release.

Lozovsky asked ingenuously whether it was correct to think that the Japanese government wanted the Soviet government to mediate. Sato formally confirmed that that was the position, and Lozovsky then asked to be sent a written text to which he promised an answer.

That same day in Potsdam the American Chiefs of Staff had been meeting alone with the Soviet Chiefs of Staff to agree on a dividing line for operations against Japan. General Alexei Antonov, of the Soviet General Staff, urged the Americans to open a southern line for shipping through the Straits of Tsushima to Vladivostok. This was agreed by the Americans with the proviso that the Russians should not rely on it until six weeks after the first landings on Kyushu because of minefields and suicide attacks on shipping in the opening phase.

On 28 July, at the tenth plenary session of the Potsdam Conference, a Soviet interpreter read a note about the renewed Japanese peace mission to Moscow. During discussion Attlee and Truman agreed with Stalin's decision not to receive the Konoye Mission and to keep the Japanese on a string.

Stalin was anxious to get into the war and make sure of extending his frontiers in the east as he had in the west. Attlee and Truman were now committed to the Potsdam Declaration's options for Japan – surrender or total destruction.

PART THREE
The Battle for Japan

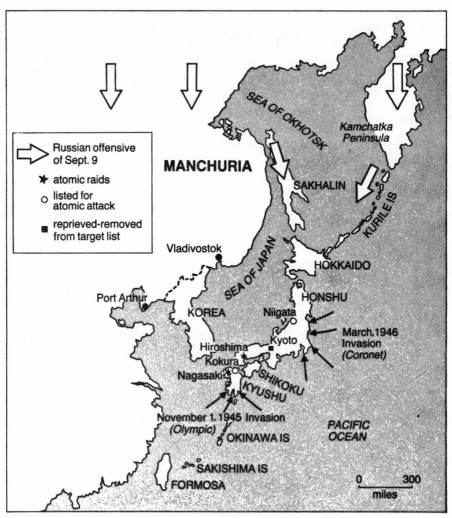

Russian offensive
of Sept. 9
★ atomic raids
○ listed for
atomic attack
■ reprieved-removed
from target list

SEA OF OKHOTSK

Kamchatka
Peninsula

MANCHURIA

SAKHALIN

KURILE IS

Vladivostok

SEA OF JAPAN

HOKKAIDO

Port Arthur

HONSHU

KOREA

Niigata

March,1946
Invasion
(Coronet)

Hiroshima

Kyoto

Kokura

Nagasaki

SHIKOKU

KYUSHU

November 1, 1945 Invasion
(Olympic)

OKINAWA IS

PACIFIC
OCEAN

SAKISHIMA IS

FORMOSA

0   300
miles

The Japanese Home Islands

1

The Battle for Japan began on 24 November 1944 when 111 Superfortress bombers raided an aircraft factory near Tokyo from airfields in the captured Marianas. It was the first time the air-raid sirens had sounded in the Japanese capital since the token Doolittle raid over two years before. In between, there had only been a few air raids on southernmost Kyushu Island by an American bomber group in India, operating at extreme range through a refuelling airfield at Chengtu in China.

The Superfortress – B29 – had been tested in the round-the-clock air offensive against Germany in which the American Air Force attacked by day and the RAF by night. It was the biggest bomber of the war, carrying seven and a half tons of bombs at 350 miles an hour at a height of 35,000 feet and a range of 4000 miles. It was used for daylight precision bombing with high explosives until General Curtiss LeMay switched his command attention from Germany to Japan. LeMay changed the tactics from precision bombing to area bombing at night with incendiary bombs instead of explosives.

In the first fire raid on the night of 9/10 March a force of 279 Superforts dropped 19,000 incendiaries on the crowded working districts of southern Tokyo with the deliberate aim of burning out an area of sixteen square miles. Strong shifting winds fanned the flames through the mainly match-wood and paper houses and 84,000 people died in the inferno.

LeMay's systematic bombing programme hit sixty-five cities with 153,887 tons of incendiaries. The number of bombers taking part increased month by month, 450 in May, 600 in June, 800 in August. In six months more than a quarter of a million civilians died and eight million lost their homes. The Emperor's palace was hit and ancient shrines were destroyed; food distribution broke down; and city populations fled to the countryside having been warned of raids to come by leaflets dropped from American planes.

After the first Tokyo fire raid in which fourteen American planes were shot down, losses to the bombing forces were negligible. At the Japanese Army's flying school at Akeno new pilots had been undergoing training since February, learning enough flying skills to enable them to ram B29 and B32 bombers. These attacks were expected to strike terror into American bomber crews, but only two such attacks were reported to have succeeded. The Japanese navy and army commanders were primarily concerned with conserving planes and precious fuel for mass attacks on the invasion fleet which they expected to appear off their shores before the end of the year. The Japanese chose to retaliate with a suicide airborne attack on Yontan airfield in Okinawa where some of the fire-raising bombers were based. Four of five troop carrier planes were shot down before they reached Okinawa, but a third got through to a belly landing on the runway. Ten commandos leapt from it tossing grenades at parked bombers, destroying seven and damaging twenty-six. They also set fire to 70,000 gallons of aviation fuel before the last of them was killed.

American submarines played a key role in crippling Japan's capacity to fight on, but did not become really effective until the last year of the war because of delays in correcting faulty torpedoes. This was the weapon that contributed greatly to Japan's early successes. Their Long Lance torpedoes carried a 225-pound warhead nearly twenty-five miles with fair accuracy, compared with the five-mile range of America's often defective torpedoes which carried only 135-pound warheads. Despite this crippling handicap American submarines had sunk 1178 Japanese merchant ships by March 1945, at which time the blockade was tightened in what was codenamed with crude accuracy 'Operation Starvation'. This involved the air drop of 13,000 mines in the waters around Japan, in the Yangtse river in China and in the Shimomoseki Straits, the main seaway between Japan and the Asian mainland. The mines took a toll of another 670 Japanese ships, and closed Japan's remaining sea communications, cutting off supplies and reinforcements from Northern China, Manchuria and Korea. All the huge overseas armies were locked up in their conquered territories, helpless to intervene in the battle for the homeland.

By the summer of 1945 Japan's position was hopeless, even though her military leaders steadfastly refused to consider surrender. Her economy, like her cities, was in ruins. The remaining warships of the once triumphant Imperial Japanese Navy were immobilized for lack of fuel. Sea blockade, which Hitler had failed to tighten around Britain, was undoubtedly succeeding against Japan. Had the war continued it was estimated that seven million Japanese would have died of starvation by March 1946.

2

The American Third Fleet sailed warily into Japanese home waters in July 1945, apprehensive of massed Kamikaze attacks. Carrier planes made exploratory strikes against airfields in the Tokyo area, and claimed that they destroyed 340 planes on the ground. The Japanese offered no serious fighter challenge, and only two of their planes were shot down in air combat. American ships then boldly sailed close inshore to bombard the Kaimaishi steel works 300 miles north of Tokyo.

The Third Fleet's tasks were to reduce the enemy's navy and army air strength, attack strategic targets, and probe the strength of Japanese defences. They concentrated on northern Honshu and the northern island of Hokkaido, where enemy reserves were thought to be dispersed out of range of the American bomber bases in the Marianas.

Planes from British carriers joined the operations and were in action for the first time over Japan on 17 July, hitting airfields south of Tokyo. The battleship, HMS *King George V*, joined American capital ships in bombarding Hitachi and Mito, some fifty miles north of Tokyo with 14-inch guns. (Since the Okinawa operations the British Pacific Fleet had withdrawn to its forward base at Manus to repair damage and restock supplies, and had been joined by the carrier, HMS *Implacable*, for operations against the once formidable Japanese base at Truk in the Caroline Islands, which had been bypassed and left far behind by the American advance.)

The American Fleet had its tail up, eager to finish off what was left of the Imperial Japanese Navy – an act of vengeance they were determined to make an exclusively American triumph. Most of Japan's major warships had been sunk in the great naval battles and two brand new carriers had been sunk by American submarines on their maiden voyages, but enough major units remained to pose a threat to the coming invasion of Kyushu. Most of the Japanese fleet, three battleships, three cruisers, two aircraft carriers and five destroyers, were dispersed around the Kure naval base in the Inland Sea, immobilized by lack of fuel. But the battleship *Nagato* (38,000 tons) was alongside a jetty in the naval base at Yokosuka in Tokyo Bay. She was chosen for the first attack.

The Americans lost twelve planes and sixteen aircrew in dive-bombing attacks through heavy anti-aircraft fire; the *Nagato* was badly damaged but still afloat.

A week later, American dive bombers attacked ships around the Kure naval base for three consecutive days, sinking the battleship *Hyuga*, the cruiser *Tone*, the aircraft carrier *Amagi*, and badly damaging most of the other ships. The Imperial Japanese Navy had been annihilated; Pearl Harbor was avenged.

While the American planes were attacking the *Nagato*, planes from the four British carriers were assigned to attack airfields and a seaplane base in the Tokyo area. While the Americans were attacking the main fleet the British planes were given targets on Shikoku on the opposite side of the Inland Sea. During raids on airfields there they spotted an escort carrier lurking in a nearby bay. Planes from all four British carriers attacked it, and left it sinking. They also sank two frigates, destroyed fifteen aircraft on the ground and damaged thirty more. The airfield at Tokushima was defended by 200 guns, and in the day's 416 sorties four British planes were shot down.

Meanwhile, Admiral William Halsey gave way reluctantly to pressure from the American Joint Chiefs and barred the Royal Navy from a role in the operations to finish off the Imperial Navy. They argued that an all-American attack would forestall a possible postwar claim by the British that they had demolished even a part of the Japanese fleet. In the British navy this was resented and regarded as a churlish way to treat an ally whose navy also had its reasons (the *Prince of Wales* and the *Repulse*) for vengeance.

During the night of 29/30 July the *King George V* joined American ships again in a bombardment, this time on the Hammamatsu railway locomotive works and two industrial plants. She poured 265 14-inch shells into the target in thirty-seven minutes. The locomotive works was severely damaged, but two key railway bridges carrying the main Tokaido railway escaped damage.

The main objective of these attacks was to hit at Japanese morale by showing that their enemy could strike hard anywhere around the Japanese coast at any time, and absenteeism caused by workers fleeing to the countryside hit production perhaps more heavily than the damage caused by the shells. Naval bombardment was far more frightening than air raids.

Before retiring to refuel, the British carriers launched another 336 sorties on 30 July against airfields in southwest Honshu and coastal shipping. They sank the frigate *Okinawa*, a large freighter, a transport and several minor vessels, and they damaged five destroyers, four escorts and a freighter. Two enemy aircraft were destroyed and six damaged for the loss of three British planes which were hit by flak.

3

The Japanese military awaited an Allied invasion with some eagerness. They looked upon it as the means to inflict an unprecedented number of casualties that would make the Americans recoil in horror. They argued with the politicians for a postponement of approaches for a negotiated settlement until this happened, believing that Japan could then end the war with honour and with much better terms than unconditional surrender.

They expected to be able to sink half the invasion ships before they reached the beaches, and withdrew 10,000 planes from current fighting to save them for massed suicide attacks. They believed that they would be able to wipe out those who managed to reach the beaches before they could establish a bridgehead. Field Marshal Hajime Sugiyame, supreme commander of the defence of the homeland, sent out orders in July which included the words, 'The key to final victory lies in destroying the enemy at the water's edge while his landings are still in progress.'

But the military chiefs in Tokyo were relying on intelligence reports which underestimated Allied manpower. These calculated that the Americans would have few reserves after committing between fifteen and twenty divisions by the end of the year. This compared with their own Home Army of over two million, plus several million militia and three million teenagers still available for call up.

They assumed correctly that the southern island of Kyushu would be the target for the first invasion attempt. It was defended by the 2nd General Army, which totalled 400,000 men. That strength was 50,000 stronger than the American intelligence estimate. In April, one of Japan's toughest soldiers, Field Marshal Sunroka Hata, was appointed to command the whole of Kyushu from headquarters at Hiroshima, the nearest major centre on the main island of Honshu. He ordered his fourteen regular infantry divisions and two armoured brigades to lead the entire population in turning Kyushu into a fortress island. They built defensive systems stretching far back from the beaches, all designed to ensure the invaders would pay the maximum price for every yard of advance inland. Teams of instructors from the Nakamo Gakko special warfare school in Tokyo were sent to every village to instruct local militias in the technique of beach defence and guerrilla resistance.

Japan had been virtually untouched by war during the first eighteen months, apart from the Doolittle raid, the bustle of war plants and memorial services to the dead of distant battles. There was no black-out and few shortages. No thought at all was given to defending Japan against attack. The possibility of invasion was inconceivable. The home islands were confidently thought to be impregnable within the distant defence rings.

All that changed from June 1943 as the Americans advanced inexorably towards them. That was the date training began in tactics to meet airborne landings, and early in 1944 a citizen defence force similar to the Home Guard in Britain was formed as a 2nd National Army to help coastal defence and resist airborne landings in every part of the home islands. By the summer of 1945 all Japanese males between the ages of seventeen and forty-one had been registered for national service and formed into a National Volunteer Combat Force numbering 28 million. They drilled with ancient rifles, swords, bamboo spears, axes, sickles and other agricultural implements. All sorts of other home-made weapons were fashioned, including crude pistols firing steel bolts. Bottles were filled with petrol to make anti-tank weapons, and with hydrocyanic acid to make poison-gas bombs. The traditional martial arts, judo and karate, were also practised; women joined in, breaking with custom to dress in peasant trousers to learn unarmed combat.

By July 1945 preparations for Operation Ketsu-go – Homeland Decisive Battle – were ready. Kamikaze planes of many types and varying degrees of airworthiness were dispersed at 200 concealed airstrips throughout Japan, supplementing seventy regular airfields and twenty-four seaplane bases. Suicide motor torpedo boats and other makeshift floating bombs were made ready at ninety-eight secret Shinyo bases. Military chiefs estimated that they would have to sink 500 key ships of the invasion fleet, and earmarked nine suicide planes against each carrier and six against each transport ship.

A last ditch redoubt was prepared for Imperial General Headquarters in the Matsushiro Mountains of central Honshu, with a separate bastion for the Emperor and his family close by at Nagano.

The woman English language broadcaster on Tokyo radio known as 'Tokyo Rose' boasted that the toll taken of American ships by Kamikaze attacks had delayed the capture of Okinawa by three months, and warned those preparing for operations against Japan, 'You just don't know what you are in for . . . you won't be seeing Mom again.'

Training courses all emphasized the glory of suicide attacks, and imbued the same fight-to-the-death spirit in every Japanese. Home Guards were trained in anti-tank tactics aimed at each defender taking out an enemy tank by sacrificing his life. The instructions specified that 'Attacks with human bullets and bombs against tanks equipped with armour and fire-power must be carried out with spiritual rigour and steel-piercing passion – a one-second delay fuse is most suitable for suicide bodies'.

The War Minister, General Amani, issued a special order in April 1945 enjoining all Japanese to 'maintain the Special Attack Force spirit at all times'. His appeal came at a time when many thousands had fled to the countryside leaving jobs in war factories to take their families to seek safety from the fire-bomb raids that had destroyed vast areas in almost every sizeable town and city. There were also severe food shortages; the official ration of low-grade rice mixed with soya beans was available only two days in three, and fish supplies were made rare by the toll taken on fishing boats by air strafing and enemy mines. But General Anami still had no serious reason to doubt that most Japanese would respond as fanatically as his soldiers to a clarion call to die in defence of their land and emperor.

The realities of Japan's hopeless situation were unknown to all but a few of the country's leaders. Most of the population were completely unaware that the once all-powerful Imperial Japanese Navy was no more. And few were perhaps aware that the air force was failing to offer a serious challenge to enemy planes because of fuel shortages and the need to conserve the few surviving experienced pilots for the struggle against the invasion fleet. Their only real strength was the Home Army, numerous, undefeated and resolute. Trust in the Emperor was largely unshaken.

All was indeed dire in Japan, with one important exception. The people's fighting spirit was as fanatical as ever. The population was mobilized to fight to the death, and slogans everywhere proclaimed 'One Hundred Million Japanese will die for the Emperor and the Nation'.

4

While Mountbatten's forces were mounting their assault on Malaya and Singapore, a special task group of the United States Air Force was preparing for an epoch-making attack from the huge air base on Tinian Island in the Marianas 1500 miles from Tokyo. The 1800 men of the 509th Composite Group were completely self-sufficient, they had their own security police, transport, communications, maintenance and support units, and crews for thirteen B-29 Superfortress bombers. The sixty-five officers and fifty-two sergeants of the flying crews had already spent ten months training to take off with a 10,000-pound bomb load and 7400 gallons of fuel, enough to fly a round trip of 3000 miles in about thirteen hours. Before coming to Tinian they had been practising the techniques of dropping a special bomb at Wendover in Utah and Batista Field in Cuba. The special bomb had to be released at 32,000 feet and aimed visually with accuracy of less than 500 feet from the aiming point. With repeated practise they had obtained an accuracy average of within 100 feet. From Tinian they made practice runs with heavy bombs over a bypassed Japanese-held island as well as over Tokyo and other cities. Three planes had already crashed in practising overladen take-offs.

Early in July, before the results of the test explosion were known, the main components for two of the special bombs were on their way to Tinian from the Los Alamos laboratories of the Manhattan District Project.

Three twin-engine Dakota transport planes carried the components and a group of specialist technicians from Alburquerque airfield near the Los Alamos laboratories across the continent to Hamilton Field, north of San Francisco. From there they went in military convoy by road to the Mare Island naval dockyard, and were immediately put aboard the waiting cruiser, *Indianapolis*.

The warship's commander, Captain Charles B. McVay, was ordered to deliver his cargo as rapidly as possible to Tinian Island. Although he was given no inkling of the nature of it, he was told that his cargo was of such importance that the components and the technicians travelling with them must have priority over the warship's crew for places in lifeboats should the ship be sunk before reaching Tinian.

It was the second time the *Indianapolis* was involved in secret weapons development. She had been the first ship to try out proximity fuses on anti-aircraft shells, developed as an antidote to Kamikaze attacks.

The *Indianapolis* crossed the Pacific at full speed, saving time by setting a direct course instead of the zig-zagging progress normally adopted to reduce the chances of a sudden torpedo attack. She docked at Tinian on 26 July, and the cargo was transferred the same day to the 509th Composite Group of the US Air Force. In the meantime, lighter components had already reached them by air cargo plane.

News of the delivery of the two bombs to Tinian was flashed to the American delegation at Potsdam, where it was still 25 July, the date of President Truman's order for the first bomb to be dropped on Japan as soon after 3 August as weather conditions permitted visual bombing.

The order, sent to the commanding general of the Strategic Air Force, General Carl C. Spaatz, laid down that the targets must include both military and industrial installations in order to put pressure on military and industrial leaders as well as the government. The cities of Hiroshima, Kokura, Niigata and Nagasaki were nominated as filling both requirements. Additional bombs were to be dropped as they became available. Within that framework all other decisions were left to the operational commanders.

The orders were to stand unless President Truman informed War Secretary Stimson that the Japanese response to the Potsdam Declaration was acceptable.

5

When the text of broadcast accounts of the Potsdam Declaration reached the Foreign Ministry in Tokyo early on 27 July, Foreign Minister Togo's first reaction was relief that the Soviet Union was not a party to it. That seemed to augur well for their peace mission. He thought it also indicated that the Western Powers were ready to back down from their insistence on an absolute unconditional surrender, and he put this down to Soviet intervention on Japan's behalf. He decided to recommend waiting for Stalin's response to the Konoye mission before deciding on Japan's attitude to the Potsdam Declaration. Members of the Peace Faction welcomed the Declaration as an indication that Japan would not be treated with complete ruthlessness. The Emperor let it be known that he considered the Potsdam Declaration to be acceptable in principle.

Togo told the Supreme War Council that the Potsdam Declaration amounted to an Allied offer of peace terms, and Suzuki, the Prime Minister, agreed that it softened the impact of unconditional surrender. But the four military members of the Council demanded its rejection, and only agreed to its publication provided the 'more lenient provisions' were deleted. They were unimpressed by the threat of 'prompt and utter destruction', believing it only meant that the air and naval bombardment would continue, devastating though it was.

The Council agreed to await Stalin's answer to the Konoye mission project, and in the meantime to treat the Potsdam Declaration with *mokusatsu*, a word that could be translated to mean to ignore, to take no notice of, to treat with silent contempt, or wise and masterly inactivity. According to the Japanese diplomat, Kase Toshikazu, the intention was merely to refrain from comment while hopes were still pinned on mediation by the Soviet Union.

Next day, 28 July, Japanese newspapers published a censored form of the Potsdam Declaration without editorial comment. Among the points omitted were those which promised that the Japanese people would not be enslaved as a race or destroyed as a nation, and that Japanese soldiers would be returned home to lead peaceful and productive lives. Inspired news reports said the government was not paying any attention to the Declaration as it appeared to be an attempt to separate the military from the people. The *Asahi Shimbun* reported that the government thought it would bolster the nation's resolve to carry on the war, unfalteringly, to a successful conclusion.

That evening American planes dropped copies of the full declaration over eleven Japanese cities along with a warning that a tremendous air bombardment would descend on them if Japan did not surrender at once on the terms in the Declaration.

Under pressure from the military, the wavering Suzuki called a press conference to speak out against the Declaration. He said it was nothing more than a rehash of the 1943 Cairo Declaration which had said the Allies would strip Japan of all the territories added to her empire since 1895. The government had no recourse but to ignore it entirely and resolutely fight on for a successful conclusion of the war. His words sealed the doom of Hiroshima and Nagasaki.

First reports of Suzuki's press conference reached America in time for the *New York Times* of 30 July to give his comments banner headlines: JAPAN OFFICIALLY TURNS DOWN ALLIED SURRENDER ULTI-MATUM.

In the War Department in Washington that afternoon, Stimson prepared the final draft of a statement in which President Truman would announce the dropping of the first atomic bomb. He incorporated some minor suggestions from the new British leaders, Attlee and Ernest Bevin, the Foreign Secretary, and sent it to Truman at Potsdam with a request to have it available for release not later than 1 August.

Meanwhile, a cruel irony in the Pacific Ocean was making 880 American sailors the first victims of the decision to drop the atomic bomb. As it was returning from Tinian after delivering the A-bomb components, the *Indianapolis* was torpedoed by the Japanese submarine L58 and sank without sending out a distress signal. Only 316 of its crew of 1196 survived to be picked up when their lifeboats were spotted from the air three days later. One of them was Captain McVay. The *New York Times* commented later, 'Her loss just before the dawn of peace marks one of the darkest pages in our naval history.'

Captain McVay, son of a former Commander-in-Chief of the American Asiatic Fleet, was court martialled. He was found guilty of failing to zig-zag, and acquitted of failing to give the order to abandon ship in time. The finding ruined a promising naval career, and he committed suicide in 1968.

The *Indianapolis* was the last major warship sunk in the Second World War. History might have been different had she been sunk on the outward voyage with the A-bomb components still aboard.

6

Japan was battered by a typhoon in the closing days of July, bringing her devastated cities respite from the mounting onslaught of air and naval bombardment. Offshore, the guns and planes of American and British warships were battened down as the fleet rode out the tempestuous seas. But any Japanese feeling that a new Divine Wind might save Japan, as it had when it dispersed an invasion fleet of Kublai Khan nearly seven centuries earlier, were soon to be brutally shattered.

The first atomic bomb was poised for operational use from 4 August when Hiroshima and the alternative targets were all obscured by cloud. Hiroshima topped the target list because it combined war factories and important military installations, and there were no prisoner-of-war camps close by. The operation to drop the first bomb was designated Bombing Mission 13.

The crews of the seven Superfortresses that were to take part were carefully briefed. In between they passed the time playing poker, reading, writing letters and dozing.

Group 509's commander, Lieut-Colonel Paul W. Tibbets, had decided to fly the plane carrying the bomb, and a few hours before take off he had his mother's given names, Enola Gay, put in huge letters across the fuselage. The Enola Gay was to be escorted by two planes carrying cameras, scientific instruments and expert observers. Three Superfortresses were to fly as weather scouts, well ahead of the others to report cloud conditions over the three potential targets, Hiroshima, Kokura and Nagasaki. The seventh Superfortress was to wait at Iwo Jima in case the Enola Gay developed technical trouble and had to transfer the bomb.

The weather scouting planes took off from Tinian just after 1.30 a.m. Little over half an hour later the Enola Gay lumbered down the extended runway carrying in her bomb bay a crude-looking apparatus 14 feet long, 5 feet wide and weighing 10,000 pounds; the crew had nicknamed it 'Thin Boy'. It contained Uranium 235 enclosed at opposite ends of the barrel with a proximity fuse to bring them into collision. As the Enola Gay and her two escorts approached the Japanese coast, Navy Captain William Parsons and his assistant, Lieutenant Morris Jeppson, clambered into the bomb bay to prime the bomb, and Colonel Tibbets told his crew that they were carrying an atomic bomb.

By that time he had received a coded message from Straight Flush, the weather scout Superfort, on conditions at Hiroshima. The message said cloud cover was less than ⅗ths at all altitudes, almost clear skies. The Straight Flush's pilot, Major Claude R. Eatherly, who later received notoriety as a man who felt himself burdened with guilt, added, 'Advise bomb primary'. The other weather scouts also reported favourable visibility over the alternative targets, Kokura and Nagasaki.

Colonel Tibbets stayed on course for the primary target, Hiroshima, with some fifty miles to go. Hiroshima (population 343,000) was the headquarters of the Japanese 2nd General Army, commanding the forces that would have opposed the November landings in Kyushu.

The approach of the weather scout, Straight Flush, caused the air-raid alert sirens to sound in Hiroshima, but when it circled and went away the 'all clear' was sounded. When three more planes approached an hour later, the local radio told people getting ready for work that it appeared to be a reconnaissance mission, but people should take shelter if they appeared over the city. The streets were crowded with people on their way to offices, factories and schools, and many glanced up at the planes glinting in the morning sunlight high above.

Soon after eight o'clock Colonel Tibbets told his crew to put on special polaroid goggles which shut out all but purple light, and begin the bombing run. As the bomb aimer, Major Thomas Ferebee, lined up his bomb sight a continuous tone signal went out from the Enola Gay to advise the military chiefs back in Tinian that the bomb was in its last fifteen seconds before release. The signal stopped just after 8.15 a.m. Hiroshima time when the opening of the bomb doors broke the circuit.

As it stopped, the Enola Gay, relieved of its heavy load, jerked upwards, and Colonel Tibbets turned steeply to get out of the area at full throttle.

Watchers below saw a cluster of parachutes fall away from one of the planes as they turned and accelerated away. Forty-three seconds later as the parachutes dropped to 2000 feet above the centre of the city there was a blinding explosion, burgeoning into an enormous fireball and a towering column of mushroom-shaped cloud.

The Enola Gay's tail-gunner, Sergeant Robert Carron, closed his eyes as the light pierced his goggles and the plane tossed in sudden turbulence. When he peered again he saw dust boiling upwards to form a mushroom cloud 40,000 feet high.

The blast of furnace heat flattened forty-two square miles of Hiroshima, and set what was left on fire. About 78,000 people died immediately, over 40,000 were horribly burned and some 14,000 were missing. Of 76,327 buildings, about 48,000 were completely destroyed and more than 22,000 severely damaged. Some 180,000 survivors were homeless, many of them soon to develop a deadly new illness they called atomic disease.

The correspondent of the Domei news agency in Hiroshima, Mr Nakamura, was caught wheeling his bicycle out of his house to ride to his office. He described what he saw several weeks later, 'There was a blinding flash, and I felt scorching heat before I was knocked to the ground and the house collapsed. I heard a booming explosion and saw a tremendous pillar of black smoke with a scarlet thread in the middle which expanded as I watched until the whole of it was glowing red.'

Mrs Futaba Kitayama, a thirty-three-year-old housewife, was working with a volunteer group to make fire breaks and limit damage from incendiary raids, just a mile from the explosion. After one of her companions shouted, 'Look, a parachute' she turned towards where the woman was pointing.

'At that moment a shattering flash filled the sky. I was thrown to the ground and the world collapsed around me, on my head, on my shoulders. I couldn't see anything. It was completely dark. I thought of my three children who had been evacuated to the countryside to be safe from air raids. When I finally struggled free there was a terrible smell and I rubbed my mouth with a towel I carried around my waist. All the skin came off my face, and then all the skin on my arms and hands fell off. The sky was as black as night, and I ran homewards towards the Tsurumi river bridge.

'People by the hundreds were flailing in the river. I couldn't tell if they were men or women, they were all in the same state, their faces puffy and ashen, their hair tangled . . . under the Kojin bridge, that had half collapsed and lost its reinforced concrete parapets, I saw bodies floating in the water with clothes in shreds.'

Mrs Kitayama eventually found a relative able to push her on a hand-cart to a first aid station, and then to relatives in a village, where her husband joined her. He bore no trace of injury, but three days after their reunion he began vomiting and died. She herself recovered, but her hands remained mutilated with the five fingers of the left one fused at the base.

Although there were no prisoner-of-war camps in the area, twenty-three American flyers from bombers shot down in attacks on the nearby port were among the bomb's victims. They were mostly killed in the destruction of Hiroshima Castle where they were held, but there were rumours that two or three survived the blast and were killed at the hands of enraged Japanese survivors.

When Bombing Mission 13 returned to Tinian Admiral William Purnell recalled that the crew of the Enola Gay had a far away look, and when they tried to talk about what they had seen, their words fell over each other.

7

President Truman was abroad the cruiser *Augusta* on the last day of his journey home from Potsdam when he received word of the Hiroshima bomb. The signal reporting 'a success even more conspicuous than the earlier test explosion' was handed to him while he was giving a farewell talk to the ship's company shortly before they were due to dock. He broke the news at once to the assembled sailors, who applauded and cheered with joyful relief at the prospect of avoiding the many months of bitter fighting they had expected to lie ahead of them. Truman recalled in his memoirs, 'I could not keep back my expectation that the Pacific War might now be brought to a speedy end.'

In Washington, a statement issued over the President's name revealed publicly for the first time that 'a new and terrible bomb' had been developed and used against Japan, dropped on 'Hiroshima, an important army base'. The statement went on, 'It is an atomic bomb. It is a harnessing of the basic power of the universe. The force from which the sun draws its power has been loosed against those who brought war to the Far East.'

The statement went on to explain that the ultimatum calling for surrender had been made at Potsdam in order to spare the Japanese people from utter destruction, and went on, 'If they do not accept our terms, they can expect a rain of ruin from the air the like of which has never been seen on this earth.'

It continued, 'Behind this attack will follow sea and land forces in such numbers and power as they have not seen, and with the fighting skill of which they are already aware.'

On his return to Washington, President Truman told the American people over the radio about the Potsdam Conference. Referring to what he called 'the tragic significance' of the atomic bomb, he said, 'Having found the bomb we have used it. We have used it against those who attacked us without warning at Pearl Harbor, against those who have starved and beaten and executed American prisoners of war, against those who have abandoned any pretence of obeying international laws of warfare. We have used it to shorten the agony of young Americans. We shall continue to use it until we completely destroy Japan's power to make war. Only a Japanese surrender will stop us.'

Truman's words would have found a receptive audience among most Americans who heard him, especially the families of the millions in uniform whose lives were still at risk. Perhaps only those who lived at that time, and were of an age to understand the stresses and single-mindedness of war, the constant fear for loved ones in peril, can fully comprehend how that could be.

8

News that a bomb of 'unprecedented power' had caused widespread devastation in Hiroshima reached Tokyo, nearly 400 miles away, in the late afternoon. It caused no great consternation. In the Supreme War Council the four military members were more concerned with renewing their demands that armistice terms must preclude any occupation of Japan, must permit the Japanese to disarm themselves and hold trials for war crimes in their own courts, as well as ensuring the retention of the Imperial Institution.

It was the following day before they had heard what had happened from Field Marshal Hata, the military commander in Hiroshima, whose head-quarters had been a mile outside the city. Although his wife was severely burned, he escaped with only minor injuries, and his headquarters was hardly damaged and only a few soldiers were killed. Because of this, he minimized the effect of the new bomb, saying it had little effect above ground level, and only those caught without protection suffered injury. The members of the Supreme War Council assumed that it had been caused by an atomic explosion, and this was confirmed by tests made by Japan's leading atomic scientist, Dr Tsunesaburo Asada, who went to Hiroshima on a flying visit and reported back on 8 August.

By that time President Truman had announced to the world that an atomic bomb had been dropped on Hiroshima and warned of the 'rain of ruin' unless Japan surrendered at once.

But the military members of the Supreme War Council were still astonishingly phlegmatic. They pointed out that the casualties and devastation the first atomic bomb had caused were by no means as great as the fire-bomb raids which Tokyo and other cities had already withstood.

They had their own latest advance in technology to report to the Council. Japan's prototype jetplane had flown for the first time on 7 August.

Togo moved to get round the deadlock caused by the Supreme War Council's attitude. After hearing Truman's statement, the cabinet gave him their backing for acceptance of the Potsdam Declaration, so long as the Emperor's position was assured. Togo then obtained an audience with Hirohito to urge him to support efforts to end the war as soon as possible. Hirohito authorized him to tell Suzuki that 'in view of the new type of weapon' Japan was now powerless to continue the war. He added that Japan must now accept the inevitable; his own personal safety was secondary to the need for an immediate end of the war. Hiroshima must not be repeated.

Suzuki decided to put the Emperor's command to the Supreme War Council immediately, but the meeting he convened on 8 August had to be postponed because one of the military members was unavoidably detained by 'more pressing business elsewhere'. This was, perhaps, the low point in the curious lethargy that gripped Japan's leaders throughout these critical days, it was partly caused by fear of assassination by the sort of military hotheads who had stalked Japanese politics for decades.

Little news of either the atomic bomb or the Potsdam Declaration was reaching most of the Japanese people. Broadcasts from Manila and Okinawa expressing the Allies' desire to end the war without destroying Japan were jammed. But gradually knowledge of the positive aspects of the Potsdam Declaration, omitted from accounts in their own newspapers, was spread as leaflets dropped from American planes were passed around.

In the first twenty-four hours after the bomb was dropped, the only official news had been an army communiqué which said that a small number of B29 aircraft had caused considerable damage in Hiroshima with a new type of bomb. But after that an idea of the real horror was unveiled in Japanese newspapers and radio broadcasts which began a campaign against the enemy's barbarity. Newspapers reported that most of Hiroshima had been obliterated. One radio broadcast said that the force of the explosion was so terrific that practically every living thing, human or animal, was seared by tremendous heat. It told of inhabitants who had been killed by blast, fire or crumbling buildings and most were so battered it was impossible to tell men from women.

The decision to use 'a barbaric weapon as a last resort' was put down to the enemy's impatience at the slow progress towards an invasion of Japan. Commentators condemned America for using such a destructive weapon, describing it as an act that would 'brand the enemy for ages to come as a destroyer of mankind'.

The Japanese government, through its embassy in Switzerland, filed a formal protest against the United States government.

When the first reconnaissance pictures of what the bomb did to Hiroshima reached Washington, Stimson was so shattered he renewed his pleas for Japan to be afforded an easier way to surrender.

9

Despite the better weather, Allied warships were ordered to stay clear of Japanese waters in the first week of August because of 'a special operation'. News on 7 August that the special operation had been the dropping of an atomic bomb on Hiroshima was received with jubilation, bringing hope that the war might end much sooner than had previously seemed likely. After the Japanese had fought on fiercely 'beyond all reason' at Okinawa, the Allies expected them to fight more ferociously still in their own homeland. There were few in the American and British ships who had any doubt that the atomic bomb was not a blessed deliverance.

Aboard the British carriers most of the pilots were newly trained youngsters, the most recent replacements lacked combat experience and had inadequate training. Of the forty-four Corsair pilots aboard *Victorious*, only eleven had made more than a dozen deck landings before joining her and fifteen had fewer than 150 hours solo flying experience.

Land-based bombers quickly resumed normal operations as bad weather cleared over their target cities. Four hundred planes bombed aircraft and ammunition stores at Tarumizu on the same day the atomic bomb was dropped on Hiroshima. The Yawata industrial complex at Kyushu and targets in Tokyo and other cities were hit on 8 August.

The Third Fleet, including the British Pacific Fleet, sailed back into Japanese waters to resume normal war operations.

On 9 August, the British ships *Newfoundland, Gambia, Terpisichore, Tenacious* and *Termagant* joined American warships in a bombardment of the coastal town of Kamaishi in northern Honshu, closing within two miles of the beaches. At the same time, carrier planes launched their first attacks for ten days. The British planes strafed six airfields in northern Honshu, beyond the range of land-based bombers, destroying forty-two aircraft and damaging twenty-two. They also attacked targets of opportunity off the coast, sinking three destroyers, a submarine chaser and a number of coastal craft; they probably sank two more destroyers, a torpedo boat and other craft, and damaged another destroyer, two escort vessels and many small craft.

British planes flew 407 sorties, and six pilots were lost. One of them was Lieutenant Robert Hampton Gray, of the Royal Canadian Navy, a veteran of the attack on the *Tirpitz*, who was posthumously awarded the last Victoria Cross of the war. The citation said he pressed home a low-level attack to sink a Japanese destroyer through heavy fire from shore batteries and five warships.

Despite the heavy toll of Japanese shipping, the main objective of the attacks had been the airfields. Intelligence reports had indicated that Kamikaze aircraft were being assembled in northern Honshu in readiness for a spectacular suicide raid. The planes were transports instead of the usual bombing planes, and they were to crash land on the B29 airfields in Saipan and Tinian with cargoes of suicide soldiers in a desperate bid to stop another atomic attack.

While this air offensive was going on in the north, American destroyers on 'Kamikaze watch' picket duty off Tokyo Bay came under heavy attack from Kamikazes. The destroyer *Borie* was badly damaged with forty-nine of her crew killed and thirty-four injured. Other Kamikazes were shot down by American fighters before they had a chance to crash dive on the ships.

These operations of normal war were quickly overshadowed by two other developments that day. The second atomic bomb was dropped on Nagasaki, and the Soviet Union entered the war against Japan with a massive offensive on the Asian mainland.

10

Stalin's long-awaited response to Japan's repeated pleas for Soviet mediation to end their war with the Western Powers was made known to the Japanese ambassador, Naotake Sato, when he was summoned to the Foreign Ministry in Moscow at 5 p.m. on 8 August. Instead of the peace moves he was hoping for, an unsmiling Soviet Foreign Minister, Vyacheslav Molotov, curtly handed him a note announcing that the Soviet Union would also be at war with Japan from the following day's date.

In the Far East, 9 August began only a few hours later. Before any warning could possibly reach them, unsuspecting Japanese soldiers in Manchuria and Korea suddenly found themselves under attack as seventy divisions of the Red Army, about 1¼ million men, smashed across the borders.

The first intimation of the Soviet move was picked up in Tokyo by a radio operator on routine duty monitoring Moscow Radio near the end of his night shift on the morning of 9 August. A transcript of the broadcast announcement of the Soviet declaration of war was taken to the home of the Foreign Minister before 8 a.m., whereupon Togo rushed across town to the Prime Minister's house to demand an immediate meeting of the Supreme War Council which had so strangely failed to assemble the previous day to hear the Emperor's demand that peace must be made before the Hiroshima experience was repeated.

The Soviet entry into the war, thought by some historians to have been more decisive than the atomic bomb in bringing Japan's acceptance of the Potsdam Declaration, certainly brought home to the divided leaders in Tokyo the fact that their last hope of a negotiated peace had gone. It could fairly be said to have been the psychological last straw. The Japanese were deeply outraged at Soviet duplicity – with the Neutrality Pact still having eight months to run – even though it was on a par with their own surprise attacks on the Russians at Port Arthur in 1904, and on the Americans at Pearl Harbor in 1941. (The Chinese were also surprised at the Russian onslaught. Stalin had promised to reach agreement on strategy and war aims with the Nationalist leader, General Chiang Kai-Shek, before entering the Far East war, and no accord had been reached.)

Suzuki now found himself under tremendous pressure to accept the Potsdam Declaration without more ado. The Lord Privy Seal, Marquis Koichi Kido, impressed upon him the Emperor's wishes. He opened a meeting of the Supreme War Council that morning by saying that Hiroshima and the Soviet intervention now made it impossible to carry on the war. Hope of getting some mitigation of surrender terms through Soviet mediation had proved abortive. There was no alternative but to accept the Potsdam Declaration with the sole condition of an assurance about the Emperor's future.

Anami, the War Minister, retorted angrily that the army was still capable of fighting off an invasion, and better peace terms would be offered when severe casualties had been inflicted on invasion forces. The army commander-in-chief, General Umezu, raised doubts as to whether the armed forces would obey an order from Tokyo to lay down their arms in surrender. He pointed out that the military code prescribed heavy penalties for men who laid down their arms, and all ranks were made to believe that suicide was the only honourable alternative to surrender.

In the end, the Supreme War Council was unable to reach a decision, being equally divided with Suzuki, Togo and Admiral Yonai ready to accept unconditional surrender, and Anami, Umezu and the Navy Chief of Staff, Admiral Toyoda, opposing it.

The question was passed to the cabinet whose meeting was called for the afternoon.

11

While the inconclusive debate continued in Tokyo, the second atomic bomb was dropped above Nagasaki, the major port of Kyushu island where the invasion was due to begin three months later. This second bomb was a more powerful plutonium version, nicknamed 'Fat Boy'. Although it fell four miles from the city centre, it still killed 23,753 people and wounded 43,000 others in a population of 260,000. Their fate was sealed by the deadly roulette of weather for, once again, as on the day Hiroshima was destroyed, Nagasaki was only a secondary target. The primary target for the second atomic bomb was Kokura, a small town at the narrowest point of the channel separating Kyushu from the main island of Honshu, linked by a recently constructed tunnel 4000 yards long. The area was shrouded in sea fog on the morning it was to have been destroyed, and after three futile passes over Kokura the B29 carrying the bomb flew on to release it over Nagasaki.

Because the bomb fell wide and because Nagasaki was built around a hill, much of the harbour area escaped the blast. On one side of the hill all was obliterated, but on the seaward side, in the lea of the hill, buildings were hardly touched. On one side stories told by the few survivors repeated the horrors experienced at Hiroshima three days before. On the seaward side a party of Allied prisoners-of-war, working in the docks, lived to tell of their experience.

One of them, Leading Seaman Thomas H. Evans of the Royal Navy, later described the explosion to a BBC correspondent, 'I can't make you understand how bright the flash was. It was blue and had a ringing sound. It went through you like the shock you get from an electric battery. It was terribly hot as well, just like solid heat coming at you.'

Two other Britons saw the flash from an American B52 forty miles away flying at 40,000 feet. They were Group Captain Leonard Cheshire, winner of the Victoria Cross for pioneering precision bombing of targets in Europe, and the physicist Dr William Penney (now Lord Penney), the only member of the Los Alamos scentific team on the Target Committee in Washington. They were at Tinian as official British observers but had been brazenly excluded from the observation party that had accompanied the attack on Hiroshima. Subsequent protests to President Truman had gained them places in an observation plane for the next atomic attack, but for unexplained reasons a rendezvous with the attack plane was not made, and they were still forty miles from Nagasaki when a blinding flash blotted out the sun, and an eerie purple radiance filled the interior of their plane. Through goggles they saw a huge, boiling fireball which gradually formed a luminous mushroom shaped cloud two miles wide, stretching up to 60,000 feet.

Cheshire told his biographer, Andrew Boyle, that on the long return flight to Tinian he could work up no honest pity for the bomb's victims, feeling that if this extraordinary bomb had claimed more than the average haphazard toll of victims that was part of the ironic fortune of war. He himself felt an overpowering sense of elation and achievement. But back at Tinian he found many Americans, most of them hard men of war, caught on an emotional rebound, full of inexpressible doubt. An American colonel spoke these doubts aloud, 'We can't undo the past, but there must be no more atomic bombs. We can't let innocent people go through that again, even Japs.'

It was not known to the Japanese, or to the world at large, that after Nagasaki the Americans had shot their nuclear bolt. There were no more bombs at Tinian. Materials for a third bomb, which could have been got to Tinian in time to be dropped about 20 August, had been held back in the expectation that Japan would by now have had demonstration enough of the atomic bomb's terrible power. It was thought that the threat of more bombs would be sufficient to bring the military diehards to heel, and President Truman advised General Spaatz that there would be no third drop unless it was specifically ordered by the President himself.

12

News of the Nagasaki bomb had still not reached Tokyo when the Cabinet met in the afternoon to listen to the latest arguments put forward by Suzuki and Togo for the acceptance of the Potsdam Declaration. They were met with the same stubborn arguments in favour of continuing the struggle as those which had been voiced in the Supreme War Council in the morning. At 11 p.m. Suzuki and Togo went to the palace to tell Emperor Hirohito that neither the Supreme War Council nor the Cabinet were able to reach a decision. The Imperial Conference, the highest council in Japan, took up the question just after midnight in the Emperor's air-raid shelter and, although it was then known that a second atomic bomb had been dropped on Nagasaki, the arguments against surrender were strenuously repeated.

Finally, at 2 a.m., Suzuki took the unprecedented action of asking the Emperor to make the decision himself. Hirohito then gave his immediate sanction to acceptance of the Potsdam Declaration with the proviso that the Imperial House should not be deposed. The Cabinet was called and gave its formal approval an hour later.

Soon after dawn on 10 August a wireless message was sent via Switzerland and Sweden to the governments of the United States, Britain and China, and a copy was sent to the Soviet Embassy in Tokyo.

It read:

In obedience to the gracious command of His Majesty the Emperor who, ever anxious to enhance the cause of world peace, desires earnestly to bring about a speedy termination of hostilities with a view to saving mankind from the calamities to be imposed upon them by further continuation of the war. the Japanese government several weeks ago asked the Soviet Government, with which neutral relations then prevailed, to render good offices in restoring peace vis-à-vis the enemy powers. Unfortunately their efforts in the interest of peace having failed, the Japanese Government, in conformity with the august wish of His Majesty to restore the general peace and desiring to put an end to the untold suffering entailed by war as quickly as possible, have decided upon the following.

The Japanese Government are ready to accept the terms enumerated in the joint declaration which was issued at Potsdam on 26 July, 1945, by the

Heads of the Governments of the United States, Great Britain and China, and later subscribed by the Soviet Government, with the understanding that the said declaration does not comprise any demand which prejudices the prerogatives of His Majesty as a Sovereign Ruler.

The Japanese Government sincerely hope that this understanding is warranted and desire keenly that an explicit indication to that effect will be speedily forthcoming.

To avoid any interference from the military, the Foreign Ministry sent the text of this message by morse code, thus bypassing the army censorship of normal telegrams. The diplomats were desperate to forestall the dropping of a third atomic bomb for which Tokyo was rumoured to be a target for 12 August. According to the Japanese Pacific War Research Society, the Foreign Office believed that once the people of the Allied countries heard that Japan wanted peace, they would be so relieved that their governments would be forced to accept Japan's one condition.

But in Japan itself the people were to be guided towards peace obliquely and gradually. The Cabinet decided that because of fears of an armed forces revolt, no announcement was to be made of the message to the Allied Powers until the time came to announce surrender in an Imperial Rescript which would have the force of a command from the Emperor.

At seven o'clock on 10 August Japanese domestic and overseas radio services broadcast two perplexing statements. The first, put out by staff officers over the name of General Anami, said that Japan had one choice, to fight on 'to win the sacred war . . . even if we have to chew grass and eat earth and live in fields – for in our death is a chance of our country's survival'. The other statement, from the Cabinet, was so oblique as to be ambiguous. It said the enemy was using a new type of bomb, unparalleled in ruthlessness and barbarity, and called on the people to 'rise to the occasion, overcoming whatever obstacles may lie in the path of the preservation of our national polity'.

Meanwhile, the message from the Japanese Government was being argued over in Washington between those who blamed the Emperor for the ascendancy of the military in Japan, and those who thought the retention of the monarchy was necessary to facilitate the surrenders of the overseas Japanese garrisons. The American response was eventually drafted, and sent to London, Moscow and Chungking for approval. It laid down that from the moment of surrender the authority of the Emperor and the Japanese Government would be subject to the Supreme Commander of the Allied Forces who would take such steps as he deemed proper to effectuate the surrender terms. It also required the Emperor and the Japanese High Command to sign the surrender documents.

In London, Attlee discussed it with Bevin and Churchill before counselling Washington not to insist on the Emperor signing the surrender documents. He argued it would be undiplomatic, and it would be better for the Emperor to be required to authorize and ensure signature of the surrender by the Japanese government and Japanese General Headquarters, and to command all Japanese forces, wheresoever located, to cease operations and surrender their arms.

This suggestion was accepted by Washington, which had already received General Chiang Kai-Shek's approval on behalf of China. Stalin raised a case for a Russian as joint Supreme Commander, but also approved the reply.

The Allied response was sent by way of Switzerland on 11 August, and was picked up by radio in the first hour of 12 August in Tokyo, less than twenty-four hours after the Emperor's decision.

In the meantime, tensions had been mounting in Tokyo. The opponents of surrender in the Cabinet had been joined by the ministers of Home and Justice, and the Allied reply brought a backlash of opposition to surrender on the basis of the version monitored by radio. It was decided to put off consideration of it until the official text arrived. It arrived just before 7 p.m., shortly after that decision, but the ministers of the Cabinet, fearful of assassination, were still not ready to grasp the nettle. The text was left for consideration on the morrow, and officially registered as being received on 13 August.

The Supreme War Council considered the Allied response throughout 13 August but had failed to reach agreement when the meeting was adjourned at midnight. Posters were already appearing on walls of government buildings denouncing those who argued for peace as traitors. There was simmering unrest in military barracks throughout the country.

13

President Truman resisted calls for a halt to the bombing from Stimson and other advisers now that the end of Japan's resistance was near. He thought a cessation of attacks on Japan might encourage its leaders to attempt further negotiations. The Americans were now impatient for an immediate surrender before the extent of the Red Army's advances strengthened Stalin's claims for a role in the occupation.

This political consideration apart, Admiral Nimitz ordered the Third Fleet to extend the time scale of its operations off Japan in order to support the Soviet offensive in Manchuria and Sakhalin. The first naval operation in Japanese waters was due to have ended on 10 August with a final series of strikes against the northern island of Hokkaido and northern parts of Honshu. The British Pacific Fleet was due to sail on that date to its main base at Sydney to prepare for the Kyushu invasion in November, and its fuel margin was already tight. The full fleet stayed on an extra forty-eight hours, and planes from the carriers flew 372 sorties against Kamikaze airfields and coastal shipping on 10 August. There was little challenge from Japanese fighters, but they were met with strong anti-aircraft fire from the ground. The approach of another typhoon caused the cancellation of coastal bombardments planned for 11 August.

Most of the British Pacific Fleet then sailed for Sydney, leaving only the battleship *King George V*, the carrier *Indefatigable* and their support ships to take part in the final operations.

The Japanese were not letting up either. On 12 August a torpedo bomber penetrated the fighter screen and severely damaged one of the major American warships, and Japanese suicide submarines sank the American submarine *Bonefish* – the fifty-first US submarine lost – the American destroyer *Callaghan* – the seventieth US destroyer lost – and the destroyer escort *Underhill*.

On 13 August American carrier planes attacked airfields in the Tokyo Plain, claiming 307 aircraft destroyed. The lone British carrier *Indefatigable* flew strikes against a chemical factory, but other targets were 'weathered in'. During these operations about twenty-five Kamikaze planes made determined efforts to find the Allied ships, and twenty-three of them were shot down.

Within twenty-four hours of the end of the war, 800 B29s escorted by 200 fighters, raided an ammunition dump at Osaka, a naval base at Hikari, an oil refinery at Atika, and the Marifu marshalling yards near Hiroshima. American planes also gave support to advancing Russian troops by bombing a major airfield at Maijo in Korea, where they also shot down sixteen Japanese fighters for the loss of one.

14

Leaflets with translations of the exchanges between the Japanese Government and the Allies over the Potsdam Declaration vitiated attempts to keep the surrender moves secret from the military diehards, and made it imperative to head off a military coup. When Marquis Kido, showed one of the leaflets to Hirohito, he immediately agreed to call an Imperial Conference – the Gozenkaigi – with the intention of demanding their acceptance of the Potsdam Declaration.

Some members of the Supreme War Council and the President of the Privy Council were summoned so hastily, they had no time to put on court dress, and had to borrow ties from their secretaries to wear with their warm weather clothing.

They assembled before Emperor Hirohito in the royal air-raid shelter just before 11 a.m. The military representatives again began to argue for their policy of holding out for better terms. They said the present terms would still endanger Japan's existence, and it would be better to carry on the struggle even at the cost of 100 million lives. They said the Soviet offensive made no difference to the situation in Japan, and dismissed the atomic bomb as causing no more damage than the big incendiary raids.

The Emperor listened to the arguments as they were put for the last time, and then declared that unless the war was 'brought to an end at this moment, I fear the nation will be destroyed'. He wept as he said his wish was that Japan should bear the unbearable, and accept the Allied terms in order to preserve the state and spare the people further suffering. He choked and rubbed moisture from his spectacles with the white gloves of his court dress as he went on to speak of the families of the war dead. He said he realized it would be a great shock to the armed forces, and he would be prepared to speak to the troops directly if it was necessary. In any case, he would face the radio microphone for the first time to broadcast his decision to surrender to the people. He ended by asking for an Imperial Rescript to be drawn up announcing the end of hostilities. The conference ended at noon with most of those present in tears.

The cabinet met immediately to give formal endorsement to the

Emperor's decision. They also authorized the foreign office to inform the Allied Powers, and then got down to drafting an Imperial Rescript for the Emperor to broadcast that same afternoon. But General Anami, made further difficulties over the wording and it was not till 11 p.m. that an approved draft was ready.

Meanwhile, a message about the Emperor's decision was sent to Berne, and telephoned from the United States embassy there to Washington, where it was still afternoon. Soon afterwards Britain, the Soviet Union and China were informed that the American Government regarded the Japanese message as a full acceptance of the Potsdam Declaration, and they wished to release it for publication at once. The Japanese government was also notified and ordered to command all Japanese forces everywhere to stop fighting.

In London, Attlee went on the BBC at midnight to break the news to a people who had been at war for twenty days short of six years. He recalled the treachery of the Japanese entry into the war at a time when Britain 'was sorely pressed in our life and death struggle with Germany and Italy', and paid tribute to the prodigious efforts of America, without which 'the Far East War would still have many years to run'.

At the same time, President Truman gave a press conference in Washington to announce that final victory had been won.

While towns and villages throughout the Allied world experienced scenes of wild jubilation, most Japanese were still unaware of their country's defeat. All they heard on Tokyo radio that evening were repeated announcements of an important broadcast that was to come at noon next day. Most listeners expected it to be an exhortation to greater sacrifices, and it was not until next morning that it was announced that the Emperor himself would be broadcasting to the Japanese people for the first time.

Emperor Hirohito was still recording his statement for the broadcast at midnight on 14 August as three separate groups of officers in the Tokyo area moved to abort any decision to surrender.

One group, which included staff officers from the War Ministry and officers from the Imperial Guards detachment at the Palace, went to the guards mess adjoining the palace to ask the guard commander, Lieut-General Takeshi Mori, to take the Emperor into protective custody. They believed Hirohito was an unwilling hostage surrounded by bad advisers, and wanted him to become a rallying point for those determined to carry on the war. At the outset of the war, Hirohito had urged the people to wage total war for 'the sacred goals of Japan'. On the eighth day of every month since, Greater Asia Day had been celebrated with solemn public readings of his exhortation to war, 'We by the grace of Heaven, Emperor of Nippon, sitting on the throne of a line unbroken through ages eternal . . . rely upon the loyalty and bravery of our subjects in our confident expectation that the task bequeathed by our forefathers shall be carried forward.' They apparently did not accept that Hirohito had been acting as a constitutional monarch complying with the wishes of a unanimous Cabinet.

General Mori refused to join the insurgents, and was shot dead when he did not sign orders for the conspirators' wishes to be carried out. His brother-in-law, a colonel who happened to be in his office at the time, was beheaded. The orders were then stamped with the general's seal, and the rebels quickly took control of the palace compound. By this time the Emperor had finished recording his broadcast and the radio station staff were arrested as they tried to leave the palace.

Word of agitation among the palace guards had reached the Emperor's attendants as he finished the recordings in the Imperial Household buildings. Hirohito left by a side door and was driven through wooded grounds to the Obunko, his library and air-raid shelter. He sipped green tea and listened to the recording with his wife, the Empress Nagako, who was in tears. The only other copy of the recording was locked in a safe hidden behind an old Chinese scroll in a bedroom in the Ladies-in-Waiting Pavilion.

The palace was in darkness because of an air-raid alert, and the mutineers had to search it by torchlight. They ransacked the apartment of Marquis Kido in the Imperial Household Building, and bullied servants who could give them no information. Marquis Kido and another court official had locked themselves in the palace vaults. Even in their desperation the rebels dared not disturb the Emperor himself. Instead they surrounded the Obunko in order to isolate him.

But the rebellion collapsed before dawn. The area army commander, General Shizuichi Tanaka, pushed his way angrily past the sentries on the palace drawbridge across the moat, and upbraided the troops inside the palace for daring to doubt a decision taken by the Emperor. Two of the principal leaders, Major Kenji Hatanake and Captain Shigetaro Uehara, killed themselves on the lawns in front of the palace during the morning; the others committed suicide elsewhere, one of them beside the coffin where the murdered commander of the palace guard was lying in state.

A final attempt to stop the Emperor's broadcast was made at the radio station. Just before it was due, a military police lieutenant on duty there threatened to kill anyone who prevented him getting into the studio where the broadcast was about to start. He was overpowered just in time.

A lesser drama in Tokyo while this was going on concerned an attempt to kill Suzuki. A captain of the Imperial Guards led a column of diehards from Yokohama to the Prime Minister's official residence, which they burned down when they found their intended victim was not there. They then went on to burn Suzuki's private home. and the homes of the President of the Privy Council and other politicians tainted with advocating peace.

At the huge Atsugi airbase near Yokohama, the control centre for 7000 Kamikaze planes poised to attack any invading armada, a naval captain persuaded pilots of 302 Air Corps to carry on the war whatever the Emperor might say in his broadcast. Later they added to the confusion in Tokyo by dropping leaflets denouncing the surrender rescript as false.

Reluctance to surrender rumbled on, punctuated by officers committing ritual suicide, and as late as 20 August army officers plotted the setting up of a 'Government of Resistance'. But by the end of the month these movements were suppressed. Japan's proud soldiers, sailors and airmen bowed to the inevitable at last.

15

At midnight on 14 August Molotov called Harriman and his aide Clark Kerr to the Foreign Ministry in Moscow. He wanted to discuss the Japanese acceptance of the Potsdam Declaration, provided the prerogatives of the Emperor would not be prejudiced. Molotov told them that the Soviet government was sceptical; they felt the Japanese were trying to impose conditions. Molotov tried to postpone the question, but Harriman insisted on making a decision that very night. Harriman noted at the time that Molotov gave every indication that the Soviet government was willing for the war to continue. At two o'clock in the morning, Molotov agreed to the American response to Japan, but raised the question of a Soviet joint supreme commander. Harriman suspected it was part of a manoeuvre to barter Soviet occupation of the northern island of Hokkaido, a question which the Russians had raised before, for agreement to an American supreme commander, and refused to consider the question. Later he was phoned by Molotov's interpreter to say Stalin had been consulted, and there had been a misunderstanding. They only wanted to be consulted on the choice of supreme commander.

Earlier on 14 August Molotov had signed a belated agreement with Nationalist China. Under threat of Soviet recognition of Mao-Tse–Tung's communists as China's government, General Chiang Kai-Shek was forced to agree to the lease of half the peninsula of Dairen for thirty years, accept the appointment of a Soviet harbourmaster at Port Arthur, and also recognize the independence of Outer Mongolia.

In the seven-day-war in North-East Asia the Red Army suffered 8219 killed and over 22,000 wounded. About 1½ million Russians attacked positions defended by 700,000 Japanese, whose numbers had been depleted by one third to reinforce the southern battle fronts. The Japanese fought delaying actions and set fire to the flat grasslands of Manchuria to hamper the advance of Russian tanks. In the fighting they lost 7483 killed and more than 70,000 wounded. After the Emperor's order to cease fire over 600,000 Japanese, including 148 generals, surrendered to the Red Army. More than 100,000 never returned home.

Soviet newspapers and radio commentaries made much of the Red Army's sweeping victories in Manchuria, but although the Hiroshima bomb had been briefly reported there was no mention at all of the second bomb on Nagasaki on the day Russia entered the war. So far as Soviet citizens were concerned, it was the Red Army that delivered the *coup de grâce* to the Japanese.

16

In the last hours of the war, the Japanese air forces which had been held for so long in reserve to await the invasion, attempted to interfere with Allied planes. A formation of eighteen planes from HMS *Indefatigable* were intercepted by twelve Zekes soon after dawn on 15 August. Four were shot down, four others were probably shot down and the remaining four were damaged. American planes were also intercepted by fighters, and a fierce dog fight took place over Tokurozama airfield on the outskirts of Tokyo in which ten Japanese and four American planes were shot down.

One of the British pilots baled out when his Seafire was hit by ground fire. Sub-Lieutenant F. Hockley landed unhurt, and was taken to the local military headquarters east of Tokyo. He was executed that evening by shooting, hours after the Emperor had broadcast Japan's surrender. Two of the officers responsible were later hanged as war criminals and a third was sentenced to fifteen years' imprisonment.

A second wave of American strike planes were recalled from more attacks at seven o'clock that morning when all further operations were cancelled. Two hours later the fleet was told that Japan had agreed to surrender and all offensive operations were to cease. Bunting flags signalled 'Cease hostilities against Japan' in the traditional way as jubilant crews crowded the decks. In the excitement some sailors threw steel helmets and other newly obsolete equipment overboard.

But it was not quite the end. At 11.20 a.m. the ceasefire signal was hauled down and the familiar flags signalling 'enemy aircraft approaching' were run up in its place. A lone Judy bomber had penetrated to the heart of the fleet, abruptly ending the feelings of relaxation. It dropped two huge bombs close to the *Indefatigable* before being shot down by an American fighter. Sporadic Japanese air activity continued by pilots probably seeking suicide. Two more planes were shot down while Admiral Halsey was broadcasting a Victory message to the fleet that afternoon, confirming the wisdom of his warning that Kamikazes were likely to have a final fling, and any 'ex-enemy aircraft approaching the fleet were to be shot down in a friendly manner'.

17

An absolute command of the Emperor was always known as the Voice of the Sacred Crane, from an ancient saying that even when the crane was hidden from sight its voice could be heard from the skies. The broadcasting debut of Emperor Hirohito at noon on 15 August brought the voice of the crane to the people of Japan, unprecedented contact with his subjects by a ruler revered almost as a deity. Tokyo's NHK radio station played the national anthem, then Suzuki introduced the Emperor and, throughout the Japanese empire, the Emperor's voice was heard by ordinary people for the first time. To Western ears the statement listened to in awe and anguish by millions of Japanese was strangely unworldly. . . 'We declared war on America and Britain out of our sincere desire to ensure Japan's self-preservation and the stabilization of East Asia, it being far from our thoughts to infringe upon the sovereignty of other nations or to embark on territorial aggrandisement . . . the war has developed not necessarily to Japan's advantage, while the general trends of the world have all turned against her interests. . . . The enemy, moreover, has begun to employ a most cruel bomb, the power of which to do damage is indeed incalculable, taking toll of many innocent lives. Should we continue to fight it would not only result in the ultimate collapse and obliteration of the Japanese nation, but would lead also to the total extinction of human civilization.'

Hirohito expressed grief for the fallen, solicitude for the wounded and the homeless, and pride in the role of the armed forces, and went on, 'We are keenly aware of the inmost feelings of our subjects . . . we have resolved to pave the way for peace for all generations to come by enduring the unendurable and suffering what is insufferable . . . cultivate ways of rectitude, further nobility of spirit and work with resolution so that you may enhance the innate glory of the Imperial State and keep pace with the progress of the world.' He also expressed 'the deepest sense of regret to our allied nations of East Asia, who have consistently cooperated with the Empire towards the emancipation of East Asia'.

The broadcast made no mention of unconditional surrender, gave no hint of what might happen to Japan and raised immediate misgivings in

Allied capitals. In the Australian capital, Canberra, it was seen as the first shot in a war of nerves that could lead to another war in the future. In London, *The Times* described Hirohito's statement on why Japan went to war as a lie, and added that while the motive might have been to try to save face, it impugned the whole moral foundation of the Allied war effort.

In the village of Karmizawa, where foreign civilians were interned, people came from outlying farms and gathered around houses with radio sets to hear the voice of their Emperor, the Son of Heaven. According to one of the internees, the French journalist Robert Guillian, they listened in a stupor. Only when an announcer explained the Emperor's words did the message get through and sobbing break out.

After the first shock of the Emperor's words, most Japanese quickly found ways to accept the reality, this was helped by the absence of any mention of defeat or the unthinkable word surrender from the broadcast. They could convince themselves that Japan was ending the war because of the inhumanity of her enemies, the Japanese army was still undefeated. The Emperor, as they saw it, was not only the saviour of Japan but of the whole of human civilization.

Soon after the broadcast ended the rebellious Kamikaze pilots of 302 Air Corps flew low over Tokyo dropping leaflets denouncing the Imperial Rescript and calling for *Gyokusai*, a final day of reckoning. But, after traumatic scenes in military camps throughout Japan and overseas, loyalty to the Emperor's wishes predominated. The diehard General Anami called on all soldiers and airmen to stand by their loyalty to the Emperor, and to refrain from rash actions, particularly 'over-hasty suicide attacks'.

After signing the surrender Anami had gone home to commit *seppuku*, the ritual suicide of samurai tradition, leaving a message saying he did so on behalf of all his officers, whom he further enjoined not to emulate his action. Vice-Admiral Ohnishi, the founder of the Kamikaze tactics, was among many senior officers who also killed themselves. He left a message expressing his appreciation of 'the brave special attackers who had fought and died valiantly with faith in ultimate victory', and added, 'In death I wish to atone for my part in the failure to achieve that victory, and I apologize to the souls of the dead fliers and to their bereaved families.'

One infantry battalion stationed near Tokyo lost all of its officers, a major, three captains, ten first lieutenants, twelve second lieutenants and a number of NCOs. The major set the example by traditional hara-kiri, opening his stomach with a dagger while kneeling on a rug, then being beheaded by his aide's sword. The other officers then killed themselves with daggers and pistols. Over thirty civilians killed themselves outside the palace gates in Tokyo during the following weeks.

The most serious defiance of the Emperor's orders came from Vice-Admiral Matome Ugaki, commander of the Fifth Air Fleet in Kyushu. He ordered three Kamikaze planes at Oita airfield to be prepared for a sortie against Okinawa under his leadership. When he arrived at the airfield he found eleven planes and twenty-two airmen determined to kill themselves in a final blow at the enemy. Four of the planes were forced to turn back with engine trouble, but the other eight continued towards Okinawa. Admiral Ugaki, crammed into a cockpit beside the observer who had refused to be left behind, sent back a message saying he intended 'to crash into and destroy the conceited enemy in the true spirit of Bushido'. The other planes also sent messages indicating they were about to crash into enemy targets. But it seems they merely committed group suicide diving into the empty ocean, because no Allied ships came under Kamikaze attack.

Carrier planes from the Allied Fleet reported sighting Japanese aircraft of several types diving one after another into the sea. It was assumed they were Kamikaze pilots inculcated with the belief that the essence of life was to die like a true samurai, and never to surrender.

Another ritual suicide came twenty-five years later when the novelist, Yukio Mishima, committed *seppuku* at the age of forty-five after haranging soldiers at the Tokyo army headquarters, accusing the Japanese people of being 'drunk with prosperity and forgetful of patriotism and the disgrace of defeat in the war'.

The Emperor's broadcast caused consternation among Japanese garrisons in the overseas territories. General Masaki Honda heard the Emperor's broadcast at his headquarters in the village of Nangala, where he was directing the attempt of his 28th Army to break out of southern Burma and regroup in Thailand. He made no comment for several hours, but finally called his staff together to hear his appeal to them to obey the Emperor's orders and refrain from committing *seppuku*. He told his chief of staff, Mitsuo Abe, 'Try to understand what is in the Emperor's mind. Neither old nor young must kill themselves. That is not the way to serve the nation. We must live and build the foundations of a new Japan. We have lost enough soldiers already.'

Unlike other Japanese generals in SEAC, General Honda made no threats to continue fighting, and began arrangements to surrender what remained of his army, 6000 men of the original 18,000 who had tried to break out across the Sittang river.

General Tomoyuki Yamashita, the commander of the 50,000 Japanese still holding out in Luzon, refused suggestions from his staff that he should commit *seppuku*. He told his young officers, 'I don't expect to see Japan again, but if I die first who takes responsibility?' Yamashita was known as the Tiger of Malaya for his conquest of Singapore. He was hanged as a war criminal for atrocities committed by his troops during the retreat from Manila.

The Japanese cabinet resigned, and the Emperor took the unprecedented step of appointing a relative, Prince Naruhiko Higashi-Kuni, as prime minister, with Prince Konoye, who was to have headed the peace mission to Moscow, as deputy. But a few days later Prince Konoye killed himself, apparently to avoid standing trial as a war criminal.

Because some Kamikaze units were still vowing to attack any Allied forces that attempted to land, steps were taken to disarm all military aircraft and remaining stocks of aviation fuel were sealed.

Members of the royal family were mobilized to ensure that the Emperor's order to surrender was obeyed. Three princes flew to the main military headquarters at Singapore, where there was a threat by the military commander to carry on fighting, to Saigon, and headquarters in China, Manchuria and Korea to explain and reinforce the Emperor's arguments on the necessity of ending the war.

Imperial General Headquarters sent out an addendum to the orders to cease fire in order to get round the requirement in the military code for a warrior to kill himself rather than face the dishonour of being taken prisoner. It said that military and civilians taken by the enemy after the proclamation of the Imperial Rescript would not be considered prisoners-of-war. It also urged 'patience and confidence in the success of the national reconstruction'.

PART FOUR

A Pyrrhic Victory

American battleships after the Japanese attack on Pearl Harbor, November 8, 1941
(Associated Press)

On the flight deck of the Royal Navy carrier, *Formidable*, seconds after a
Kamikaze crash dive (Imperial War Museum)

A Japanese Kamikaze plane begins its suicide dive on an American carrier off Okinawa

Bombs dropped by carrier aircraft from the British Pacific Fleet burst on the runway of a Japanese airfield in the Sakishima Islands

Right: View from the bridge of LST 380 approaching the Zipper Beaches, D-Day.

Below: Close-up of stranded landing ship showing a vehicle stuck in mud and blocking the exit of tanks (Photo courtesy of Stanley Skinner)

Landing ships and transport bogged in the mud on Morib beach, D-Day for Zipper
(Photo courtesy of Stanley Skinner)
Landing ships and craft marooned on the beach at Morib, September 9, 1945
(Photo courtesy of Stanley Skinner)

Right: A Japanese sentry guarding Dutch internees at Padang, Sumatra, presents arms to the author, September, 1945

Below: The Japanese destroyer, *Kamikaze*, flying the White Ensign over the Rising Sun, heaves to beside the destroyer *Petard* in the Malacca Straits, August 30, 1945

Above: The atomic cloud rising over Hiroshima, August 6, 1945 (Associated Press)

Left: A mushroom cloud billows to over 20,000 feet above Nagasaki, August 9, 1945 (Imperial War Museum)

Men from the Royal Indian Navy ship, *Sutlej*, look out over the ruins of Hiroshima after docking at Kure naval base, fifteen miles away (Imperial War Museum)

Lady Edwina Mountbatten, President of the St John's Ambulance Brigade, talks with emaciated prisoner of war, Gunner I. Taylor, soon after his release in Singapore (Imperial War Museum)

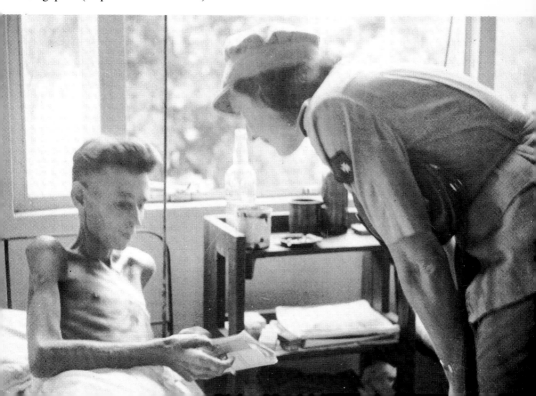

General MacArthur presides as Japanese leaders arrive to sign the surrender document aboard the US Battleship *Missouri* in Tokyo Bay, September 3, 1945 (Associated Press)

General Itagaki, Japanese commander in Singapore who had broadcast threats to defy the Emperor's order to surrender, signs the Singapore surrender document (Imperial War Museum)

1

The Emperor's order to surrender was received with angry disbelief at the headquarters of the Japanese 7th Army in Singapore. General Seishiro Itagaki, whose command covered Malaya, Sumatra and Java, suppressed all news of it for four days. When it was released on 20 August officers argued to defy the Emperor and carry on fighting. General Itagaki himself announced that any Allied ships that tried to land troops would be fired on, and orders to that effect were sent out to shore batteries and coastal defences.

Preparations to mount Operation Zipper had reached a stage where the plans could not be accelerated or abandoned, nor even much changed without causing chaos. Supply ships were loading heavy weapons, tanks, vehicles and stores, and men of six divisions were concentrated for embarkation in five ports in India and two in Burma. The assault troops had spent two days rehearsing landings on beaches at Conanada and Mandapan on the east coast of India, and an attack force of three aircraft carriers with supporting ships was on its way to pound Japanese airfields and bases covering the approaches to the invasion zone on the eve of the cease fire. The vast harbour at Trincomalee was crammed with ships of the invasion force, ready to sail. Admiral Mountbatten, who returned to his Kandy headquarters on the day the Japanese accepted unconditional surrender, decided that Zipper had to go ahead in sufficient strength to ensure success should Japanese forces in Malaya defy the surrender order.

Appeals to help internees in Japanese camps in the occupied territories flooded into SEAC headquarters the moment news of the Japanese surrender reached European governments and relief agencies. There were fears of wholesale massacres and the starvation of whole populations. Every day more people were dying for want of proper nourishment, drugs and nursing care.

The SEAC Land Forces Commander, General Slim, described the background to the decision to carry out Zipper in his book *Defeat into Victory*: 'Our first decision was immediately to carry out the Zipper landings as planned, as though the war were continuing. It would have caused immense confusion to unload and redistribute troops and stores. Besides the Japanese commanders were still breathing defiance and it was possible resistance would be encountered. To treat the landings as an operation of war was the quickest way to disembark the force, and should that go peaceably, we could then direct its later echelons elsewhere.'

Alternative plans for an early occupation of Singapore, either through the Zipper bridgehead or directly by sea, were ready for execution when Mountbatten arrived back at the Kandy headquarters. They provided for an initial occupation of the offshore island of Penang by Royal Marines – Operation Jurist – for use as an air staging post and a base for small craft. Another party of marines would occupy the Dutch island of Sabang off the north of Sumatra – Operation Beecham.

The plan for the direct occupation of Singapore – Operation Tiderace – meant the diversion from Zipper of a convoy carrying the 5th Indian Division from Rangoon. It was to sail straight past the invasion beaches and land directly in Singapore. Ships carrying the 3rd Commando Brigade were also taken out of Zipper, and given orders to proceed via Singapore to Hong Kong. This move was given high priority because of intelligence reports that General Chiang Kai-Shek, with American acquiescence, was planning to rush Chinese forces there and integrate the colony back into China before the British had a chance to reassert their authority.

The main force of the British East Indies Fleet sailed from Trincomalee to carry out initial Operation Zipper tasks on 15 August after joining in VJ-Day celebrations. Two days out across the Indian Ocean they received confirmation of the Japanese surrender in Admiralty General Message 243A, which said that HM Government had announced the surrender of the Japanese and, as a result, all offensive operations were to cease forthwith. The message added, 'Some time may elapse before it is clear that Japanese forces have received and intend to carry out the instructions of their High Command. Accordingly, danger of attack by individual enemy surface craft, U-boats and aircraft may persist for some time to come.'

Contingency plans made in response to Mountbatten's warning from Potsdam of an early end of the war were put in hand at once. It looked as though the British would be back in Singapore in a few days.

But General MacArthur, who had been appointed Supreme Commander for the Allied Powers for acceptance of the Japanese surrender, signalled Mountbatten to hold back the British Fleet. He said the Royal Navy should not reach the Penang area prematurely as cease-fire instructions would not reach Japanese units throughout the area until 22 August. As a result, Operation Jurist was delayed for three days.

Then came what General Slim described as a 'bombshell'. On 19 August

General MacArthur laid down that no surrenders were to be signed and no landings made on enemy occupied territory until representatives of Emperor Hirohito and the Imperial General Staff surrendered to him in Tokyo, probably at the end of the month. General Slim explained why it was a bombshell, 'The first ships of the Malaya force were already at sea when a considerable spanner was thrown in the works. The British and American Combined Chiefs of Staff had, ignoring their Supreme Commander on South-East Asia, entrusted the overall control of the Japanese surrender to General MacArthur, the Supreme Commander in the Pacific. He decreed that the formal surrender in SE Asia could take place only after it had been ceremonially completed in his own theatre. This, though inconvenient, might not have mattered had he not ordered, also, that no landings would be made until after he, personally, received the surrender of the Japanese Empire.'

The British found themselves in the humiliating position of not being permitted to reoccupy their own colonies until the Japanese High Command had formally acknowledged defeat to an American general on an American battleship in Tokyo Bay.

Mountbatten's protest was so strongly worded that MacArthur signalled back, 'Keep your pants on,' drawing a further riposte from the SEAC supremo, 'Will keep mine on if you take Hirohito's off.'

MacArthur's caution was not really a manoeuvre to hog the spotlight as victor over the Japanese. It was based on real worries that Japanese armies garrisoning the occupied territories would fight on unless the surrender was clearly and formally signed in the Emperor's name.

In his report on his period as SEAC Supreme Commander to the British Chiefs of Staff, presented in 1956, Mountbatten commented more coolly on the MacArthur bombshell, 'This was the first instruction I received that my plans for the reoccupation, which were being urgently proceeded with, would have to be postponed – a great blow at a time when the utmost speed was imperative. Ships, landing craft and forces were already at sea, and if these were recalled and had to start again, the delay might mean the difference between life and death for prisoners-of-war at starvation level. Since many craft were, in any case, incapable of turning back into the south-west monsoon, then at its height, without incurring severe damage or even total loss, I agreed with Admiral Power to hold them at sea in the forward area.'

Marking time at sea raised many difficulties. The minesweeping flotillas huddled in the lee of Simular Island off the west coast of Sumatra, supplied with fresh water and rations from bigger ships. The main naval force under Admiral H.T.C Walker anchored off the Great Nicobar Islands, but a cruiser, two escort carriers and four destroyers had to return to Trincomalee to refuel. The 3rd Commando Brigade was held aboard troopships in the great harbour at Trincomalee, and the 5th Indian Division waited in troopships at anchor in Rangoon.

The author was aboard the destroyer, HMS *Petard*, anchored in the sultry heat of Trinkat Chomplong Bay, in the Nicobar Islands, close to a picturesque jungle-fringed beach, conserving fuel, slipping out at intervals to take turns at escorting the heavier ships which had to stay at sea. No lights were allowed, and smoking was banned on the upper deck as a precaution against poison darts from a local tribe of head hunters. By day there was no sign of life on the untrodden beach, and steam rose from the brooding lush-green thicknesses of the jungle. A week after the joyous celebration of VJ-Day in London crews were called to action stations several times. It was still uncertain whether the Zipper invasion might yet have to fight its way ashore. Singapore radio was still bragging of the Japanese army's supremacy, and threatening attacks on British ships in the Nicobars area. Japanese reconnaissance planes approached the Fleet, but raced back to base when aircraft took off from carriers to intercept them.

Mountbatten sent a message to his Japanese opposite number, Field Marshal Count Juichi Terauchi, at his headquarters in Saigon, instructing him to send a plenipotentiary to Rangoon for preliminary discussions on surrender. The meeting was called for 23 August, but it was three days after that before Lieut-General Takazo Numata, Terauchi's chief of staff, reached Rangoon. He immediately requested the British to tell him the whereabouts of Japanese formations in Burma so that he could send orders to them to cease fire. He claimed there were about 150,000 troops still in Burma, compared with a British estimate of 60,000, and it turned out that Japanese casualties in Burma were around 300,000, half of them killed. Fighting continued along the Mawchi road and in the Sittang Valley late into August, and it was not until 13 September that a formal surrender of the Japanese remnants in Burma was signed.

Describing the meeting with Terauchi's delegation, General Slim wrote that after 'an initial tendency to argue was promptly and firmly suppressed', the Japanese showed 'proper submissiveness' and readiness to obey orders.

Preliminary arrangements for surrender were signed in Rangoon at 1 a.m. on 28 August. They covered Allied minesweeping, relief for Allied prisoners-of-war and internees, air reconnaissance and the entry of Allied ships into Japanese-controlled waters.

That same day Mountbatten's headquarters established direct contact with Terauchi's headquarters through All-India Radio and, finding the Japanese ready to cooperate, he decided to take some risks in getting immediate succour to Allied prisoners-of-war. Planes dropped leaflets explaining the situation over all known prison camps. They were followed hours later by air drops of 950 tons of supplies and 120 medical personnel.

They found many prisoners at the limits of endurance, had it not been for the prompt deliveries of supplies many more would undoubtedly have died.

That day, too, minesweeping flotillas began sweeping the approaches to the Malacca Straits, and British naval forces arrived off Sabang and Penang, the two naval bases on each side of the entrance to the straits. In Saigon, immediately after his return from Rangoon, General Numata broadcast orders forbidding suicide planes and craft to make attacks on the British ships.

Next day the Japanese commander in Penang, Rear-Admiral Uzumui, went aboard Admiral Power's flagship, the cruiser *Cleopatra*, in response to instructions broadcast over All-India Radio. Wearing his British Distinguished Service Cross and First World War victory medal, he signed the arrangements for the British reoccupation of the island. Next morning, 30 August, marines went ashore, and soon afterwards two squadrons of Spitfires and two squadrons of Mosquitos flew in from Rangoon.

Meanwhile, aboard the troopships, unit commanders opened sealed orders and learned that Exercise Button had become Operation Zipper, the British return to Malaya and the long-awaited reconquest of Singapore. They were still left in doubt as to whether the Japanese would hold to their earlier defiant refusal to accept the Emperor's order to surrender, and braced themselves to carry through the invasion under fire. The D-Day passwords – Soo Bar and Sharm – and codenames for all features and places in the landing areas were memorized, and troops received British Malayan currency at pay parades. A tourist guidebook, *Return to Malaya*, with Malayan phrases was also given to each man. The 41 Beach Group learned they were responsible for 'the prompt disposal of civilian dead by burning or mass burials' in specified locations.

General Roberts noted in his diary, 'Few commanders can have been in command of troops of such high morale and one feels that with them nothing can stop us. Many of them were sorry that the Japanese have surrendered, and so am I in many ways, but I thank God that no more of our men are going to be killed.'

Aboard some of the older LSTs, veterans of landings in North Africa, Italy and France, engineers were struggling to keep overworked engines functioning. There were several breakdowns, but all caught up with their convoys in time. Many of the troops, including the commanding general, suffered severe sea-sickness as monsoon storms swept the Indian Ocean.

While Penang was being secured and another force of Royal Marines was raising the Dutch tricolour beside the White Ensign over Sabang, the destroyer *Petard* was leading the flagship *Cleopatra* and the Royal Indian Navy's *Bengal* through a narrow channel marked by the three minesweeping flotillas up ahead, sweeping a way down the straits to Singapore.

Spotters on the *Petard*'s upper decks fired rifles and pom-pom guns at bobbing mines which the sweepers had cut loose, these then sank or exploded in high spouts of water. It was a risky passage. Scuttles, hatches and watertight doors were all closed, and lifeboats were swung out on davits in case the ship hit a mine the spotters had failed to see. All the ship's company, except engine room and wireless staff, were on the upper decks wearing lifebelts.

In the afternoon a smudge of smoke was spotted directly ahead, and a strange looking warship hove into view. Under orders from *Cleopatra*, the *Petard* raced to intercept the 'enemy', crew closed at action stations, bobbing mines ignored. The ship was the elusive Japanese destroyer *Kamikaze*, survivor of several close calls in recent actions with the East Indies Fleet. She was flying a large White Ensign above a smaller Rising Sun flag of Japan. The only movement on her decks came from an officer in spotless white uniform carrying a leather despatch case. As the ships hove to some twenty yards apart, scores of stocky figures in green uniforms and soft peak caps crowded the *Kamikaze*'s fo'c's'le. A moment of panic came as a shot rang out, firing a line from the *Petard* across the Japanese warship's bows. An order was shouted and men in green uniforms hauled in the line.

A murmur of hate grew into growling jeers from British sailors until stilled by a crisp order from the captain on the bridge. A despatch case was quickly hauled back over the line and delivered to the *Cleopatra* before the destroyer resumed her position behind the minesweepers as far as the Singapore roads.

Next day she sailed back through the swept channel and anchored at the Penang entrance to it, acting as a floating buoy for five days and nights, watching convoys sail through, occasionally scrounging much needed food supplies from passing supply ships. The troopships carried the 5th Indian Division and XV Corps headquarters from Rangoon, diverted to occupy Singapore from their role in Zipper. Others carried the 3rd Commando Brigade, embarked for the Zipper beaches at Bombay, but diverted to Hong Kong.

The reluctant General Itagaki, whose earlier threats to oppose any landings had been silenced by a peremptory order from Field Marshal Terauchi to accept surrender, put his signature to the surrender of the 77,000 Japanese garrison of Singapore. He did this aboard HMS *Sussex* on 4 September and British troops went ashore at eleven o'clock next morning.

The Japanese Imperial Navy insisted on surrendering to the Royal Navy, and the destroyer *Rotherham* sailed under the silent guns of the two crippled cruisers in the Johore Strait to occupy the naval dockyard some two hours before the main landings took place in the commercial harbour.

2

News of the end of the war and their imminent liberation was slow in reaching the prison camps where Allied captives were employed as slave labour – although General MacArthur was broadcasting daily warnings to the Japanese people of the consequences of harming prisoners. The first hint of a change in the situation came at Camp 21 at Nakarma in Japan when the usual work detail was not called upon to go to a nearby coal mine. Prisoners had also noticed a lull in air raids and Japanese people crying in the streets. Otherwise things seemed much the same. On 20 August prisoner number 39, a Dutchman, died from injuries he had received in a beating at the coal mine a week before. It was 22 August before the camp commandant announced that hostilities had ceased on 18 August, and the prisoners would soon be going home. A huge sign was painted saying 'PW Camp 21 – 608 men' and hoisted across the roof. Then out of the blue came two huge planes with the white stars of the American air force on their wings, and forty gallon drums, stuffed with supplies, crashed down. They were dropped too low for the parachutes attached to them to open properly, and three Japanese civilians were killed and two injured in the nearby village.

That was the beginning of regular drops to camps throughout Japan during the last days of August.

3

A sixteen-man delegation led by Lieut-General Torashiro Kawabe, deputy chief of the Japanese Army General Staff, arrived at Clark Field, near Manila, on 19 August to receive General MacArthur's instructions for the surrender. They had left Tokyo in great secrecy to avoid risks of assassination by military diehards, flying to the island of Ie-shima near Okinawa to transfer to an American plane for the flight to the Philippines. They carried details about the location of prison camps, and of military establishments in the Tokyo Bay area and at Kanoya in Kyushu, two areas chosen for the initial landing of occupation forces.

Next morning, Kawabe was handed a copy of the Instrument of Surrender and other documents, and told what preparations were to be made for the reception of the occupation forces. After looking over the documents, Kawabe asked for ten days to complete the preparations. He said this would be necessary to ensure the fullest control of Japanese forces. MacArthur agreed, and Kawabe and his party flew back to Japan that night.

The Allied advance party was due to fly into Atsugi airfield, twenty-two miles from Tokyo, on 26 August, but typhoons delayed their arrival for forty-eight hours. In the meantime the Allied Navy had made contact with representatives of the Imperial Japanese Navy in a destroyer which rendezvoused with them off Sagami Bay.

The British flagship, HMS *Duke of York*, was among the major Allied warships which took on Japanese pilots to drop anchor in the bay. Coastal forts commanding Tokyo Bay and the Yokosuka naval base were occupied without incident on 30 August. General MacArthur arrived in Tokyo that same afternoon.

The impatiently awaited surrender ceremony began at 9 a.m. on 2 September. Representatives of all the Allied nations gathered on the quarterdeck of the American battleship *Missouri*, eighteen miles offshore in Tokyo Bay to receive an eleven-man Japanese delegation: the military men in uniform, the ministers in tall silk hats and cutaway coats. Even now the Japanese raised a quibble. The two plenipotentiaries chosen by

Emperor Hirohito wanted to sign 'by command of and on behalf of the Emperor of Japan'. But they were made to sign the way MacArthur wanted it, the new Foreign Minister, Mamoru Shigemitsu, 'by command of and on behalf of the Emperor of Japan and the Japanese government', and General Yoshijiro Umezu, one of the arch opponents of surrender, signed dutifully 'by command of Imperial General Headquarters'.

General MacArthur signed on behalf of all the Allied Powers, Admiral Nimitz for the United States, Admiral Fraser for Britain, General Sir Thomas Blamey for Australia, Air Vice-Marshal L.M. Isitt for New Zealand, General Hsu Yung-chang for China, General P. LeClerc for France, Admiral C.E.L. Helfrich for the Netherlands and Lieut-General K.N. Derevyanko for the Soviet Union. The failure to invite an Indian representative caused indignation in Britain as well as India.

After the formalities of surrender were completed, the skies above Tokyo Bay filled with a roaring cloud of Allied destructive power as 400 Superfortress bombers and 1500 carrier planes took part in a massive fly-past.

So it was that, with a finale like a Hollywood movie, the Second World War came to an end.

4

While a pack of more than 600 newspaper correspondents watched the formal surrender ceremony aboard the *Missouri* in Tokyo Bay, Wilfred Burchett of the *Daily Express* was on a train journey that lasted thirty hours. He travelled alone from Yokosuka naval base where he had landed with an advance naval party, braved the scowls of besworded Japanese officers, was sustained by friendly curiosity of civilians and newly demobilized soldiers, and eventually dropped among the ruins of the railway station at Hiroshima. 'There was devastation and nothing else. Lead grey clouds hung low over the city, vapours drifted from fissures in the ground, and there was an acrid, sulphurous smell. The few people to be seen wore white masks covering mouth and nostrils. . . . Buildings had dissolved into grey and reddish dust, solidified by rain . . . it was just less than a month since the bomb had exploded. . . . In the only hospital still functioning the effects on humans I saw was a thousand times more horrifying . . . a terrible wasting disease had stricken thousands of people. . . . Dr Gen Katsube said something was killing off the white corpuscles in the blood and they could do nothing about it. . . . These people are all doomed to die. . . . How can Christians do what you have done here? Send at least some of your scientists who know what it is so that we can stop this terrible sickness.'

A city health official explained to Burchett that most of the terribly disfigured people in the hospital had been untouched by the explosion, but had been digging in the ruins for relatives and possessions. It was thought some sort of ray had been released into the soil, and digging had been stopped for an estimated 30,000 bodies still under the rubble.

Burchett's story appeared in the 6 September edition of the *Daily Express* under the banner headline 'THE ATOMIC PLAGUE – a warning to the world'. By contrast, reports on a visit to Nagasaki about the same time by the *Chicago Daily News* correspondent, George Weller, were never published. They disappeared in the censor's office at General MacArthur's headquarters.

Official efforts were made to discount the *Daily Express* story which had been repeated around the world. A scientist in brigadier-general's uniform told a press conference in Tokyo that there could be no question of atomic radiation causing the deadly disease. He explained that the bombs had been exploded at sufficient height to obviate any risk of residual radiation. An attempt to expel Burchett from Japan failed because he was accredited to the US Pacific Fleet, not to MacArthur's headquarters.

Efforts to suppress the truth about the continuing horrors of the atomic bombs continued, and it was many months before deaths were officially confirmed as being due to atomic radiation.

According to the Japanese Council Against A and H Bombs, the Hiroshima bomb accounted for over 130,000 deaths by the end of 1945 and the Nagasaki bomb more than 60,000. By 1950 the joint count had risen to about 300,000, and in 1980 370,000 people were officially listed as A-bomb victims. In the worst conventional air raid on Japan, the 9 March fire-bomb attack on Tokyo, 84,000 people were killed and 40,000 wounded. In the heaviest air raid of the European war, on 13 February 1945, 2000 British and American bombers dropped 3000 tons of high explosives and incendiaries on the German town of Dresden in support of the advancing Red Army. Estimates of the dead range from 35,000 to 100,000.

5

Meanwhile in SEAC, the destroyer *Petard*'s duties as a floating buoy ended on 8 September when she led the armada of D-Day ships on the last perilous stage of their voyage to stand off the Zipper beaches. The line of ships stretched back forty miles, a combination of four fast and three slow convoys which had made the ocean crossing from India and Ceylon through monsoon gales.

The early tropical night came down as the lead ships headed from the wide gulf around Penang into the narrows of the Malacca Straits, shutting out the brooding smudges of enemy-held shores on either side, Malaya to port, Sumatra to starboard, still harbouring the suicide planes and motor-boats which might, but for the A-bomb, have exacted a high price for the intrusion. The ships followed a channel six cables wide, swept already for the earlier convoys to Singapore and Hong Kong. They sailed in line astern, two cables' distance between each ship. After the stormy crossing the water in the Straits was flat calm.

It was still dark when the ships dropped anchor at their allotted assault stations three miles off the Morib beaches, troops clambered down into landing craft, ships' crews closed up at action stations.

The cruisers *Nigeria* and *Ceylon*, the destroyers *Petard*, *Paladin*, *Tartar* and *Nubian*, the Indian sloops *Cauvery* and *Narbada*, were at bombardment stations, but because of a breakdown that impaired her steering, the battleship *Nelson* stayed in reserve with the French battleship *Richelieu*. The 15-inch, 6-inch, 4.7-inch and 4-inch guns were manned and ready, but stayed silent as the landing craft headed for the beaches in the grey smudge of first light. Attack planes from carriers circled watchfully over them with silent wing cannon.

The first assault waves of the 25th Indian Division hit Love Red and Love White sectors in the centre of Morib beach at 6.47 a.m. – two minutes late. Instead of enemy fire they were met by a curious crowd of Malay civilians and a party of Chinese-Malay guerrillas. A senior Japanese officer waited with agents of Force 136 in a resthouse above the beach, anxious to cooperate with the commander of the invading forces.

More waves of infantry came in at fifteen-minute intervals to secure the beach area and move on inland. The first wave of landing craft carrying tanks beached ten minutes early in just the right place; they disembarked in good order only to get stuck on the road above the beach. One LST anchorage was marked two miles from the correct position and by the time this was sorted out valuable high-water time had been lost.

The commander of 46 Indian Beach Group, whose unit totalled 1260 men, landed on Love White beach with the first wave of infantry. This was to have been the main beach for the build-up of supplies at the Seaview Rubber Estate above the shoreline. But the beach commander quickly discovered that, while hard enough for infantry, the beach was too soft to carry vehicles, and a beach roadway would have to be laid before any more were disembarked. His orders to hold vehicles aboard landing ships were overruled by a senior officer, unnamed in official reports, who impatiently ordered vehicles to proceed ashore without delay. All of them sank into the mud that lay just below the surface sand, and although many lighter vehicles were manhandled across the beach by every available hand from field officer to private, many were stuck and swamped by the next tide. The Beach Group itself, whose job was to facilitate the passage of succeeding waves of troops and supplies over the beaches, had its own recovery vehicles bogged down and swamped, and most of its personnel were several hours behind schedule in getting ashore.

The beach commander commandeered an Indian Army engineers unit which was part of the 459 Forward Airfield Engineers detailed to repair the airfield at Kelanang and make it ready for Spitfires to fly in there. The unit's heavy construction equipment and vehicles were carried in three LSTs which hit the neighbouring Love Red beach six minutes after H-hour.

Stanley Skinner, then a 22-year-old lieutenant in the Royal Engineers, was second-in-command of the commandeered unit. The confusion when they beached had put them more than an hour behind schedule when they began disembarking, and he recalled, 'Vehicles were breaking through the thin crust of sand and sinking into the underlying mud all along the beach, often as soon as they came off the ramp, and that meant they blocked the exit for all the following vehicles. Immediately we started disembarking, we had several of our vehicles deeply bogged. However, we were able to get the unit's tractors from the other two LSTs that carried our equipment, and begin recovering those of our own vehicles that were bogged. While this was going on, the Beach Commander told us he was commandeering our services because the REME Beach Recovery Unit had already lost all its tractors, and a Naval Beach Unit's armoured bulldozer was hopelessly deep in the mud. By that time we had heard that the airfield was undamaged, and there was consequently no longer any urgent need for us to go there.

'We spent the rest of D-Day hauling out vehicles until we had to stop because of the incoming tide. I had to borrow the services of an amphibious Weasel to rescue two truck drivers from the tops of their cabs and the driver of a tractor we had not managed to recover. Through the next weeks we worked our equipment ten hours at a stretch, taking breaks only at high tide. We must have recovered several hundred vehicles which had been covered by one or more tide.'

Mr Skinner still remembers his relief at seeing a diminutive Japanese officer on the beach pestering a very large Scottish engineer officer to accept his sword in surrender. 'Although there had not been the planned bombardment on the assumption we would be unopposed, we were not entirely sure that the Japanese would not fire on us until then. But Jimmy Scorier, the Scottish engineer, had other concerns. Several of his vehicles were stuck in the mud, so eventually he booted the Japanese officer up the backside with a few Scottish oaths. The Jap sat down on the beach with his sword across his lap and waited for a more receptive officer.'

Several months after the landings Lieutenant Skinner sent transporter vehicles back to the area to recover several tracked cranes, and noted, 'Our drivers returned with the story that some 800 vehicles were written off as well as several smaller landing craft which could not be towed back to sea as they had settled in the mud.'

(Mountbatten visited the beach in 1972 and expressed amazement at the apparent firmness of the sand, commenting that he could hardly blame his intelligence for their misleading reports. The author was there in 1961, and found the beach looked firm enough, though children building sand castles were digging up mud just below the dry sand surface.)

Mr Skinner summed up Operation Zipper: 'This was a terribly badly planned operation, apart from the naval organization which was remarkably efficient. It ended in such chaos that it would have been catastrophic if the atomic bombs had not been dropped and we had, therefore, faced an opposed landing. The result is really unimaginable. So far as I can see there would have been wholesale slaughter.'

By 7.30 a.m. LSTs were beaching with a water gap of 300 yards and eight feet of water at the ramp, and thirty-two vehicles were bogged. Amphibious craft called DUKWEs were also in trouble. Three were lost at sea, apparently because of overloading, but all the personnel were rescued. Another four were bogged down on the beach.

Major Roland 'Slim' Iliffe, then commanding the leading company of the 2/2 Punjab Regiment, was in a landing craft that beached on the offshore sandbank. He recalled, 'We went over the top of the sandbank into eight foot of water with 40 lb. packs on our backs and weapons in our hands. Getting up that beach after that would have been very difficult under enemy fire. It would have been an extremely bloody landing, much worse than some of the battles in Burma. We understood that the Japanese engineering general commanding the area was still refusing to surrender, and we felt like sitting ducks out there on the sandbank. From the Japanese point of view we presented a dream target for the light artillery pieces – 75s – they had dotted along the coast.

'Soon afterwards, LCTs (landing craft-tanks) began beaching on the sandbank, and one three-ton lorry after another was driven off into the sea before somebody stopped them. It was absolute, total chaos, but once ashore our only difficulty came from one or two awkward incidents with Japs in roadside pillboxes who were bewildered and without orders. At one point staff cars went by with fluttering pennants, and I automatically whipped off a salute before realizing they were Japanese officers. Eventually we commandeered some civilian lorries and went on to Kuala Lumpur.'

Mr Ronald Day, of the 96th Field Regiment, Royal Artillery which landed at Morib fifteen minutes after the last wave of the 2/2 Punjab Regiment at H45. He recalled, 'I drove the first vehicle off our landing craft, towing a 25-pounder. Water came up to my waist as I sat behind the steering wheel, but I stayed in bottom gear and made it to dry land. There were a lot of other vehicles floundering, but all four guns of my troop got clear of the beach in fairly good time.

'At the top of the beach two Japanese officers were standing by an old Chevrolet car flying a white flag, and we were amused to see the lieutenant in charge of our landing craft pinch the car and put it aboard his craft. As we moved inland we found roads lined with women and kids waving little Union Jacks, and I remember wondering how they came by them after so long under Japanese occupation.'

Captain Jim Bowes, who was a Royal Artillery Liaison Officer with 25th Division's headquarters, says there is a special niche in his memories of Zipper for the words of the first lieutenant of the LST (landing ship-tanks) in which he made the voyage from Madras. Pointing at a thin line off the landing beaches on one of his charts, the Navy man said, 'I wouldn't give odds on you getting over that bar.' Mr Bowes recalled, 'None of us saw any great drama in the warning because the war was officially over and any opposition we might expect would be from such Japanese who wanted to indulge their passion for "no surrender" or suicide missions.

The first lieutenant was right for we became stuck fast on the sandbar, and when we tried to get our vehicles ashore at low tide many were inextricably bogged down.

The tide turned and came in again, and we made frantic attempts to salvage stores and equipment. As the water lapped around the vehicles we took to diving in to haul anything we could get out of the vehicles back onto the LST. I took off my jacket to join in, and when I went back for it my wallet had gone!

'Ultimately we got some vehicles ashore, but the scene on the beach was pathetic. Apart from a feeling of embarrassment there was also a tinge of anger the serviceman always feels when there's been a bog up. By the time we got things together it was dark.

'It was common to hear remarks like, "My God, one sniper would have done for the lot of us!" '

Captain Rex Waite, who was beach liaison officer for the 18th Field Regiment, Royal Artillery, went ashore with the infantry assault landings. He recalled, 'Our LCA (landing craft-assault) stuck on an offshore sandbank in about four feet of water, and I tried to get the Indian soldiers to push it clear. It was no use, and we had to struggle ashore from there. The water became deeper and we had to swim a few strokes before we could touch bottom again and eventually wade ashore. Fortunately, there was no opposition, because we were very vulnerable for a long time and even small arms would have picked off a lot of men.

'The landing craft-tanks carrying the regiment's vehicles grounded directly on the beach, more or less on schedule. They included 105 howitzers on Sherman tank chassis, and they and all our guns came out dry. But a lot of 3-tonners from other units were becoming bogged down, and a good many LCAs were missing the tide and getting stranded.

'The landing of our supply vehicles and baggage was badly delayed, and I was stuck on the beach for.seven days instead of the thirty-six hours we had expected to take getting all our kit ashore.

'I think the invasion would have succeeded even against Jap resistance, but it would have been very difficult and would have meant heavy casualties – as at Anzio and Salerno.'

Lieut-Colonel Teddy Lock then commanded a troop of self-propelled guns of the 18th Field Regiment. Their LCTs grounded directly on the main beach, and they were able to drive their tracked and four-wheel drive vehicles off without great difficulty after waiting for the tide to go out. He recalled, 'There was a chaung or stream at the top of the beach which was giving two-wheel drive vehicles a lot of trouble, but we managed to tow each other across it and left the beach about midday. I remember I didn't like it at all having to dry out on the open beach where we would have been sitting ducks for aircraft. It was still very much in the air whether the Japs were going to surrender or fight, and when we passed an airfield a few miles inland we were all very greatly relieved when the Japanese sentries presented arms. In the next few days we saw an awful lot of Japs, and I've always had the impression it would have been a bloodbath if they had still been fighting. It was a shambles that, luckily, we didn't have to pay for.'

Gunner, Captain Frederick Field was at Morib as a conducting officer with correspondents from the army newspaper, *SEAC*, and other service information personnel. He recalled seeing 25-pounders with their muzzles sticking out of the water and gun crews cursing the Navy for bad intelligence about the condition of the beaches.

However, correspondents of the national newspapers and radio missed the story of the chaos on the beaches. They had been embarked on ships at Rangoon which sailed straight down the straits to Singapore. The sports writer Frank Rostron, who was then a *Daily Express* war correspondent, told the author that the Fleet Street men only heard about the shambles on the beaches several days later. He said, 'Every effort was made to hush it up, and the story was censored. We had plenty of things to write about, and it was weeks before we heard just what a disaster Zipper would have been. If the Japs had still been in their foxholes – as they would have been but for the surrender – our troops would have been mown down as they floundered in the quicksands. It would have been the most grisly story of the war, the most ghastly failure.'

Dr John Gordon-Brown, a medical officer with an advance unit of the 5th Parachute Brigade, said that as paras they had had no previous experience of a beach landing. 'When our landing craft grounded a few hundred yards offshore we waded almost up to our necks, such was the rotten nature of the bottom. Had there been opposition I would not, of course, be writing this letter since a single machine gun would surely have accounted for us. We were told the beach was chosen because it was unsuitable and warnings by those who knew the coast were ignored. Once ashore, we marched up a long road fringed by palm trees for about ten miles, camped the night in a jungle clearing, then, like the Grand Old Duke of York, marched back to the beach to re-embark for Singapore next day.'

A veteran of Akyab and the fiercely opposed landings at Myebon beach and up tidal creeks at Ru-ywa, Kangaw and Tamandu in the Chaung War, Mr Clifford White was at Morib as a Royal Signals cipher operator attached to the 53rd Indian Brigade.

He recalled, 'The approach to the beach in the LCA seemed to take a very long time, and Royal Marines piloting the craft had trouble finding a suitable stretch of beach after three LCAs had already grounded on a sandbank. I wondered what would have happened to us had the landings been opposed. As it was we knew some of the Japanese were opposed to the surrender, and I remember looking back for reassurance at the ships of all kinds that filled the horizon. It helped balance our worries over the landing problems.

'Eventually the ramps went down and we went into water about waist deep, and again I felt glad there was no opposition because we couldn't have run until we got into shallow water.

'Our equipment, wireless sets, batteries etc. was put on hand-carts. These proved – not unexpectedly – to be completely useless. The wheels buckled at the first stretch of bumpy ground in the rubber plantation, and the equipment had to be manhandled. It took fourteen hours to cover six miles. Local people seemed friendly, but there were a lot of sullen-looking Japs. I was amazed there was no opposition, if there had been, the consequences would have been dreadful.'

For Mr Len Goddard, then a twenty-three-year-old able seaman manning an oerliken anti-aircraft gun on LST 410, Zipper was an operation of the kind he had experienced many times before, at landings in Italy, Normandy and more recently at Ramree Island and Rangoon. 'For me Morib was a near disaster. We landed on a very untidy beach of mud and sand, and after the infantry went ashore the 3-ton Bedford lorries, carrying their stores, became bogged. I was told to leave my oerliken gun and join other members of the crew in helping soldiers who were trying to push lorries up the beach. It was no good, and the tide came in so quickly I found myself stranded on the roof of a lorry with a British driver and a crowd of very frightened Indian soldiers. It was heartbreaking to see bodies floating among the crates and crates of stores that covered the surface of the sea. I was eventually picked up by one of the motorboats sent to rescue those who needed help.'

Canon Pat Magee took part as a chaplain in the D-Day landings at Morib and the D3 landings on Si Rusa beach near Port Dickson. He recalled, 'We didn't know what to expect as the Japanese C-in-C in Malaya had earlier refused to surrender. I well remember the messy landings on that swampy beach at Morib, and the confusion as LCTs and other craft got stuck in the mud, thus preventing those behind them landing. I found a bicycle and rode up and down the road which ran along the top of the beach telling commanders where other units were. There really was more confusion than I witnessed in any other operation. In contrast, the landings at Si Rusa were excellent. There was a fine, firm beach and communications by road were good. We should have established a bridgehead there in the first place.'

Mr C.R. Coleman, an RAF armourer also heading for Kelanang airfield, recalled having to swim about 500 yards after his landing craft beached on the offshore sandbank. By that time the beach was littered with stranded vehicles, and Mr Coleman, a veteran of the Burma advance, told the author, 'But for the atomic bombs I don't think we would have stood a cat in hell's chance. We would have been murdered in the biggest massacre of the war. They would have annihilated the lot of us.'

Mr Coleman went on to Japan with the British Commonwealth Occupation Force, and visited Hiroshima. He has no doubt it was right to have dropped the bomb. 'Nothing else would have made them give in.'

Mr Colin Sharman, a former RAF fitter, was also aboard a landing craft which hit the sandbar. He recalled going down the ramp with an 40-lb pack on his back, canvas mosquito boots and rifle in hand, 'I am five foot six inches and it came up to my chest . . . as we waded towards the shore – which seemed a hell of a way off – the water became deeper and the waves were going over my head. When we finally reached the beach I remember very clearly glancing to left and right and having a good laugh at the antics of the army transport drivers jumping out of their sinking wagons and wading ashore half drowned. I still laugh at the events of that landing, but often wonder what would have happened if the Japs had been awaiting our invasion. I doubt if I would have been here now.'

Mr E. Saunders, then a Royal Navy petty officer motor mechanic with Combined Operations, went into Morib beach with his tool box to repair engine breakdowns which dogged the landing craft. He recalled that they were more frequent in SEAC than elsewhere because of a lack of spare parts – especially water pumps, dynamo belts and fan belts. They went into Operation Zipper with fan belts made in an Indian factory, and they needed to be changed frequently since they quickly became shredded. At dawn on D-Day when Indian soldiers scrambled down the nets from troopships to board them, all the craft of his 548 flotilla were in A-1 condition. Petty Officer Saunders and his men had worked on them throughout the passage across the Indian Ocean. 'I remember thinking as I looked on some of the disasters on Morib beach that morning "Thank God there's no opposition".'

Another member of Combined Operations, Mr Frank Humphris, recalled thinking that the Zipper landings would be a 'piece of cake' compared with his earlier experiences in the Normandy and Rangoon landings. They had been shown aerial photographs of the beaches as HMS *Glenroy*, carrying LCA flotillas 546 and 547, sailed past the Nicobar Islands.

'Alas, the photos showed no obstruction for the run into the beach – it looked perfect. As our flotilla went in on D-Day, the leading LCA came to a sudden shuddering halt on an underwater obstruction. We were waved off and had to wait while frogmen were called and a way was blown for us to put our troops ashore.'

Mr Humphris added, 'I spent the next few weeks working on the beach, and had a good chance to see what lay behind the peaceful-looking coconut palms that fringed the beach. The gun pits and bunkers reminded me of the gun positions behind the Normandy beaches. We would have been sitting ducks waiting to get past the offshore barrier, and I'm certain most of us would not have survived had it not been for the Japanese surrender.'

An account of the landings was published in the newspaper *SEAC* about a week later: 'A few days ago we landed our troops in Malaya. It was a magnificent sight. Scores of ships lying off the beaches, every kind of warship present, and hundreds of landing craft lying squatly in the water as they wallowed inshore laden with troops and equipment. This was no invasion over a small distance like the English Channel, but the biggest Combined Op we ever carried out. A vast invasion force had to be convoyed hundreds of miles from numerous bases and put ashore, maintained there by the Navy. I was able to get ashore a couple of hours after the first troops touched down. A splendid scene, with every kind of supply and equipment pouring ashore.'

The War Diary of the 25th Division, the spearhead of the assault, tells a different story: 'The LCMs (landing craft-mechanized transport) were late in grounding, missed the best state of the tide, and of the first twenty vehicles out none reached the beach across the hundred-yard muddy gap without assistance, and only two without assistance from recovery vehicles and DUKWEs. At the end of the first day about fifty vehicles were drowned, and only the first flight of LSTs had been offloaded. Divisional headquarters was particularly unlucky in that only one of its vehicles – a jeep – was offloaded on D-Day.'

Vehicles that succeeded in reaching the Casuarina trees at the top of the beach were soon in fresh trouble. The tracks leading through the rubber and coconut plantations to the tarmac of the coast road were bordered by deep drainage ditches and a water-pipe raised a foot above ground level. This meant vehicles could not get off the roads to carry out de-waterproofing and we were having to halt on the track to do it, causing a tailback of vehicles. Vehicles and tanks that tried to get by on grass verges were bogged down and added to the bottleneck.

LCT 1060, in which Sikhs, Muslims and Hindus of the Indian Army had been crammed together for a month, hit the beach at the height of the chaos. Midshipman Kenneth McCaw wrote in the ship's log, 'No attempt seemed to have been made to clear the beach of stranded vehicles, tree trunks and other debris; also there was a sort of muddy bar to get across to the beach and it was extremely difficult to get in and even more to get out.' He added that welcoming parties of local women took the crew's minds off their grumbles – in return the ship's stores were soon minus tins of milk and other rations.

On the left flank a special task group, Peggy Force, landed on schedule high up the Langat River and quickly secured the bridges and crossroads over which the main force of the 25th Indian Infantry Division later moved towards Port Swettenham and Klang airfield. Peggy Force comprised infantry from the 16th Punjab and the Hyderabad regiment, a half squadron of the 19th Lancers, and self-propelled guns and field guns of the Royal Artillery. They were carried in amphibious tracked vehicles known as Buffaloes with a capacity for thirty men, launched from parent ships off the river entrance at 4.10 a.m. They crossed the river bar at H-Hour just as dawn was breaking, crawling against a strong ebb tide and went three abreast in an unbroken line up seven and a half miles of river to the landing beach, a firm surface of rocks dumped from barges when roads were being built before the war. But space proved to be more limited than anyone had expected and only one boat could be unloaded at a time instead of the simultaneous unloading of three at a time as planned.

Major George Mowat Slater, who commanded B company of the 7/16 Punjab at the head of the convoy, retains vivid memories of the painfully slow passage upriver in the shadow of a dominating jungle-covered hill called Jugra.

He recalled, 'After the operation I am sure I am right in saying that we all felt that Peggy Force was a forlorn hope. The Jugra feature commanded the river with clear lines of sight from almost half-way up. One light calibre anti-tank gun properly sighted and dug in, would have caused havoc in the convoy of LVTs. There were twenty-eight carrying the 7/16 alone. If opposition was met on the river, the plan was for the 7/16 to disembark and clear the enemy from the shore and if necessary attack and secure the Jugra feature.

'If Jugra had been occupied and direct fire brought to bear while the force was in the Buffaloes the operation would, I think, have failed and casualties would have been high. Even if some had managed to reach the riverside, movement thereafter would have been next to impossible in the thick mangrove swamps. As for an attack from the river on Jugra itself, having seen the country I would rule it out as impossible.'

Major Mowat Slater commented, 'It is difficult to assess the effect of considerable fire power from fleet and air, but having taken part in the closing stages of the Singapore fiasco, followed by two years in Burma, my experience left me in no doubt that we always over-estimated the effect of our bombing and gunfire on the Jap. His skill in digging in and his ability to "take it" allowed him to withstand levels of bombardment that we would have thought beyond the limit of human endurance.

'It would have required only one gun to have survived on the Jugra feature, for with that tide running we were sitting ducks. Incidentally, when we occupied Port Swettenham we found a squadron of Kamikaze at Klang airfield. I think we were very lucky that Zipper was not for real, and for that we have to thank the atomic bombs.'

On the right flank 20 miles away the 37th Brigade of the 23rd Indian Division landed on How and Easy beaches and quickly secured the Sepang road junction. But these beaches were later judged unfit for vehicles to land from LSTs, and attempts to do so ended at noon. They were resumed further north at first light next day.

Despite the problems of getting heavy equipment ashore, the infantry advanced quickly inland and by 4.30 p.m. Port Swettenham and Kelanang airfield were in British hands. Pilots aboard the ferry carrier *Trumpeter*, who had waited since dawn to fly their Spitfires into a captured airfield ashore, had been stood down until the following day because of the chaos on the beaches. The chronicler of 19th Squadron noted that 'Zipper seemed to have come slightly unzipped'. But the ship's Tannoy called all pilots to a briefing at 2 p.m. where they were told that they would be off that afternoon after all. Fifteen Spitfires took off despite lack of wind over the flight deck, and landed at Kelanang an hour before dusk. Next day the advance headquarters of 224 Group managed to get from the beach to join them, and more aircraft flew in.

The headquarters staff of 224 Group had spent an uncomfortable first night ashore with the Army divisional headquarters, without vehicles or equipment, on Morib beach. Their diary entry read, 'Conditions on the beach were chaotic, vehicles drowned in scores as there were no decent exits from the beaches, and the roads became choked with ditched tanks which had torn up the road surfaces and grass verges. A lack of vehicles ashore made movement of stores an impossible undertaking.'

The commander of the amphibious force, Rear-Admiral Martin described the Morib beaches as 'a convincing example of the most disadvantageous discharge conditions'. He reported that the gradient was so slight that landing craft were neaped (left high and dry), and LCTs could dry out only during the spring tide. Runnels (crevices and gullies) crisscrossing the beach caused damage to craft, and the sandbar running parallel with the beach a mile offshore presented an obstacle over which even minor landing craft could not pass at low water. In most places on the beach only a foot of soft sand covered muddy subsoil. He summed it all up in one word – 'vile'.

Advance troops of the 23rd Division, who had landed on the southerly Morib beaches, quickly moved on from securing the Sepang road junction to occupy Port Dickson. There they released nearly 1200 Indian Army prisoners-of-war, and were met by an officer of one of the two missing beach reconnaissance parties who had hidden out with guerrillas since landing by submarine in June.

The breakdown of the landing schedules on the Morib beaches was overcome by adopting a transfer line principle which the Americans had developed to solve the problem of offshore coral reefs. This involved the transfer of loads from landing craft to amphibious craft for the last stage to the beach. By the end of the third day 21,400 men and 2043 vehicles were landed across the Morib beaches, and on D3 the second invasion transports arrived to open another beachhead near Port Dickson. The beaches there were known to be good, but troops ashore reconnoitred them to make sure there were no snags of the kind they had met at Morib.

The new landings went smoothly despite a heavy monsoon downpour that drenched the assault troops who otherwise enjoyed a mainly dry landing. Mr Frank Head, who went ashore there with Naval Landing Party 2423, recalled finding 'a large number of suicide boats ready for use had the war not ended'.

Mr Dick Evely, was then a sergeant with 73 Mechanical Equipment platoon which landed with heavy equipment including 22-ton Caterpillar bulldozers. He recalled, 'The freighter used its own derricks to offload into LCTs, and I remember it literally standing on her beam. On one transshipment the slings broke and a bulldozer ploughed its way through the flat-bottomed LCT and is probably still on the seabed. We went ashore almost dry, the LCTs going well up the fairly deeply shelving beach. The jungle came almost to the water's edge, and if the Japs had been firing from it I wouldn't have been writing to you.'

While the new landings began at Port Dickson, advance patrols of the 25th Division were establishing themselves in Kuala Lumpur, Malaya's main city. They were helping prevent looting and preparing for a ceremonial entry the next day.

Five days later, on D8, nine more convoys arrived off the beachheads to complete the massive build-up for what would have been the drive south to Singapore.

When the Morib beaches closed on D17 a total of 44,474 personnel had been landed over them as well as 4305 vehicles and 11,671 tons of stores. The Port Dickson beaches were also used for a period of seventeen days, and when they closed on D20, 19,364 personnel, 3032 vehicles and 14,000 tons of stores had been landed across them.

These combined totals were well below the 97,506 troops, 9157 vehicles and 81,910 tons of stores that should have been put ashore under the original assault plan in combat conditions.

A succession of later convoys sailed straight into ports for unloading.

The authors of the *Official War History* wrote, 'Despite the chaos on the beaches there is little doubt that, had it been necessary to take Malaya by force of arms, Operation Zipper would eventually have achieved its object. It was, however, equally certain that, had the Japanese offered any resistance to the landings on 9 September at Morib and the Sepang beaches . . . the invasion forces would have been very roughly handled and at least pinned to the beaches for some time. It is even possible, in view of the chaos depicted and the fact that there were some 6000 Japanese only about thirty miles away at Kuala Lumpur, that the troops landed on the Morib beaches might have had to be withdrawn. Although it was realized that the information about the beaches might not be accurate, a risk was accepted that might have proved unjustifiable had the Japanese opposed the D-Day landings with even a few battalions. There would in any case have had to be a quick and sound revision of the plan when it turned out there was no possibility of the follow-up division being able to land at Morib as planned.

Only good generalship could have avoided the delay that would have given the Japanese time to concentrate their available forces to oppose a break-out from the beachheads.'

Thirty-nine years later, the commander of the Zipper land forces, General Sir Ouvry Roberts, a sprightly eighty-six, told the author, 'The unexpected difficulties on the beaches would have added considerably to our casualties. As the commander I would have had to have sorted things out on the Morib beaches myself, and I don't suppose I should have been here today.'

Sir Ouvry Roberts knew more than most generals about casualties. In the epic battles at Kohima he had commanded troops holding the vital Shenam positions where the casualty rate on both sides was higher in proportion to the numbers involved than in any other action in the Second World War. In notes for his memoirs, he wrote this about Zipper, 'I was indeed happy from every point of view that we were not involved in fighting. Had the Japanese defended Malaya it is more than probable that our operation would have been a failure. Troops with no experience of fighting in the jungle or against the Japanese went in across beaches that were nothing like as good as the intelligence reports led us to believe.' But penned at the bottom of the typescript he added second thoughts, 'I believe we would have succeeded, but only after tough fighting.'

On the morning of D-Day General Roberts had watched from a DUKWE offshore as the first echelon of LCAs beached exactly at high water. He noted in his diary later that day, 'The assault would definitely have been a success as the troops had only a few feet to go to get under cover.' But the diary entry went on, 'The beach turned out to be far worse than anticipated, having deceptive patches of soft mud under the firm layer of sand. Though troops were not getting ashore as ordered, no one appeared to be lost and there was little confusion. Forty-seven vehicles were bogged and drowned.'

An entry in the diary a few days later described the view from Morib beach, 'The sea was an amazing sight at high tide the first two days with the tops of every imaginable kind of vehicle sticking up.'

In his Oxford garden on a summer's day in 1984 Sir Ouvry was still blaming himself. 'I should never have accepted the intelligence reports about the beach. I knew intelligence was generally unsatisfactory. I was told that the beach was absolutely firm – that a car could be driven over it. This may have been true when the sand was dry, but when it was under water vehicles sank a foot and more into it. The result was that even though we landed at high tide, all the amphibious vehicles got stuck before they reached dry land. . . . From the beginning I wasn't happy about Morib because there were only two exits from the beach. I argued for simultaneous landings at Morib and Port Dickson, but we just didn't have the resources to do the two landings at the same time.'

Sir Ouvry also recalled that the job of ironing out the difficulties was compounded by serious communications difficulties. The Naval Force Commander, Admiral Martin, had taken the communications headquarters ship HMS *Bulolo* to Singapore, and the landings had to be directed by staff transferred to the standby headquarters ship HMS *Largs*.

This was only one cause of contention between the service commanders. Mr Bill Clarke was on the staff of the naval commander-in-chief, Admiral Sir Arthur Power, watching events from the quarterdeck of the flagship *Cleopatra*. The report he wrote for the Admiral is still among classified Cabinet papers, but he said that Zipper was a shambles in many ways.

Little more than forty-eight hours after the first troops went ashore, three VIP planes landed at Kelanang airfield. One of them was Mountbatten's personal York command plane. The others brought the RAF and Army Commanders-in-Chief. Among the troops they inspected was a party of communist guerrillas described in General Robert's diary as 'little chaps, but quite smart and impressive with their clenched fist salutes'.

While the second beachhead was opened nearby, General Roberts visited a prison camp at Port Dickson where Indian soldiers put on a smart guard of honour and festooned their liberator with 'more garlands than I've seen anywhere'. He noted that every man in the camp had resisted every form of coercion to join the Indian National Army to fight the British.

Four days after the landings had begun, General Roberts took the surrender of the commander of the Japanese 29th Army, General Ishiguro, in Kuala Lumpur. His diary entry for that day reads, 'I opened the proceedings by making it clear that this was an unconditional surrender following on the utter defeat of the Japanese. The Japanese commander signed without demur. He said he wanted to cooperate with their old allies in restoring world peace. They are a despicable, deceitful race, but I couldn't help feeling sorry for the old man, thinking what I should feel like had it been the other way about. But one's sympathy soon turns to anger when one listens to someone who has suffered at their hands.'

There were, as General Roberts noted in his diary en route for the Zipper beaches, some regrets that British forces were robbed of the chance to make a fighting comeback to Malaya and wipe out the shame of Singapore – the biggest surrender in their history. The Conservative politician, Julian Amery, a staff officer in SEAC at the time, believed, 'It was a tragedy that the atomic bomb saw to it that Mountbatten never had a chance to show himself as a great commander.' Richard Hough wrote, 'There was no decisive and final battle for Mountbatten – no Agincourt to be told "The day is yours". At first forgotten, later denied supplies, right to the last wickedly ironical denial while it was already at sea for its own

D-Day, Mountbatten's command was also deprived of its climactic last triumph.'

In his own autobiography, General Slim made no mention of the beaches at all, dismissing this biggest British amphibious operation in the Far East in a single paragraph which described the welcome his troops received from the local people. He even got the spelling of Port Dickson wrong, referring to Port Dixon!

Brigadier Michael Calvert wrote that there had been grave deficiencies in planning, particularly in selection of the beaches. 'The opening phase of a true assault would have been a nightmare. Determined opposition even from a few Japanese battalions might have been disastrous.' He also observed, 'The scheming and musical chairs of the High Command in South-East Asia, from which Slim does not emerge unmuddled, must have been partly to blame for this bad planning.'

Most of those who took part in Operation Zipper felt at the time that the atomic bombs were the only factor that saved them from being embroiled in a bloodbath. All those contacted by the author during the last twelve months hold to the belief that their chances of being alive today would have been slim indeed if the Japanese had opposed the landings. To them Churchill expressed the Allied development of the atomic bomb exactly right – for them it was a miracle of deliverance.

6

Just a week after the British reoccupation of Singapore, Mountbatten accepted the formal surrender of the 680,879 enemy forces in South-East Asia at a ceremony in the council chamber of the Municipal Buildings in Singapore. He was driven there in an open car, chauffeured by a released prisoner-of-war, through streets lined by sailors and Royal Marines. Bands played 'Rule Britannia' as he inspected honour guards of the Royal Navy, Australian paratroops and the Indian Army, while a seventeen-gun salute thundered over the city.

Officers of all the Allied Powers except the Soviet Union witnessed the signing of the documents by seven Japanese admirals and generals. Field Marshal Terauchi, however, sent a medical certificate saying he was too ill to attend, still suffering from the stroke he had had when told that Mandalay had fallen. He was to hand his two swords to Mountbatten at Saigon ten weeks later.

Mountbatten told the gathering, which included released civilian detainees, prisoners-of-war and guerrillas, that the Japanese were surrendering to superior forces established ashore at Port Dickson and Port Swettenham. He said, 'When I visited the beaches yesterday men were landing in an endless stream. As I speak there are 100,000 men ashore. This invasion would have taken place on 9 September whether the Japanese had resisted or not. I wish to make this plain – the surrender today is no negotiated surrender, the Japanese are surrendering to superior forces now massed here.'

The thoughts of General Itagaki and his staff officers at this dubious assertion can only be guessed. They sat inscrutable. General Slim later wrote of his feelings as he sat on Mountbatten's left facing them. 'I looked at the dull, impassive faces of the Japanese generals and admirals opposite. Their plight moved me not at all. For them I had none of the sympathy of soldier for soldier that I had felt for Germans, Turks, Italians or Frenchmen that by fortune of war I had seen surrender. I knew too well what these men and those under their orders had done to their prisoners. They sat there, apart from the rest of humanity.'

Mountbatten read his Order of the Day from the steps of the Municipal Buildings, congratulating the Allied forces on the completeness of their victory, adding a warning that the Japanese would try to wriggle out of the terms of the first defeat in their history.

Then, as the bands played 'God Save the King', a Union Jack which had been kept concealed in Changi prison camp through the dark years of defeat, was hoisted.

The British in South-East Asia ignored General MacArthur's instructions that the 'archaic ceremony' of the surrender of swords was not to be enforced. General Slim had already sent out his own orders, and these were not countermanded. Slim laid down that all senior Japanese officers were to surrender their swords to appropriate British commanders in front of a parade of their troops. However, it was laid down that instead of being regarded as prisoners-of-war, the Japanese were to be referred to as JSPs – Japanese surrendered personnel. This terminology was considered to involve less loss of face.

When some of his staff officers queried the wisdom of insisting that Japanese officers surrendered their swords, arguing that many might prefer to go on fighting or commit suicide to such public shame, Slim retorted that if they liked to go on fighting he was ready for them, and any who wanted to commit suicide would be given every facility. He wrote later, 'I was convinced that an effective way to impress on the Japanese that they were beaten in the field was to insist on this ceremonial surrender of swords. No Japanese soldier who had seen his general march up and hand over his sword would ever doubt that the invincible army was invincible no longer. We did not want a repetition of the German First War legend of an unconquered army. . . . I'm afraid I disregarded General MacArthur's wishes . . . in South-East Asia all Japanese officers surrendered their swords to officers of similar or higher rank, the enemy divisional and army commanders handed theirs in before large parades of their already disarmed troops . . . General Kimura's is now on my mantelpiece, where I always intended that one day it should be.'

Mountbatten was deeply and permanently affected by the condition of Allied prisoners. He confessed to Richard Hough that he had never liked the Japanese from the time of his first visit to Japan in 1921, regarding them as hard people with hard eyes.

He went on, 'Now I knew just how horrible they were after seeing such terrible things in Singapore and in the camps. It was the one thing during the war that seared my mind. There were no extenuating circumstances, and I could find no compassion for them at all. I loathed them. That was why I didn't go to the Tokyo Bay surrender – I just could not have stood the sight of them all there. My own ceremony at Singapore, well, duty obliged me to be there, but I didn't like it.'

The attitude of the Queen's uncle caused some embarrassment when Emperor Hirohito was in London on a State Visit in October 1971. At first, Mountbatten planned to boycott all the functions he would normally have been expected to attend, and only on the Queen's express command did he attend a Buckingham Palace reception, though he left before the official banquet. Despite all the publicity about this, he did have a discreet private audience with Hirohito during the visit, as Mountbatten revealed to the author shortly afterwards, 'I wanted to discuss the United World Colleges [an international educational organization of which he was then president] and felt that the committee recently formed in Japan would need his blessing. There was absolutely no moral problem because we are not concerned with ideologies or past wrongs. I am not going to comment on the past behaviour of the Japanese about which I naturally have strong views. I am interested in the future and getting youngsters from different countries educated together and growing up with a real international understanding so that mistakes which led to two World Wars may be avoided.'

Mountbatten also told me that he would not rule out a visit to Japan, but he never got round to it in the eight years before he was killed by an IRA bomb in 1979. Japanese representatives were pointedly omitted from the invitation lists which Mountbatten himself drew up as part of the meticulous arrangements he made in readiness for his own state funeral.

After the main ceremony in Singapore, other big ceremonial parades for Japanese troops to see their officers hand over their swords were held in Ipoh, Kuala Kangsar and Bidor, and the occupation of Malaya was completed by 25 September. But in the bypassed islands of the Andaman and Nicobar groups, the formal surrender had to wait till 8 October.

With the Tokyo ceremonial surrender at last out of the way, the occupation of Siam began on 4 September. Here the Regent had been working with British agents for some months despite a state of war as Japan's ally. All available air resources lifted the 7th Division into Bangkok from Burma where it had been waiting to take part in phase two of Zipper. From 11 September Bangkok airport was used as a staging post for the lift of the 20th Division into Saigon where fighting had broken out between Viet Minh nationalists and French officials who had come out of internment camps and taken back the running of the country. There was also a nationalist uprising in the Dutch East Indies aimed at preventing the return of the Dutch. A British naval force arrived at Tanjong Priok, the port of the capital of Java, Batavia (now Jakarta) on 15 September, and the Japanese headquarters there was ordered to move troops into the city to maintain order until British troops arrived from Singapore. For weeks after that, Japanese forces throughout the islands kept their arms and stood guard at internment camps where the unhappy Dutch still had to stay for their own safety. But the Japanese were suitably subservient to their victors, presenting arms to all British servicemen without regard to rank.

From the moment of the Tokyo surrender, the SEAC area of operations was enlarged to include much of the southwest Pacific. Mountbatten commented, 'Suddenly I was responsible for 1½ million square miles of territory and 128 million people, many of them starving, many more in degrees of political unrest.

'I had threequarters of a million Japanese prisoners-of-war to house and feed and employ until I could get them home, and 123,000 of our ex-prisoners-of-war and internees to house, feed, and get home, and there was the world's worst-ever shortage of shipping.'

In fact, the problem was even bigger. The figure of Allied POWs and internees in Japanese hands turned out to be nearly 300,000 of whom 140,000 were caught up in new turmoil in Java. Apart from 36,000 in Singapore the rest were scattered in small numbers and some have never been accounted for.

By the time of the Zipper landings, Force 136 had infiltrated 371 agents into Malaya to organize the guerrilla forces to advance from the north and cut off road, railway and telephone communications and attack radio stations and Japanese headquarters. Their leaders made cease-fire agreements with many local Japanese commanders, and by 24 August, despite continued threats by General Itagaki to fight on, the Union Jack and guerilla flags were flying from many police stations. There were some isolated attacks by guerrillas, and Force 136 officers had to intervene and organize a truce when the Japanese mounted a counterattack on one police station.

E Group of Force 136 had located most of the prison camps – there were about 200 throughout the SEAC area – and made plans to try to prevent the massacre of prisoners which it was feared the Zipper landings would precipitate. Immediately after the Emperor's call for surrender, Force 136 organized air drops of doctors and 650 tons of medicines and food to the camps.

Most of the camps were little more than barbed wire enclosures with huts and palm leaf basha shelters, guarded by Japanese and Koreans who were at best indifferent to their prisoners, at worst bestial sadists. The food supplied was scarcely enough to keep westerners alive, much less sustain them for hard labour in a debilitating climate. Many died from tropical illnesses while drugs and medicines sent in by the Red Cross were withheld from them by their captors. (Medical advances like penicillin, sulphonamides and blood plasma had meanwhile reduced the proportion of non-battle casualties among the British forces in Burma from 129 to 1 in 1943 to 7 to 1 in the last year of the war. In the same period mepacrin tablets cut the incidence of malaria from 628 per 1000 to 128 per 1000.)

General Slim noted this reaction to a visit to several of the camps. 'There can be no excuse for a nation which as a matter of policy treats its prisoners-of-war in this way, and no honour to an army, however brave, which willingly makes itself an instrument of such inhumanity to the helpless.'

As British troops moved into the occupied territories, the Supreme Commander's wife, Lady Edwina Mountbatten, often went ahead of them on a tour of prison camps in her role as head of St John's Ambulance. She reported later, 'There is no doubt that had the war gone on a few more weeks there would have been no prisoners left alive. They were absolutely at their last gasp in the Dutch East Indies area, and the tragedy is that so many did die in the last weeks before the surrender, and even after it.'

Mrs Vivian Skinner was a Queen Alexandra nursing sister with the Relief Agency for Prisoners-of-War and Internees – RAPWI – working from Raffles Hotel in Singapore since the first days of British reoccupation. She told the author, 'The internees in the Sime Road camp were comparatively better off than those up-country, but even they had hardly any clothing, not much more than G-strings. Many were at the point of death and only survived because of the sudden ending to the war. There is no doubt many of those who died in the last weeks would have still been alive had the Japanese not hoarded drugs and insulin. There were plenty in their stores.'

(Mrs Skinner met her husband, whose account of his landing in Operation Zipper has been told earlier, when he eventually reached Singapore and was in hospital as one of her patients.)

The survivors of the battleship *Prince of Wales*, sunk on the outbreak of the Far East War, were still what the Royal Navy calls 'pusser' when they greeted their liberators – parade smart in camp-made uniforms with the ship's name on their caps and wire badges of rank.

British, Australian and Indian POWs were evacuated by river boat to the coast, where they transferred to landing craft which risked minefields to speed them to Singapore. A small number of the urgently ill were taken out in Dakota transport planes – the air mule of the Burma war. By the end of September, 54,000 POWs and civilian internees had been evacuated through Singapore to India and Australia, almost all of them by sea. The total quickly reached 80,410 POWs and 16,156 internees, but a year later there were still about 30,000 Dutch internees stranded in the interior of Java.

7

The inhuman treatment meted out to Allied nationals who fell into Japanese hands was widely known long before the war was over. It had been deliberately used to bolster fighting spirit in Allied ranks by inflaming hatred for the Japanese enemy. But the full extent of Japanese brutality and atrocities emerged only with the liberation of the prisoners in the camps. Their stories about how they had become so physically emaciated must surely have tempered any moral scruples over the atomic bombs, had any then existed amid the overwhelming relief at having the war finished.

Japan had signed the Hague Convention of 1907 on the law and customs of war, but had refused to sign the more detailed 1929 Geneva Convention on the treatment of prisoners-of-war. The idea of treating men who surrendered as worthy of consideration was alien to their thinking. In most of the territories they conquered, the Japanese even refused facilities to the International Red Cross. Captured Allied servicemen were forced to sign certificates promising not to escape, were deprived of proper food, drugs and medical care, and crowded into insanitary camps. They were forced to work for the Japanese war machine, often till they dropped.

Of 61,000 Allied prisoners detailed to work on the infamous Siam railway, more than 16,000 died from malnutrition, ill-treatment and sickness. So did more than 100,000 of the 270,000 labourers from Malaya, Siam and Burma who also worked on the railway. Another 6000 British and Dutch prisoners were sent from Singapore to build airfields in the Flores and Moluccas islands of the Dutch East Indies, where conditions were less well known but just as arduous.

In a diary of his captivity published by the Imperial War Museum, Dr Robert Hardie has described life in a camp on the railway at Takanum in Siam on the border with Burma, which the Japanese regarded as a medical centre:

> May 15, 1943. Tents are crammed, but still men have to sleep in the open (some prefer to) under such primitive shelters as they can improvise with bamboo and little attap and perhaps a groundsheet. . . . They parade after a

hasty breakfast threequarters of an hour after dawn . . . until an hour or two before sunset, bamboo cutting, tree felling, bridge building, embankment building and making cuttings, pile driving and so on, all in blazing sun under constant pressure backed by violence. . . . 240 out of 400 men are unable to work . . . many are desperately ill with dysentry, beriberi and pellagra, malaria and exhaustion. The Japanese are having a 'speedo-speedo' – driving all possible men out to work, ruthlessly cutting down the numbers of people available to do the water carrying and cooking, and as often as not refusing to allow us a single man or spade for the needs of camp sanitation. . . . The Nips keep demanding more men for the railway and launch into furious tirades against us because so many are sick.

So we live, lying at night on the bare ground or on a hastily constructed frame of flattened bamboo with no lights, our food little beyond rice and the utterly unappetizing and probably dietarily useless dried vegetables looking like seaweed. The conditions in the hospital are really terrible. The few tents are overcrowded, six or seven people on each side on roughly flattened bamboo. Most of them are severe dysentaries, and they are helpless. There is a lot of rain now, and the tents leak. There is only one bedpan in the whole hospital, and three enamel pots. The weather is too wet to get the patients out every day – even if there were stretchers to carry them on – and even if they could be got out we have no soap and cloths to clean the tents up. The stench and squalor is shocking.

The Burma railway became strategically vital to the Japanese because of enormous shipping losses on the long sea route to Burma via the Malacca Straits. A route for a railway to link Burma with Bangkok had been surveyed by the British years before, but the project was never pursued because of the inevitable cost in human life of constructing it through fever and plague stricken mountains.

The railway workers received their first direct contact with the outside world on 5 September 1944 when leaflets, obviously dropped by an Allied plane, were picked up by working parties beside a nearby river. The leaflets told of the war going well in Europe, and added the exhortation, 'Hold on! We are coming'.

Two months later Allied planes began bombing the railway, and in one attack near the Wampo viaduct in March 1945 the Japanese overseer refused to allow prisoners to take cover and several were killed and wounded.

Rumours of heavy air raids on Japan, spectacular Allied advances and expectations of an imminent end to the war reached the prison camps within a week of the atomic explosion over Hiroshima, and on 17 August the Japanese officially told the prisoners the war was over. They were told to control camp discipline themselves until the Allied forces arrived.

Dr Hardie's diary entry for 1 September read, 'Sick men from up-country are coming down as fast as they can be brought, and the shocking condition of many of them revives one's feelings of animosity against the

Japanese, which had sunk quite low, seeing them so submissive and orderly and now harmless.'

John Fletcher-Cooke, who wrote his experiences as a prisoner-of-war in *The Emperor's Guest*, believed that 'few, if any POWs would have got out of Japan alive if the atomic bombs had not been dropped on Hiroshima and Nagasaki.' He thought news of them rekindled in the minds of the guards at Miyata camp, sixty miles from Nagasaki, 'that dormant and indefinable fear of the POWs they all possessed.' He added, 'If the Allies had been forced to make an opposed landing the Japanese would undoubtedly have liquidated the POWs, if for no other reason than that to guard them and feed them would have interfered with the task of repelling the invaders "polluting the sacred soil of Nippon".

'There is no doubt in my own mind that these atomic bombs saved many more lives than the tens of thousands they killed. They saved the lives of tens of thousands of POWs, of hundreds of thousands of Allied servicemen, and almost certainly of millions of Japanese – for let there be no mistake, if the Emperor and his Cabinet had decided to fight on, the Japanese would, literally, have fought to the last man.'

Unlike Mountbatten, Fletcher-Cooke, who later became a diplomat at the United Nations, returned to Japan and even looked up some of the men who had guarded him years before. He wrote, 'I have found it impossible to be bitter against the Japanese.'

Immediately after the reoccupation, Allied investigators began putting together a casebook of Japanese atrocities, and bringing some of their perpetrators to trial. They heard of the machine-gunning of nurses and soldiers as they waded through the surf at Banka Island after surviving the sinking of the ship in which they were escaping from Singapore in February 1942. From the surviving prisoners on the Dutch East Indies island of Amboyna came this horrifying statistic: of 549 Australians and Dutch captured there in 1942, seventeen had been executed and 386 had died of cruelty and neglect, ninety-two of them only weeks before their camps were liberated. In Borneo, more than 2500 prisoners-of-war, mostly Australians, died on three forced marches through the jungle.

On 9 March 1944 the British motor vessel *Behar* was sunk by the Japanese cruiser *Tone* north of the Cocos Islands, but managed to send out a radio signal which forced the Japanese cruiser force to withdraw after this single sinking. The *Tone*'s commander, Captain Mayusumi, picked up 104 passengers and crew, but was later ordered to 'dispose' of them by the force commander, Vice-Admiral Sakonju. When Captain Mayusumi questioned the order he was sternly rebuked, and after putting thirty-two of the rescued ashore at Batavia (Jakarta), the twenty-seven Europeans and forty-five Indians still aboard when he sailed from there on 18 March were lined up on the decks at midnight, made to kneel and then beheaded.

Some Japanese paid the penalty at the hands of Allied troops later. When the Australians landed in Borneo in July 1945 they took savage revenge for the death marches three years earlier. No efforts were made to take prisoners during the fighting, and after the Emperor's order brought about a general surrender, 6000 Japanese were disarmed and marched 150 miles through an area where they had earlier burned villages suspected of contact with Allied submarines. Only a few hundred Japanese survived attacks on their columns by head-hunting tribesmen.

8

Japan was totally defeated, stripped of her conquests, her cities laid waste, her economy devastated. But it quickly became evident that Japan had achieved one major war aim. Their early military triumphs had blown apart the myth of invincible European power, and it was this that brought an abrupt end to European colonialism in the Far East. While General MacArthur's occupation forces met a politely submissive population as they moved into the Japanese home islands, Admiral Mountbatten's SEAC forces returned to the colonial territories which the Japanese had overrun to face a seething tide of nationalism.

The first Allied force to return to the Dutch East Indies – an advance party of seven – dropped by parachute at Kematoran airfield, near Batavia, on 8 September, and sent back a misleading report to Mountbatten. They dismissed the nationalist movement as a concern of a 'few intellectuals'. Once again British forces blithely stepped ashore to be beset by unanticipated difficulties, not muddy beaches as in Zipper, but a quagmire of tricky, explosive politics. The Japanese had made preparations to leave behind a booby-trap on an immense scale when, as they anticipated, Allied pressure forced them to withdraw from the Dutch territories.

They had kept news of a Dutch declaration about plans to end the old colonial rule from reaching the people of the territories. This declaration was made by the Dutch government, exiled in London during the German occupation of Holland, to square its colonial possessions with the principles of self-determination embodied in the Atlantic Charter, the Holy Grail of Allied war aims. The Dutch declaration promised to replace the colonial regime with an administration based on partnership. While censoring all word of this, the Japanese encouraged the independence movement of Dr Soekarno, and helped him build up a formidable new army. They supplied arms, including light tanks, armoured cars and artillery and provided training.

On the day the second atomic explosion hit Nagasaki, 9 August, Dr Soekarno and the Japanese Commander-in-Chief, Field Marshal Terauchi, attended an elaborate ceremony at Dalat, a hill station in South Vietnam, to sign a document making Indonesia an independent sovereign state. It was to be made public on 7 September, but immediately he heard of the Japanese surrender Soekarno decided to bring it into force at once. He read the Independence Declaration at a public ceremony in Batavia on 17 August, and the red and white flag of Indonesia was raised for the first time. At that time only the huge northern island of Sumatra came within the boundaries of South-East Asia Command, and by the time Mountbatten's authority extended to the whole of the Dutch East Indies on 2 September, Soekarno's armed volunteers numbered 250,000. Many Japanese units had been forced to hand over weapons and arsenals to them.

A Dutch civil affairs chief arrived with the British naval force on 15 September, but after just one day ashore attempting to set up office in the capital he was forced to seek safety back aboard the cruiser *Cumberland*. Soekarno's government announced it would oppose by force any attempt by the Dutch to reimpose their rule. The British ordered the Japanese to send troops into the city to keep order until the arrival of an advance party of 1000 Seaforth Highlanders, whose job was to begin disarming the 230,000 Japanese in the Dutch island empire. British forces also had the task of rescuing 80,000 internees and 6000 Allied prisoners-of-war. The British soldiers and sailors received a wary welcome in a capital plastered with quotations in English from the American Declaration of Independence.

Mountbatten made it clear that their role was to disarm the Japanese and evacuate Allied prisoners-of-war and internees. They were to stand apart from any political role. The Commander-in-Chief in India, General Auchinleck, had laid it down that Indian troops were not to be used against any nationalist movement 'save only in the most exceptional circumstances'.

These exceptional circumstances erupted in the port of Sourabaya on the east coast of Java in October. The Japanese commander there had persuaded the leader of an Allied team sent to contact prison camps to accept his surrender, passing the buck of responsibility by thrusting his sword into the hands of the team leader who happened to be a Dutch naval commander. Misunderstandings arising from this led to heavy fighting, and the commander of the British forces landed in the area, Brigadier A.W.S. Mallaby, and several of his officers were killed by a mob on their way – under a white flag – to discuss a truce. Mobs also attacked a convoy carrying 200 Dutch internees, killing their escort of Indian Mahratta soldiers, and all but twenty women and children.

The British reacted strongly. Every available warship was ordered to Sourabaya, and a cruiser and several destroyers supported troops with gunfire while Mosquitos and Thunderbolts bombed and strafed the Indonesian positions. In the month-long battle the Indonesians suffered 4697 casualties, including 1618 dead. Allied casualties in two months in Java, mostly in this battle at Sourabaya, were 608, including 98 killed and 197 missing. The British destroyed or captured fifteen armoured cars, forty-seven field guns, thirty-six anti-aircraft guns, seven anti-tank guns, eleven mortars, seventy-five heavy machine guns, forty-four light machine guns, 794 rifles, 580 miscellaneous firearms and 400 tons of ammunition.

The Japanese were themselves caught up in the whirlwind of chaos that sprang from the seeds they had sown. Eighty Japanese were massacred in one incident at Bekasi, and another seventy at Semerang. Altogether about 1000 Japanese were killed in the troubles, about the same number as had been killed in capturing the Dutch empire more than three years before.

Dutch forces were held back by 'shipping shortages' until the tasks of SEAC were accomplished. This caused great bitterness in Holland particularly against the British. The Dutch felt abandoned by Allies with whom they had fought hard against the Japanese invaders. Their efforts to regain control were met with sporadic fighting which continued until November 1949 when a formal transfer of sovereignty of all the Dutch Indies, except Western New Guinea, was made. Later Western New Guinea was invaded by Indonesian forces and renamed Irian Jaya.

In Indo-China, fighting had broken out in March 1945 when the Japanese ordered the governor general, Admiral J. Decoux, who had supported Vichy, to put all French forces under his command to face an expected American invasion. Decoux said he could only consider this in the actual event of invasion, and was promptly arrested. French forces were attacked, and some were killed after surrendering. SEAC flew in supplies and ammunition to the beleaguered French soldiers, but American forces were under orders not to send aid to them even though they were fighting for their lives. General de Gaulle, by this time firmly in power in Paris, warned of consequences to American interests in Europe, and after nine days Roosevelt agreed that American forces in China, the nearest Allied troops, could fly aid to the French so long as it did not interfere with other operations. Seven thousand French soldiers managed to retreat into China and were flown to India.

On 10 August leaders of the Viet-Minh guerrillas, who had cooperated with American agents, declared Tongking and Annam to be an independent republic of Vietnam under the leadership of Ho Chi Minh. When British troops arrived to take the surrender of the Japanese they had to stand between the French, who had come out of internment to attempt to take back control, and the Viet-Minh. The Japanese turned a blind eye to attacks on Europeans although they were still responsible for law and order, and the British commander, General D.D. Gracey, had to intervene with firm measures. More than sixty Viet-Minh were killed in attacks on British forces occupying the radio station and other installations.

After the departure of the last British troops in May 1946 the French made determined efforts to restore their position in Indo-China, but they suffered a decisive defeat at Dien Bien Phu in 1954. This led to a peace settlement at Geneva in which Vietnam was partitioned and Cambodia and Laos became independent kingdoms.

In neighbouring Siam, the pro-Japanese government was overthrown on 16 August, just one day after Japan offered to surrender, and the declaration of war was withdrawn. SEAC forces were welcomed when they arrived in September, the king returned from Switzerland and the leader of the exiled Free Siam movement became prime minister. The territories gained as Japan's ally – two Shan states of Burma, parts of Cambodia and Laos and the four northern states of Malaya, were all given up.

The hard-fought British return to Burma was to be short-lived. After the independence of India and Pakistan in 1947, a British handover of sovereignty in Burma became only a matter of negotiation. The battles which had been fought as the Japanese advanced in 1941, and again as the British 14th Army pushed them all the way back again, left deep scars. When independence came in January 1948 the new Republic of Burma cut all ties with Britain and chose to stay outside the Commonwealth, the only former territory to do so. Burma to this day has virtually shunned the outside world, and for a long time was almost a forbidden land to foreigners.

The immense British victory in Burma, Japan's biggest land defeat, brought little gain. Even the reopening of the Burma road, remembering that the original Japanese objective was to close it, turned out to be futile in view of the sudden end to the war. The new section from Ledo in Assam, so dear to the Americans, carried only 38,000 tons of supplies before the liberation of Chinese ports made both it and the recaptured route from Rangoon superfluous. The airlift over the Himalayan 'hump' from India had carried as much as 39,000 tons in a month.

Throughout the war Britain and America were at loggerheads over the role of Chiang's China. The British could never understand what they regarded as a strange American ju-ju, an obsession with China which amounted to a touchstone by which all British efforts were judged. They resented resources – which they felt the neglected SEAC could have better used – being poured into 'a bottomless pit of oriental inefficiency and corruption'. The Americans believed that Britain looked at China through 'treaty port eyes', and that Britain's only interest in the war against Japan was to recover her lost colonies while leaving America to do most of the fighting. They snidely dubbed SEAC as standing for 'Save England's

Asiatic Colonies'. Mountbatten's nominal deputy in SEAC's early period was the American General 'Vinegar Joe' Stilwell who was also Chiang Kai-Shek's Chief-of-Staff. He was quoted as saying 'The more I see of Limies, the more I hate them', and often referred to his chief as a 'pisspot'. For a time he convinced the military chiefs in Washington that 'the British simply won't fight in Burma'.

At the same time, Mountbatten's Chief-of-Staff, General Sir Henry Pownall, was noting in his diary, 'Chiang has been perfectly bloody. American-trained forces at Ledo are not out to fight, and its certain the Yunnan forces won't go a yard. So any plan built on their doing their share is built on sand whether Chiang agrees to it or not. So its better he keeps up his intransigent attitude. Then at least we can plan the best we can without reliance on rotten allies.'

At the very time the decisive Kohima-Imphal battle was beginning, the American press, led by *Time* magazine, featured a contest between Mountbatten and Stilwell. This presented accurate details of the competing SEAC plans on a plate to Japanese intelligence. Churchill had to speak out strongly against attacks on SEAC and on the British Pacific Fleet in the American press. Official American documentary films on the Burma campaign were so unbalanced that they were rejected for showing in Britain, and a Hollywood film starring Errol Flynn in an American victory in Burma brought a storm of protest.

President Roosevelt, had he lived, would doubtless have been delighted at the demise of the European empires in the East. He openly chided Churchill over his imperial pride, and was determined to do nothing to help the French and Dutch regain their lost colonial territories. Churchill made his retort publicly when he said, 'I have not become the King's first minister to preside over the liquidation of the British Empire.'

In strange contrast, Roosevelt passed lightly over his agreement to the Soviet's blatant territorial aggrandisement in the Far East by saying, 'Stalin was only asking for what the Japanese had taken from them.' His obsession with the need to sustain General Chiang Kai-Shek's armies went beyond the early American plan to build up a huge American-trained Chinese army to clear the Japanese out and use China as an air platform to bomb Japan into oblivion. He also believed that China would dominate the area as America's protégé in the postwar world. This early China strategy was a classic example of politics winning out over sound military considerations, for from the beginning, the American naval chief-of-staff, Admiral Ernest King, had urged the ocean strategy favoured by Churchill. It was the impetus of the ocean advance that made the China strategy obsolete long before most of King's political colleagues recognized it.

Despite the huge volume of supplies which the Americans delivered to Chiang Kai-Shek's forces, when British forces in SEAC were being ironically starved of them, the Japanese armies in China were never under pressure there. When the Allies were advancing on every other front in 1944 the last Japanese offensive in China (by troops from the Manchurian border with the Soviet Union) overran the American airbase at Kweilan in November and had a clear road open to Chungking. It forced the withdrawal of Chiang's troops from northern Burma and, much more critically, the withdrawal of American air support.

The Japanese began to pull back only in the last months of the war, and then only from positions of minor importance to save manpower. Chiang Kai-Shek was saving his forces and supplies for a renewal of his clash with the communists of Mao Tse-Tung who had sat out the war in Yunnan on the borders of Mongolia.

With the general Japanese collapse, the Americans airlifted Chiang Kai-Shek forces into Shanghai, Nanking and Peking, but by 1949 Mao Tse-Tung's Peoples' Army, which took over Japanese weapons surrendered to the Russians in Manchuria, had driven their nationalist rivals right off the mainland. General Chiang Kai-Shek's forces took refuge in the island of Taiwan (Formosa) where they remain to this day. In 1950 the Chinese Peoples' Republic signed a treaty of alliance and friendship with the Soviet Union, and all American hopes of her China protégé were dashed. President Harry Truman refused to recognize the Peoples' Republic and continued to regard the refugee Chiang Kai-Shek as Chinese head of state. Two decades passed before America eventually recognized reality.

Back in 1945, the sudden Japanese collapse caused urgent worries in London over the future of Hong Kong. Intelligence reports indicated that Chiang Kai-Shek forces, with American connivance, were planning to move into the colony and proclaim its restoration to China.

American backing for a return of Hong Kong to China went back to before the war; in the summer of 1941 a State Department official, Harry Dexter White, drew up a draft basis for a settlement with Japan. It involved America in considerable financial, economic and military concessions to get Japan's agreement to withdraw from China and Indo-China. Britain was to hand Hong Kong back to China, and French Indo-China was to be placed under a joint commission run by America, Britain, France, Japan and China. Nothing came of that, but in January 1943 the State Department prompted Britain to sign treaties with Nationalist China for an end of the extra-territorial treaties. The Americans claimed the kudos, but in fact twelve years before Britain had taken the lead in trying to negotiate a gradual surrender of extra-territorial rights with the newly formed Nationalist Government. They had hoped to improve trading conditions by removing the causes of potential conflict. At the end of the 1943 negotiations, the Chinese reserved the right to raise at a later date the question of the Kowloon leased territory, clearly foreshadowing a claim for sovereignty over all Hong Kong. The Foreign Office then expressed readiness to discuss this within the context of a United Nations security system for the area as a whole.

President Roosevelt believed he would have no difficulty in getting China to agree to Hong Kong becoming a free port 'if only the stubborn British would surrender it to Chiang Kai-Shek in the first place'. But Britain's attitude hardened, and Churchill truculently told Roosevelt and Stalin at the Teheran summit the following November that 'nothing would be taken away from Britain without a war'.

During a visit to Chungking in June 1944, Vice-President Henry Wallace told Chiang Kai-Shek, 'Churchill is old. A new British government will give Hong Kong to China and the United States expects that China will next day make it a free port.' During this visit Wallace pointedly snubbed the British ambassador, and he agreed to a joint statement which proclaimed 'the right of self-government for Asiatic peoples now dependent'.

The British government were conscious that 1860 of Hong Kong's garrison of 10,000 British and Indian troops had died putting up a stubbornly heroic seventeen-day defence of the hopelessly beleaguered colony less than four years before, in sharp contrast to the shameful surrender of the huge garrison at Singapore. On 23 August they sent a message through clandestine channels ordering civilian internees to set up a British administration at once, and not to hand over to any other authority without the express approval of the British government. This crossed with a message sent to London via the Portuguese enclave at Macao saying the Secretary of the Colonial Government of Hong Kong, Mr F.C. Gimson, had come out of internment and had set up a British administration again.

However, the Japanese refused to recognize this move, insisting that they could only surrender to the Chinese military commander because the colony was part of the China theatre of war. When two internees from the Public Works Department unfurled a long-hidden Union Jack on the Peak on 18 August, the Japanese sent troops to haul it down. It was not until 28 August that Mr Gimson was able to announce over Hong Kong radio that a British administration had been re-established.

As early as 13 August the Admiralty had sent instructions for the Royal Navy to re-establish British power in Hong Kong. The Commander-in-Chief of the British Pacific Fleet, Admiral Bruce Ramsey, was told to despatch a force to Hong Kong as soon as possible. But American reluctance to be any part of the recovery of colonial territories caused a long interchange of signals before the British warships were released from American command. The Hong Kong task force under Rear Admiral H.J. Harcourt, comprising the battleship *Anson*, the aircraft carrier *Indomit-*

able, the cruiser *Swiftsure*, four light carriers and numerous support ships, was delayed in Subic Bay in the Philippines until 27 August.

As they headed north, Admiral Harcourt sent a message to Mr Gimson asking him to tell the Japanese that they were to send an envoy to meet a British aircraft when it landed at Kaitok airfield, Kowloon, to pick him up. The Japanese responded truculently, telling Mr Gimson they were not proposing to comply, as they had no orders from their own authorities empowering them to do so. Either second thoughts prevailed or orders came through from Tokyo, because a Japanese official was at the airfield to meet the plane, and was taken to the *Indomitable* to receive British instructions.

It was against this background of Japanese reluctance to hand back the colony to a European power that the British naval force arrived off Hong Kong, crews closed up at action stations, on 30 August. Because of dangers from mines, Admiral Power transferred from the *Indomitable* to the cruiser *Swiftsure*, to sail into harbour, accompanied only by the *Euralyus*, the Royal Canadian Navy's *Prince Robert* and several smaller ships.

As they approached the southerly island of Lamma spotters aboard the warships reported a 'concentration of motorboats' coming out of a known Shinyo suicide motorboat base on the island. Because their intentions were uncertain, Admiral Harcourt took no chances, and planes were scrambled from the *Indomitable* and *Venerable* to attack them. Three were bombed and sunk, and their base inside the bay was plastered with bombs. Japanese casualties were reported to be heavy.

According to Japanese accounts only one boat left Lamma Island, and it was unarmed, despatched to naval headquarters with a message because of a technical breakdown in normal communications. A Shinyo boat was used because nothing else was available.

Birtish records are taciturn. After passing reference to this last British action of the Second World War fifteen days after the cessation of hostilities, official reports go on blandly, 'The British re-entry was not marked by any incidents.'

In fact there was considerable sniping by diehard Japanese before they were overcome or committed suicide. An unknown number of Japanese were also killed by Chinese mobs, and looting was on a grand scale, leaving many buildings looking like bombed-out ruins.

Admiral Harcourt announced that the formal ceremony of surrender would take place on 12 September, but it had to be postponed because of objections from General Chiang Kai-Shek. It was eventually held on 16 September when Admiral Harcourt accepted surrender on behalf of Britain and China.

Although the Japanese march on Delhi was halted in the hills around

Kohima and Imphal, the leaders of the Indian National Army, Subhas Chandra Bose, declared himself leader of a Free Indian government (Azad Hind) in Singapore in October 1943. Bose, an admirer of Hitler, was killed in an aircrash in the final months of the war. Although Gandhi's 'Quit India' agitation vexed the British in India throughout the war, few Indians wanted British rule to be merely replaced by Japanese domination. Thousands of Indian soldiers captured in Singapore joined the INA in the belief that it gave them a better chance of survival than they would have in prison camps, but many also thought of it as a way of escape. Many more stayed in POW camps, remaining faithful to what Indians called 'the salt they had eaten'. When Pandit Nehru visited Singapore soon after the surrender, Mountbatten persuaded him to cancel his plan to place a wreath on an INA memorial that had been erected there.

The one colonial territory the Japanese occupied which was never promised independence was Malaya. They intended to keep tight control there, using Singapore as the sheet anchor of their domination of the puppet regimes established in the southern resources area. Four of the northern states of the Malay Federation, which the Japanese had given to their ally Siam, were handed back immediately after the surrender. For years afterwards Chinese communist bands which had fought the Japanese in cooperation with the British made a bid for power. They were stamped out by the British in a skilled jungle campaign before Malaya became independent in 1957.

When British rule ended in Singapore and in the North Borneo states of Sarawak and Sabah in 1963, these territories joined Malaya in a new Federation of Malaysia. But after only two years Singapore seceded to become an independent island republic.

Today, Singapore has a Japanese business community of nearly 20,000, the strongest foreign group living there. Both Singapore and Malaya now look to Tokyo for their economic ideas, and relations with Britain have deteriorated to a point where the Malay government ordered a boycott on dealings with British firms.

Japan's victims in the period of military expansion are now her partners in Asia's bid to dominate the economies of the West. The Greater Asia Co-Prosperity Sphere is a going concern.

The Americans, despite their anti-colonialist stance, made sure that they secured a strategic stranglehold over the Pacific in the postwar arrangements. The Philippines, which the Americans took from Spain in the war of 1898, had been given independence by Japan in 1943, but became officially independent from the United States on 4 July 1946. However, the Americans extracted guarantees of military bases, and a Trade Act continued American privileges and tied the currency to the dollar. Most of the other islands captured by Americans in the Pacific were transferred to

American trusteeship. Okinawa and several other islands close to southern Japan were handed back to Japanese control in the years up to 1972.

For Britain the fruits of victory soon turned sour. She had won the survival of her way of life by her own exertions, but her place as a world power was quickly taken by the new global ambitions of the United States. The voluntary winding up of the Empire, so much feared by Churchill, was one reason, but the main causes stemmed from the disparity of economic resources and population, and also the disproportionate burdens Britain had carried in two world wars. In the Second World War British casualties in dead and missing, while much fewer than in the earlier war, were proportionately three and a half times higher than America's. Britain also mobilized 55 per cent of her labour force compared with 40 per cent in America; her industry suffered three times the deterioration in plant; she had spent thirty-five times as much of her foreign investments; consumption of civilian goods in Britain had decreased by 16 per cent while in America consumption increased by 16 per cent; her merchant fleet was reduced by half while America's quadrupled. Altogether the proportion of British expenditure on the war effort was 50 per cent higher than that of the United States, and the resulting national debt was higher by the same proportion.

The ambivalence of American policy makers, demonstrated so clearly in the SEAC area and over Hong Kong, played a major role in bringing about Britain's decline, whether or not that had been the intention. In the postwar settlement of Lend–Lease the Americans generously wiped out 20 billion dollars owed by Britain, they transferred six billion dollars of property and Lend–Lease goods in the United Kingdom for 532 million dollars, and accepted 118 million dollars for goods still in the pipeline. But in order to obtain a 3.75 billion dollar postwar loan at 2 per cent Britain had to ratify the Bretton Woods agreement, and agree to there being no restrictions on United States imports. This commitment to end tariffs had always been feared by Conservatives as the price Churchill might be making Britain pay for vital American aid. It did in fact achieve Wall Street's ambition and destroy the imperial economic bloc which had been set up at Ottawa to pull Britain out of the 1930s recession.

The real winner in the war against Japan was the Soviet Union, whose armies fought for only seven days. The port of Dairen, now called Luda, and Manchuria were subsequently handed to the People's Republic of China, but the Soviet Union annexed the Kurile Island chain, promised by Roosevelt as inducement to enter the war against Japan and the southern half of Sakhalin Island. (The latter is now part of a special military zone in which an off-course South Korean airliner was shot down with the loss of 269 lives in September 1983.)

Soviet forces landed on the most northerly island of the Kuriles, cover of heavy bombardment four days after Japan had announced acceptance of the Potsdam Declaration, and the Japanese garrison fought back until ordered to surrender from the mainland. Besides securing the eighteen islands of the Kuriles proper, the Soviet forces also occupied the two southerly islands of Etorufu and Kunashiri which had always belonged to Japan. They also took the three islands of the Habomai group and Shikotan Islands which lie just off the coast of northeast Hokkaido. These islands, known to the Japanese as the 'northern territories', have always been regarded as an integral part of Japan.

When the Japanese Peace Treaty was signed by forty-nine nations at San Francisco on 8 September 1951 the Soviet Union, with Poland and Czechoslovakia, refused to sign on the grounds that the treaty failed to specify Soviet title to Sakhalin and the Kuriles. They remained technically at war with Japan until the Soviet Union and Japan signed a joint declaration in October 1956, formally terminating the state of war between them. At that time the Soviet Union was ready to return the three Habomai islands and Shikotan to Japan on the signing of a formal peace treaty, but positions hardened as Japan continued to insist on the return of Kunashiri and Etorofu islands as well.

Forty years after the seven-days war Japan has still not signed a formal treaty of peace with her giant neighbour.

Epilogue
The Moral Question

Today, when both sides in the East-West confrontation have huge arsenals of nuclear weapons with press-button delivery capability, resort to their use has become generally regarded as 'unthinkable'. Not simply on moral grounds, but because of the mass destruction that would be sure to result on all sides. This balance of terror has preserved the world from war between the superpowers for forty years. Neither wants the destruction of civilization. The nuclear strikes against Japan in 1945 demonstrated clearly that nuclear weapons can only be used if one power has achieved an exclusive monopoly of them. Otherwise their use means national suicide.

In that sense these weapons of mass extermination have brought peace for two generations, to the children and grandchildren of survivors of the world wars that decimated the two preceding generations.

Sadly this nuclear stalemate also created an open season on small wars, sometimes being the cause of them in situations where the rival power blocs have used client states as catspaws in their global struggle for dominant influence. A world community divided by the hanging sword of rival nuclear arsenals has been unable to act collectively to prevent them, as the major powers were able to do in the pre-nuclear age and under the earlier Pax Britannica.

The moral debate about whether the atomic bombs should have been dropped on Japan was a feature of the postwar years, and continues still in a world under the shadow of gigantic nuclear armouries. There is debate, too, about the destruction of Dresden when Germany was clearly on the brink of defeat. But it is the death and mutilation of entire city populations in one huge explosion that has redefined society's conception of atrocity.

In defeat, the Japanese government's protest to the Swiss at the use of a weapon that they said 'would brand the enemy for ages to come as a destroyer of mankind' was forgotten. It was never put before an international court.

Crimes against humanity by the Axis powers were never taken to the international courts either. Instead, the perpetrators were tried in special war crimes courts set up by the victorious powers. Winston Churchill was entertaining his chief wartime adviser, General Sir Hastings Ismay, at his Chartwell home when news came of the death sentences passed on the Nazi leaders at Nuremburg. Churchill remarked ruefully, 'Nuremburg shows that its supremely important to win. You and I would be in a pretty pickle if we had not.'

To wage total war all the warring powers had blatantly ignored the key principle of the Rules of War drawn up to protect non-combatants from direct attack. This was formulated in Article 25 of the Hague Convention of 1907, of which Japan and the other warring nations were signatories. It states, 'The attack by bombardment, by whatever means, of towns, villages, dwellings or buildings which are undefended is prohibited.' This was broken eight years later by the German Zeppelin raids on London during the First World War in which 741 Londoners were killed. In 1938, just a year before the Second World War began, the British government initiated a protocol, passed unanimously by the League of Nations, which extended Article 25 specifically to air raids. It said, 'The international bombing of civilian populations is illegal . . . objectives aimed at from the air must be legitimate military targets and must be identifiable.'

In June 1940, at the height of Hitler's blitzkrieg in Western Europe, the British government was still trying to stand by the protocol it had put forward two years before. It instructed the Air Ministry that air attacks must be carried out 'with reasonable care to avoid undue loss of life in the vicinity of the target'.

But that same month Churchill was already evolving the plan to destroy Germany by bombing. In a note to Lord Beaverbrook he wrote, 'When I look around to see how we can win the war, I see that there is only one sure path. We have no continental army with which we can defeat the German military power. The blockade is broken and Hitler has Asia and probably Africa to draw from. Should he be repulsed here, or not try invasion, he will recoil eastwards and we have nothing to stop him. But there is one thing that will bring him back and bring him down, and that is absolutely devastating, exterminating attack by very heavy bombers from this country on the Nazi homeland. We must be able to overwhelm them by this means, without which I do not see a way through.' Later he told the Cabinet that Hitler's advances might take him far, even to the Great Wall of China, adding, 'but we shall bring him back to find a fire in his own backyard and we will make Germany a desert, yes, a desert.'

Even so, Churchill expressed moral scruples in the following December, when London was under heavy attack, against a RAF plan, Operation Abigail, to single out a German town for complete destruction, and then publicly announce a list of other towns destined for the same fate.

Officers of the forces were still being handed an Oxford University pamphlet in which Professsor A.L. Goodhart described the separation of civilians from combatants as 'the greatest triumph of international law'. He added that there was no need to despair because the Nazis had ignored it in destroying cities like Rotterdam and Coventry because 'International law as recognized by the civilized nations will not cease to exist because one state has deliberately violated its provisions . . . it is to re-establish the law of war in a world threatened by barbarism that this war is being fought'.

By the spring of 1942 the RAF had enough bomber squadrons to deliver a heavier tonnage than the Luftwaffe was capable of, but because of Germany's internal communications a superiority of two to one was thought necessary. Most RAF bombing raids were then still connected with the vital Battle of the Atlantic with U-boat bases in Brest, Kiel and Hamburg as the main targets. When extra squadrons became available the great night bombing offensive began against oil stocks, industries and transport systems with the by-product of the lowering of morale when bombs fell wide into residential areas. On 16 June 1941, Lieut-General Pownall, Vice-Chief of the Imperial General Staff, noted in his diary, 'Morale may later become our primary target.'

Early inhibitions against bombing civilians were swamped by calls for revenge as the bombing spread from London throughout the industrial cities and even to spa towns like Bath. Most Britons approved the RAF bomber offensive which eventually carried brutal destruction to German cities on a far greater scale.

At the Casablanca Conference in January 1943 the Anglo-American Combined Chiefs of Staff issued a directive stating the objectives of Allied bombing policy as 'primarily, the progressive destruction and dislocation of the German military, industrial and economic system, and the undermining of the morale of the German people to a point when their capacity for armed resistance is fatally weakened'.

The Chief of RAF Bomber Command, Air Chief Marshal Sir Arthur Harris, suffered postwar disfavour when the horrors of his saturation bombing policy became fully known. He was thought by many to have carried it out 'with warped apostolic fervour' in making his command an overwhelming instrument of destruction. At the time it was happening, however, there was no doubt he had the complete support of the War Cabinet. Those who questioned saturation bombing were regarded as unpatriotic cranks, and the air crews themselves generally supported it for the few weeks or months most of them survived operations. Group Captain Leonard Cheshire, who carried out more raids than most, gave this interpretation of the attitude of the young men who carried out the raids, 'I doubt if any of us ever felt squeamish. On the actual attack itself we were far too concerned with getting through the defences and dropping the bombs to think about the people on the ground.'

It was in this climate of total war, near the end of a global struggle that had already lasted nearly six years and cost more than 50 million lives, that the atomic bombs were dropped on Japan. Any weapon that hastened victory was welcome, and its fearful consequences were looked upon as a natural part of war, for as everybody knew, 'War is hell!' The enemy had to be destroyed, the one objective, even the one morality, was victory. In his speech to the American nation on the evening of Pearl Harbor, President Roosevelt had said modern war was a dirty business and promised that Americans would fight 'with everything we've got'. In a Gallup Poll at the end of 1944, 13 per cent of the Americans questioned favoured Japan's extermination, and another in 1945 had 54 per cent of those questioned approving the dropping of the atomic bombs, and 23 per cent said more should have been dropped before Japan had a chance to surrender. In the heat of war sensibilities are hardened to an extent that seems incomprehensible in later years. Few doubted that Germany or Japan would have used atomic bombs had they developed them first. The dominant factor was that more of our own people were dying every day the war lasted.

In Britain, people's attitudes had been stiffened not only by memories of the blitz, but even more by the later V-weapons, frankly named the revenge weapon – Vergeltungswaffen – by the Germans. Intelligence gathered from Japanese communications between their Berlin embassy and Tokyo indicated that the Germans planned to destroy the whole of Britain with V-weapons.

Feelings had been hardened by casualties among relatives and friends, propaganda about enemy atrocities and particular deep loathing for the Japanese for attacking when Britain's hands were full fighting off German invasion. There was no pity for the enemy, rather delight that he was getting back what he had started, tenfold and more.

Among many thousands of Allied servicemen who felt that they owed their survival to the Hiroshima and Nagasaki bombs there was little or no argument about whether or not they should have been dropped. Paul Scott caught the mood in his novel *Division of the Spoils*, 'An atomic bomb – the ultimate weapon, the question whether Hirohito would now surrender to save other cities, Tokyo itself, from devastation. Moral reservations would come later. At the time you could only feel glad. Awestruck by its power and the miracle it seemed sure to produce – an end of the slaughter. I never met anyone who felt otherwise for a long time. Doubts about it were very long term. The short term for us was the important thing.'

One of those who changed their minds, Lord Jenkins of Putney, later became a leading campaigner for nuclear disarmament. He told the House of Lords in October 1983, 'I was one of those whose lives were supposed to have been saved by the dropping of the atomic bombs on Japan. I was in the Royal Air Force in Burma at the time, and at first I fell for the story. I have since found it to be untrue. That war could have ended without a single atomic bomb being on America's conscience. The bomb was dropped on people rather than in the sea to demonstrate to the Russians who was boss.'

In another debate in November 1984 Lord Jenkins said the Allies had broken the rules of war more barbarously than the Germans, for Coventry was followed by Hamburg and Dresden, finally by Hiroshima and Nagasaki 'which perhaps marked the end of our civilization'.

In 1945 the London Agreement on War Criminals reasserted the rules of war by specifying the wanton destruction of cities, towns and villages to be a war crime. But it was not until 1960 that the General Assembly of the United Nations got round to a declaration that the use of nuclear or thermonuclear weapons would be 'a crime against humanity and civilization'.

It was certainly true that by August 1945 there was nothing at all to be gained by carrying on the war, and Japan had few resources left to back up a fanatical last stand. Despatches from newspaper correspondents who landed with the occupation forces made this clear. After seeing the devastation in Tokyo and Yokohama they reported that Japan could not have carried on the war for more than another three months even without the atomic bombs and Russia's entry into the war.

Immediately after the surrender the generals in command of the American bombing offensive, flew a low-level reconnaissance tour of the main target cities to survey their achievement. General Curtiss Lemay reported that the damage was greater than had been estimated. He gave some detail, 'Especially memorable was the aircraft assembly plant on the east side of the river at Nagoya. We had estimated 60 per cent damage, but actually there is not a thing there. The Mitsubishi plant at Nagoya was estimated at 95 per cent gone; nothing is there but the steel framework and some concrete.'

Unlike the Germans, the Japanese had made little effort to repair damage and get bombed factories back into production; the Americans found them stupefied, helpless to do anything about it.

The new prime minister, Prince Higashi-Kuni, enumerated ten factors that had contributed to defeat in an address to both houses of Parliament in Tokyo two days after the surrender. He said air raids had reduced production by 75 per cent long before the atomic bombs were dropped, and factories that were still in production were on the point of closing because of a coal shortage. Bombing had reduced the carrying capacity of the railways by half. Imports had been cut to a quarter of prewar supplies by shipping losses and the sea blockade. Supplies of industrial salt from the

Asian mainland were inadequate for the needs of munitions production. Air raids had also disorganized city life, killing or injuring hundreds of thousands, and wrecking 2,100,000 houses. He said the military defeat became inevitable with the loss of the Marianas, and the loss of Okinawa had sealed the blockade. By May, or at least June, he said Japan's resources had been so undermined it was impossible to carry on a modern war.

The argument that the dropping of the atomic bombs was unnecessary because Japan had been on the point of surrender anyway was taken up by some conscience-stricken Americans soon after the war ended. They claimed that with nine–tenths of Japanese shipping sunk or disabled, air and sea forces crippled, her industries wrecked and her people scattered in the countryside and starving, Japan would have had to give in before long.

A strategic bombing survey by the USAF claimed that air supremacy could have exerted sufficient pressure to bring about unconditional surrender, certainly before the end of 1945, probably in time to obviate the need for invasion, without using the atomic bombs.

Admiral Ernest King, the US Navy Commander-in-Chief, said that, given time, the naval blockade alone would have starved the Japanese into submission.

Admiral William Leahy, who had been Roosevelt's closest military adviser, was totally opposed to the use of the atomic bombs. He said, 'The use of this barbaric weapon at Hiroshima and Nagasaki was of no material assistance in our war against Japan. The Japanese were already defeated and ready to surrender because of the effective sea blockade and successful bombing with conventional weapons.' Admiral Leahy also alleged that 'the scientists and others wanted to make this test because of the vast sums of money that had been spent on the project' (some two billion dollars).

Other military leaders who opposed the use of atomic bombs included General Henry Arnold, the Air Force Commander and General Dwight Eisenhower, the Supreme Allied Commander in Europe, who later became President.

Soon after news of the successful atomic test explosion reached Potsdam, General Eisenhower told Henry Stimson that he hoped the United States would not be first to use it. He said it would be unnecessary to use it against the Japanese as they were so nearly beaten and ready to surrender. By dropping the bomb on Japan, he said, the United States would risk the condemnation of the world. But Stimson spoke of the heavy casualties in the invasions of Iwo Jima and Okinawa, and of fears that many more suicide planes and surface craft would be used against the coming invasions of Japan if they had to go ahead as planned. Unless the bomb was used he feared that very heavy losses of American lives might be suffered before Japan was ready to admit final defeat.

Stimson's agonized response to Eisenhower went straight to the heart of the Allied dilemma. Japan's defeat was sure, but her leaders were refusing to admit it. They looked determined to take their people into national suicide – together with perhaps hundreds of thousands of Allied lives in a hopeless fight to a finish.

American military chiefs were influenced by their military academy lectures on the Civil War when the Conferate army fought on long after their cause was lost. More recently – barely six months before Potsdam – the Germans had prolonged the war in Europe by their desperate last fling offensive in the Ardennes. German industries had carried on with war production despite round-the-clock bombing that had left most of their cities and towns in ruins.

The decision to use the atomic bombs was made on this one overriding consideration: to save countless thousands of Allied lives that were bound to be the price of having to overwhelm the Japanese in their own land. That it would also be bound to prevent the deaths of many more Japanese than died at Hiroshima and Nagasaki was unlikely to have figured much, if at all, in the consideration of military leaders hardened by years of total war. But apart from the battle casualties involving civilians on a huge scale, millions would probably have died from starvation had every yard of Japanese territory been fought for and won.

A panel of civilians appointed by President Truman to advise him on whether or not the atomic bomb should be used could not agree. Several were against its use but most of the others were for it, with restrictive conditions. About the same time three separate groups of scientists involved in nuclear development drew up petitions opposing the use of an atomic weapon. The chief of the Manhattan District Project, General Leslie Groves, withheld them from Truman. From the time of his appointment in October 1942, General Groves had no doubt that the bomb would be used as soon as possible. He told the Oppenheimer Congressional hearing after the war, 'The aim from the start was to produce an atomic bomb at the earliest date to bring the war to a successful conclusion.'

In his memoirs, *Year of Decision*, President Truman wrote, 'I regarded the bomb as a military weapon and never had any doubt that it should be used.'

Churchill wrote in his memoirs, *Triumph and Tragedy*, that at Potsdam the Allied leaders had had no doubts about the need to use the atomic bombs to bring the Japanese to an early unconditional surrender. 'The decision whether or not to use the atomic bomb to compel Japan to surrender was never even an issue,' Churchill noted. 'There was unanimous, automatic, unquestioned agreement.'

The question has been posed on racialist grounds. Had the atomic bomb been developed earlier, would it have been dropped on Germany, or was the decision to use it made easier because its victims would be orientals who had made themselves widely regarded as subhuman because of the savage way they fought and treated prisoners. However, the total destruction of German cities like Dresden leave little doubt that had atomic bombs been available at the time of the Ardennes offensive or earlier they would certainly have been used.

It has also been argued that the new weapon of mass destruction had to be used against real targets in order to demonstrate its full horrific capabilities as a weapon. There is little doubt that some American chiefs welcomed the exclusiveness of the power which possession of the atomic bomb gave them to restrain growing Soviet assertiveness. Stalin had steamrollered the West into acceptance of his plans for Poland, the Baltic States, Finland and the rest of Eastern Europe. After that, Western hands were strengthened to resist not only his ambitions in the Bosphorus but also his desire for a share in the occupation and control of Japan – the same desire which was even then causing problems in Germany.

But the Soviet charge that the Truman administration planned to indulge in atomic blackmail from the beginning is without foundation. Truman rejected Churchill's proposals to oppose Stalin's expansion far into Europe, and ignored his concern at the rapid redeployment of American army divisions from Europe to the Far East. Churchill argued that, until the future of Poland was settled, American and British troops should stand fast at the furthest points of their advances beyond the boundary agreed for the Soviet Zone of occupation. They should also ensure that the Soviet occupation of East Germany was only temporary. At Potsdam, Truman saw himself as a 'friendly mediator' between Churchill and Stalin. Then, and for long afterwards, the Americans worked patiently for compromises that would establish a stable international order.

Some Americans saw that the atomic weapon might have political advantages. They saw its potential for enforcing the peace, since resort to war was likely to mean destruction on a scale that might end all life on earth. The new United Nations Organization, founded by the victors in San Francisco, would thereby be the means of settling international disputes by negotiation. Civilized values would no longer be subverted by the brutalities of war.

In the real world it has been the balance of fear, not idealism, that has kept the major powers in check for the past forty years. Would it have worked so well if the atomic bomb had not been dropped on Japan, if Hiroshima and Nagasaki had not been put through their agonizing sacrifice? The test explosion in the New Mexico desert had provided a spectacular bang, but it had killed only such insect and reptile life that existed there, and melted a large patch of sand.

Back in the circumstances of 1945 could a public demonstration have convinced the Japanese that they had no alternative but surrender or cease to exist? The atomic scientists urged that a harmless demonstration explosion would have been sufficient to end the war if Japanese witnesses had been present. The arguments against it were that there was a real risk that a test explosion might not work and such a failure would only strengthen Japan's resolve to fight on; that it would be a waste of valuable fissionable materials which could be used to gain operational advantages; that it would take a great deal of time to arrange an international test with Japanese among the witnesses, and in the meantime Allied lives were being lost every day the war continued.

Stimson accepted the arguments against an international demonstration, and after the war he explained his reasons this way, 'The atomic bomb was more than a weapon of terrible destruction; it was a psychological weapon. . . . So far as the Japanese could know, our ability to execute atomic attacks, if necessary by many planes at a time, was unlimited.'

Some experts argued that it was not the two bombs that were dropped on Hiroshima and Nagasaki that brought surrender, but two experiences of what one bomb could do and fear of many more that might be dropped that was decisive. Certainly, rumours that Tokyo itself was to be the third atomic target seemed to have impelled the Emperor's decision to step in and end the last week of prevarication.

Should a preliminary warning have been given so that the target cities could be evacuated? This was considered, but rejected for good military reasons. It would have enabled the Japanese to move Allied prisoners into the target area as hostages. A warning would also have invited the Japanese to concentrate a major effort on intercepting the plane carrying the bomb.

The SEAC Supreme Commander, Admiral Mountbatten spoke many years after the war of his own mixed feelings about the atomic bombs, which robbed him of his hopes of military glory in the campaign to recapture Singapore. In *Mountbatten – Hero of Our Time* Richard Hough quotes Mountbatten: 'My feelings about the dropping of the atomic bombs were mixed ones. On the one hand I was afraid this would mean the end of the war without the defeat of their armies in the field, just as the Germans had claimed in 1918. Against this was the colossal saving of human lives. As many Japanese had been killed defending the small island of Okinawa as at Hiroshima. Imagine what the invasion of the Japanese mainland in 1946 would have led to! You didn't count Japanese casualties – you counted their dead. They would blow themselves up rather than surrender. Millions would have been killed, civilians and soldiers.'

In a later role as Chief of the Defence Staff, Mountbatten was one of the strongest proponents of Britain having its own nuclear deterrent, but after his retirement he made disarmament his main cause.

The military historian, Major-General J.C. Fuller, was one of the leading British critics of the dropping of the atomic bombs on Japan. He believed that all Truman and Churchill need have done at Potsdam to bring the war to an immediate end was to remove the obstacle of unconditional surrender. He thought that if it had been made clear to the Japanese that their Emperor would not be tried as a war criminal, there would have been no need 'to revert to a type of war that would have disgraced Tamerlane.'

The details of how the controversially uncompromising policy of unconditional surrender became the ultimate Allied war aim only emerged after the war. The phrase was apparently first uttered at a press conference at the end of summit talks between Roosevelt and Churchill in Casablanca in January 1943. Roosevelt told his aide, Harry Hopkins, that it arose because he had been likening the efforts they had been making to get two French generals to meet in North Africa to the difficulties of arranging a meeting between Grant and Lee in the American Civil War. He explained, 'Suddenly the press conference was on and Winston and I had no time to prepare for it, and the thought popped into my mind that they called Grant "old unconditional surrender" and the next thing I knew I said it.' The expression, curiously, seems to have been with us far longer.

It is unlikely that it was, in fact, as unpremeditated as Roosevelt seemed to indicate. His notes for the press conference contained an explanation of what he meant by it: 'Unconditional surrender means not the destruction of the German populace, or the Japanese populace, but does mean the destruction of a philosophy in Germany, Italy and Japan which is based on the conquest and subjugation of other peoples.'

Churchill later told Hopkins that the statement had been made in a spirit of defiance at a moment when the war was going so badly that no one could claim that victory was assured.

He added, 'I would not myself have used these words, but I immediately stood by the President and have frequently defended the decision. It is false to suggest it prolonged the war. Negotiation with Hitler was impossible. He was a maniac with supreme power to play his hand out to the end, which he did; and so did we.'

Long after the war, in a document presenting Japan's case for the return of islands off her northern coast still occupied by the Soviet Union, Japan has used the argument that she did not, in fact surrender unconditionally. The document, 'Japan's Northern Territories' issued in 1974, says, 'Japan lost the war, to be sure, but did not surrender unconditionally. It surrendered on the terms of the Potsdam Proclamation, through which it also accepted the Cairo Declaration.' (The Cairo Declaration laid down that Japan would be stripped of all territories taken by force.)

One thing that can, perhaps, be laid on the conscience of the Western powers is their failure to be more explicit in the warning carried in the Potsdam Declaration about the nature of the cataclysm in store; the only reference was a vague 'prompt and utter destruction'. A clear statement about the intention to use atomic bombs with detail of their explosive force might have induced more precipitate action from Emperor Hirohito to overcome the stalling of the military diehards. But this argument is a rather frail one against the indisputable fact that the war went on for another nine days after the first atomic explosion over Hiroshima.

Some guilt for Hiroshima and Nagasaki must surely attach to Stalin and his aides for their cynical, self-seeking rebuff to Japan's persistent appeals for their mediation to end the war. Also, and more particularly, for the slaughter on both sides in their seven-days offensive – a heavy toll in lives for Soviet territorial gains already agreed to by the Allies. It rates, perhaps as one of the most unnecessary military campaigns in history, an appalling example of token compliance with a promise made in different circumstances; a fear that the war they were joining might end before they had grabbed a lion's share of the spoils as they had done in Europe.

In view of Russia's failure to advise Washington and London of Japan's peace approaches, the Western Allies might have found it diplomatically embarrassing to take any action over their own secret intelligence information that the Emperor was trying to make peace. Ways could have been found to explore the Japanese peace move had there been any desire to do so, but it seems clear that the doctrine of unconditional surrender, so impetuously born at Casablanca, had become compulsive thinking – an Allied blindspot.

The shroud of secrecy which inevitably surrounded all wartime activity was another handicap to any chance there may have been to end the war without resort to the atomic bombs. While the American State Department knew every move the Japanese had made to get peace contacts going before Stalin officially passed on the information at Potsdam, they knew nothing about the development of the atomic bomb until they were brought in to draft the Potsdam Declaration. Churchill's deputy, Clement Attlee, only learned of the atomic bomb when he returned to Potsdam after the general election result which put him in Churchill's place as Prime Minister. By that time his participation was limited to discussion over the wording of the press release to be issued after the first bomb was dropped. The scientists working on the atomic bombs, while deeply worried about the human consequences of their scientific achievement, had no knowledge at all that the Japanese had put out peace feelers.

None of these might-have-been factors were relevant in view of the Japanese government's decision to let the Potsdam Declaration lie on the table. Even the Hiroshima bomb failed to prevail on a split government to reach a decision, and it was only after the Nagasaki bomb and fears that

Tokyo would be the third atomic target that Emperor Hirohito intervened decisively to end the war.

The atomic bombs were probably necessary to provide the military diehards in the government with a face-saving excuse to agree to the Emperor's decision to surrender, and put down the efforts to defy it. Japan in 1945 was perhaps the one nation that would have been prepared to fight to the death of most of its people. Defeat had been inevitable for at least a year, but the Japanese were the kind of people who would have carried out the sort of battle cry Churchill had proclaimed for Britain in 1940, 'We shall fight on the beaches, on the landing grounds . . . in the streets . . . in the fields . . . in the hills . . . we shall never surrender.'

Ironically, it took a weapon which drew its awesome power from the elements of the sun to subdue the Land of the Rising Sun, ruled over by an Emperor believed by his people to descend from Amaterasu O-Mikami, the Sun Goddess.

Thirty-nine years after the atomic bombs were dropped on Hiroshima and Nagasaki, a past president of the Japanese Medical Association, Dr Taro Takemi, expressed his belief that the atomic bombs saved Japan from a worse fate. In an article in the *Journal of the American Medical Association* in August 1983 he wrote, 'The military had driven Japan to a stage that if it could not win, it would never surrender. Japan would have lost the war and many people would have starved if the atomic bomb had not been dropped. When one considers the possibility that the Japanese military would have sacrificed the entire nation if it were not for the atomic bomb attack, then this bomb might be described as having saved Japan.' Dr Takemi went on to say that it was regrettable that the development of atomic power was used for war, and he doubted the need for the second bomb on Nagasaki.

Commenting on Dr Takemi's observations, Edwin O. Reischauer, a postwar ambassador to Japan, thought few Japanese were ready to agree with Dr Takemi's conclusion. He himself had thought that dropping the bomb was a mistake at the time, but had later changed his mind, 'The Japanese would have had to go on fighting, and there would have been an absolute massacre with attendant starvation. I feel certain that many people would have died.'

The men who must surely carry the major share of guilt for Hiroshima and Nagasaki were those in the government of Japan who prevaricated for more than two weeks after the Potsdam Declaration laid down the terms for surrender, and warned that the alternative was 'prompt and utter destruction'.

But whoever carries guilt – and its significant that though Pope John Paul has made the pilgrimage to Hiroshima and Nagasaki, no person of political power in a nuclear state has felt able to visit either city – Japan emerged from the war she had started with infamy and brutality in the role of victim, not perpetrator, of inhumanity.

An International Military Tribunal of the victors sat in judgement over Japanese leaders from May 1946 till November 1948, and sentenced General Hideki Tojo, the prime minister who ordered the attack on Pearl Harbor, and six other former leaders to be hanged. Eighteen others were jailed. (The condemned were cremated with orders from General Mac-Arthur that their ashes were to be scattered at sea, but crematorium workers kept Tojo's ashes and handed them to his widow after the occupation ended. Since then the names of Tojo and others hanged as war criminals have been discreetly placed in the inner sanctum of the Yasakuni shrine, the national memorial to Japan's 2,500,000 war dead.)

The Soviet Union, Australia and some organizations on the American West Coast made strong demands for the Emperor to be tried as a war criminal, and some Japanese newspapers, liberated from military censorship, took up the call. Hirohito put on top hat and tails and drove in his Rolls-Royce to General MacArthur's headquarters to surrender himself. He told MacArthur, 'I come to you, General MacArthur, to offer myself to the judgment of the powers you represent as the one to bear sole responsibility for every political and military decision made, and action taken, by my people in the conduct of this war.' A political decision to take no action against Hirohito had already been taken, and MacArthur sent him away with a gift of a box of chocolates.

Generally, there was by then a feeling that the terrible retribution of Hiroshima and Nagasaki had wiped the slate clean.

So it was that Japan was able to establish a unique role in the postwar world. On the first New Year's Day of peace, Emperor Hirohito was prompted by the Occupation Authorities to issue an Imperial Rescript which denied two basic beliefs that had set Japan on the path of conquest. He denied the divinity of the Imperial House and Japanese superiority over other races which destined them to rule the world. In 1947 a new constitution committed Japan to peace. Article 9 declared 'The Japanese people renounce war as the sovereign right of a nation' and pledged that Japan would not maintain land, sea or air forces. In 1967 the Prime Minister, Aisaku Sato, was awarded the Nobel Peace Prize for his government's decision never to possess, manufacture or allow nuclear arms in Japan.

The economic benefits of Japan's peace constitution have been enormous. Freed from the kind of defence budgets that continued to burden the victor nations as they split into hostile camps, Japan's industry has risen from the wartime ashes like an economic phoenix. Today Japan's economic domination extends far beyond the Greater Asia Co-Prosperity Sphere for which she went to war in 1941. The new samurai is the successful technocrat, the new philosophy is to invade other countries with Japanese manufactured goods. Her new overseas bases are factories built abroad by the international Japanese companies, welcomed in supplicant terms for the jobs they provide, however short-term the benefits in the wasteland of Britain's recession-hit industrial areas.

The idealism that inspired the search for a new Japanese identity after the trauma of atomic bombing, defeat and occupation is still largely intact forty years later. Fears that Japan had made a tactical peace in what some Japanese officers took comfort in calling a reverse in the first stages of a war that would perhaps last a hundred years have so far appeared groundless.

Pressure on Japan to resume an international political role in line with her position as the second economy among the industrial democracies, to take a share in defence of the free world, have come from outside, mainly from America. Many influential Americans see their country's future in a technological partnership with Japan that would be able to dominate the modern world. They favour moving the main thrust of American foreign policy from the transatlantic relationship with Europe to a kind of economic condominion with Japan over the Pacific basin.

The Allied occupation of Japan ended with the signing of a peace treaty at the San Francisco Conference in September 1951. But the Soviet Union refused to sign the peace treaty and their forces still occupy all the islands they took over in 1945. On the same day as the peace treaty was signed Japan signed a security treaty with the United States under which American troops have continued to be stationed in Japan to ensure regional security.

For a few years, Japan's own security force was limited to armed police, but the idyll of a land without military forces was short lived. In 1954, a pragmatic decision was made that 'armed forces of a non-offensive character' would not breach the spirit of the Peace Constitution, and Self-Defence Forces were formed. Gradually over the years Japan has developed a defence establishment on a scale commensurate with her position as the second largest economy of the non-communist world. Today she has the eighth biggest defence budget of all nations, and armed forces totalling 250,000. She rates fourth in naval tonnage, fifth in submarines, eighth in combat aircraft and fifth in armour and artillery. The Self-Defence Forces have a higher proportion of officers than any other military force, and could be expanded rapidly. Her high-tech industries, already making war planes under US licence, could be switched to full war production almost overnight.

Japanese forces hold regular exercises with American units on land, sea and in the air. Japanese officers attended as observers when American marines re-enacted the assault on Okinawa in 1983. To mark the eightieth anniversary of the Japanese victory over Russia in 1904 British and French warships, as well as American, joined Japanese warships in a review off Kagoshima. America is putting Japan under increasing pressure to extend self-defence to protection of her sea lanes to a distance of 1000 miles.

There is growing resentment against the Soviet Union for its occupation of the northern territories, as the occupied islands are known. Youths in anti-soviet groups have taken to wearing military-style uniforms, and singing old wartime songs about dyeing the Japanese flag red with blood and conquering the world. Recent films about the war have shown the men who took Japan into the war as having no other choice in view of American oil sanctions; they also portray British and American troops as despoilers of Japanese dead.

But a storm of protest came in 1982 when new school textbooks played down the policy of military expansion and excused the actions taken with 'law breakers' in the occupied territories. Tokyo's biggest newspaper, the *Asahi*, called for the new text books to be amended to make it clear that 'aggression is aggression'.

Every 15 August Emperor Hirohito attends silent prayers to the spirit of those who died in the war at the National War Memorial in Tokyo. But Hirohito, who is eighty-four in his fortieth anniversary of defeat, has not put on uniform or attended a military parade since the war. Public distaste for the military remains sufficiently strong to preclude Japan from taking part in a formal military alliance, despite the powerful Soviet forces poised close by in the occupied islands off her northern shores.

Forty years after Hiroshima and Nagasaki, Japan relies for her national security on the American nuclear umbrella.

Select Bibliography

Little was put on record about the last invasion of World War Two, Operation Zipper, and the author has had to rely mainly on personal accounts and the incomplete files in the Public Record Office at Kew.

The general background has been compiled with the help of a wide range of books, including:

The War Against Japan (six volumes) edited by Major-General S. Woodburn Kirby and Associates (HMSO, 1957); *Grand Strategy, Volume VI*, by John Ehrman (HMSO, 1956); *The War at Sea*, by Stephen Roskill (HMSO, 1977); *British Foreign Policy in the Second World War*, by Sir Llewellyn Woodward (HMSO, 1970); *British Intelligence in the Second World War*, by F.H. Hinsley (HMSO, 1979); *British Military Administration in the Far East, 1943-46*, by F.S.V. Donnison (HMSO, 1956); Report to the Combined Chiefs of Staff by the Supreme Allied Commander, South-East Asia, 1943-45, by Vice-Admiral, the Earl Mountbatten (HMSO).

Command Decisions, edited by K.R. Greenfield (Office of the Chief of Military History, Department of the Army, Washington, 1960); *The United States Army in World War Two* (Office of the Chief of Military History, Department of the Army, Washington, 1962).

Japan's Longest Day, compiled and published by the Pacific War Research Society of Japan (Transworld, 1969).

Allen, Louis *Japan, The Years of Triumph*, Macdonald, 1971, *The End of the War in Asia*, Hart Davies, 1976
Barber, Noel *Sinister Twilight*, Collins, 1968
Barker, A.J. *The March on Delhi*, Faber and Faber, 1963
Bateson, Charles *The War with Japan*, Ure Smith, 1968
Bergami, David *Japan's Imperial Conspiracy*, Heinemann, 1971
Boyle, Andrew *No Passing Glory*, Collins, 1957
Braddon, Russell *The Naked Island*, Evans Bros, 1961
Burchett, Wilfred *At the Barricades,* Quartet, 1980
Butow, R.J.C. *Japan's Decision to Surrender*, Stanford University Press, 1967

Calvert, Brigadier Michael *Slim*, Valentine, 1973

Chapman, Spencer *The Jungle is Neutral*, Chatto and Windus, 1949

Churchill, W.S. *Secret Session Speeches*, Cassell, 1946, *The Hinge of Fate*, Cassell, 1951, *Triumph and Disaster*, Cassell, 1954

Collier, Richard *The War that Stalin Won*, Hamish Hamilton, 1983

Connell, John *Wavell – Supreme Commander*, Collins, 1969

Costello, John *The Pacific War*, Collins, 1981

Cruikshank, Charles *Deception in World War Two*, Oxford University Press, 1979, *SOE in the Far East*, Oxford University Press, 1984

Ellis, John *The Sharp End of War*, David and Charles, 1980

Falls, Cyril *The Second World War*, Methuen, 1948

Feis, Herbert *Japan Subdued*, Princeton, 1961

Fletcher-Cooke, John *The Emperor's Guest*, Hutchinson, 1971

Frankland, Noble and Christopher Downing *Decisive Battles of the 20th Century*, Sidgwick and Jackson, 1976

Fuller, Major-General J.F.C. *The Second World War, 1939-45*, Eyre and Spottiswoode, 1948

Gallagher, Thomas *Assault in Norway*, Harcourt Brace, 1975

Gilchrist, Sir Ian *Bangkok Top Secret*, Hutchinson, 1970

Grew, Joseph C. *Ten Years in Japan*, Simon and Schuster, 1944

Groves, Leslie R. *Now it Can be Told*, New York, 1962

Guillian, Robert *I Saw Tokyo Burning*, John Murray, 1981

Hachiya, M *Hiroshima Diary*, University of North Carolina, 1970

Hanson, Norman *Carrier Pilot*, Patrick Stephens, 1979

Harriman, W. Averell *Special Envoy to Churchill and Stalin*, Hutchinson, 1976

Hart, Liddell *History of the Second World War*, Cassell, 1970

Hashimoto, Lieut-Cdr Muchitsura *Sunk, The Story of the Japanese Submarine Fleet, 1942-45*, Cassell, 1954

Hastings, Max *Bomber Command*, Michael Joseph, 1979

Hough, Richard *Mountbatten, Hero of Our Time*, Weidenfeld and Nicolson, 1980

Huie, William Bradford *The Hiroshima Pilot*, Heinemann, 1964

Inogushi, Capt. Rikikei and Cdr. Tadashi Nakajima *The Divine Wind*, Hutchinson, 1959

Kase, Tushikazu *Eclipse of the Rising Sun*, Yale University Press, 1950

James, D. Clayton *The Years of MacArthur*, Houghton Mifflin, 1975

Ladd, J.D. *Assault from the Sea, 1939-45*, David and Charles, 1976, *SBS – The Invisible Raiders*, Arms and Armour, 1983

Lewin, Ronald *Slim, The Standard Bearer*, Leo Cooper, 1976

Lord, Walter *Day of Infamy*, Holt, Rinehart and Winston, 1976, *The Incredible Victory*, Harper and Row, 1967

Lund, Paul and Harry Ludlam *The War of the Landing Craft*, Foulsham, 1976

MacIntyre, Donald *Fighting Admiral*, Evans, 1961

McKelvie, Roy *The War in Burma*, Methuen, 1948

Masters, John *The Road Past Mandalay*, Michael Joseph, 1961

Mayo, Lido *Bloody Buna*, David and Charles, 1975

Miller, Nathan *The Naval Air War*, Conway Maritime, 1980

Mosley, Leonard *Hirohito, Emperor of Japan*, Weidenfeld and Nicolson, 1965

Mzarek, James E. *The Glider War*, Robert Hale, 1975

O'Neill, Richard *Suicide Squads*, Salamanader, 1981

Pocock, Tom *The Dawn Came Up like Thunder*, Collins, 1984

Pownall, General Sir Henry *Diaries of a Chief of Staff*, Leo Cooper, 1972

Roskill, Stephen *The Navy at War, 1939-45*, Collins, 1960, *Churchill and the Admirals*, Collins, 1970,

Scott, Paul *Division of the Spoils*, Heinemann, 1975

Sherwood, Robert *The White House Papers of Harry Hopkins*, Eyre and Spottiswoode, 1948

Short, Antony *The Communist Insurrection in Malaya, 1948-60*, Muller, 1975

Sinclair, Dr Robert *The Burma-Siam Railway – Secret Diary*, Imperial War Museum, 1984

Skidmore, Ian *Escape from the Rising Sun*, Leo Cooper, 1973

Slim, Field Marshal Sir William *Defeat into Victory*, Cassell, 1956

Spurr, Russell *A Glorious Way to Die*, Sidgwick and Jackson, 1982

Stewart, Adrian *The Battle of Leyte Gulf*, Robert Hale, 1979

Stokesbury, James L. *A Short History of World War Two*, Robert Hale, 1979

Swinson, Arthur *Four Samurai*, Hutchinson, 1968, *Kohima*, Cassell, 1966

Thomas, Gordon and Max Morgan-Witts *Ruin from the Air*, Hamish Hamilton, 1977

Thorne, Christopher *Allies of a Kind*, Hamish Hamilton, 1978

Truman, Harry S. *Year of Decision*, Hodder and Stoughton, 1955

Trenowden, Ian *Operations Most Secret*, William Kimber, 1978

Winton, John *The Forgotten Fleet*, Michael Joseph, 1969

Appendix I

Order of Battle for Operation Zipper

British units: 2nd West Yorks, 1st Seaforth Highlanders, 1st South Wales Borderers, 9th Royal Sussex, 13th Lancers, 19th Lancers, 11th Cavalry, 45th Cavalry, 25th Dragoons, 5th Brigade, 6th Parachute Division, 3rd Commando Brigade, 34th Amphibious Support, a Regt Royal Marines, 18th (Self-Propelled) Field Regt, RA, 208th (Self-Propelled) Field Regt, RA, 6th Medium Regt, RA, 86th Medium Regt, RA, Field Squadrons, bridging troops, workshops, Royal Engineers and REME, 1st Heavy Anti-Aircraft Regt, Hong Kong and Singapore, RA.

Indian Army: Gurkha Regt, Punjab Regt, Jat Regt, Madras Regt, Burma Regt, Hyderabad Regt, Patiala, Rajputana and Mahratta Light Infantry, Baluchistan Regt, Royal Garhwal Rifles, Ajmer Regt, Frontier Forces, 2/4 Bombay Grenadiers, 1st Indian Medium Artillery, 8th Sikh Light Anti-Aircraft Regt, 9th Rajput Light Anti-Aircraft Regt.

Support Forces Navy:

close gun support	2 battleships
	2 cruisers
	4 destroyers
	4 sloops
naval air support	8 assault carriers
	(100 Hellcats,
	20 Wildcats,
	60 Seafires)
	1 cruiser
	destroyer screen
assault	81 assault ships
	111 major landing craft
	276 minor landing craft
general	8 destroyers

14 frigates and sloops
3 fighter direction ships
3 minesweeping flotillas
18 auxiliary minesweepers
112 merchant ships

Support Forces RAF:

8 Thunderbolt squadrons
2 Spitfire squadrons
2 Beaufighter squadrons
5 Mosquito bomber squadrons
1 photo-recce squadron of
  Mosquitos and Spitfires
1 fighter recce squadron of Spitfires
½ squadron of Mosquito night fighters
5 Transport Dakotas
3 Sunderland Flying Boats
1 Air observation squadron
44 Light aircraft
  Balloon and ancillary units

Appendix II

The war had lasted just one day short of six years for Britain, two months short of four years for America. Its battles had been fought in every quarter of the globe, bringing death to over 53 million people, some in battle, some in bombed homes, others by execution or extermination, many by starvation and exposure. The economic cost was put at 1600 billion American dollars. The human cost was calculated at 38,573,000 civilians and 14,904,000 killed in battle. Another 25,218,000 carried scars and disabilities into the postwar years and few alive at the time escaped without any sort of mental scars.

The Soviet Union suffered by far the most in lost lives, with around 15 million military dead, and an estimated 10 million civilians. The death toll during seven years of war in China was estimated as high as 15 million, but most authoritative sources put battle losses at around 500,000 and civilian deaths due to war operations at about one million. Germany lost 2,850,000 military dead, and about 500,000 civilians were killed in air raids. About three million Poles died in the repeated ravaging of their land and in military units fighting away from home with the British and Russians.

British Empire forces lost 397,762 military dead, and 65,595 civilians were killed in air raids and rocket attacks on Britain. The United States lost 292,100 killed in battles overseas, Yugoslavia lost 1,700,000 dead – one tenth of the population. The Greeks had 360,000 dead, including 50,000 executed. France lost 210,671 military dead, including some who fell fighting the British in Africa and Syria, and 108,000 civilians, some fighting with the resistance and in prison camps. Italy lost 360,000 dead, first against the British, then against the Germans, and 40,000 civilians. The 232,000 Netherlands dead included 104,000 Jews, 20,400 civilians killed in war operations, and 16,000 who died of famine in the last months of the war. Belgium lost 22,651 servicemen and 90,000 civilians. Denmark had 6400 dead; Norway 1598 military and 3638 civilians.

Britain had entered the war at 11 a.m. in 3 September, 1939 – six hours before France – on the expiry of an ultimatum requiring Hitler to withdraw troops which had begun invading Poland on September 1. At the end her immense wealth was gone, spent on cash-and-carry supplies from America when she fought alone, and she was deeply in debt. Her imperial power, thanks to Japan, was at its last gasp. Most of her cities were scarred with bomb ruins, and 456,000 houses had been destroyed and another 4,073,000 damaged. Despite crash wartime replacements the British merchant fleet was down by half because of U-boat sinkings.

The tiny British Isles put six million men under arms, of whom 264,443 were killed and 277,077 wounded. The 60,595 civilians killed in air raids and rocket attacks included 25,399 women and children. Another 86,182 civilians were wounded in air raids. Over 35,000 merchant seamen were killed or missing and 4707 wounded.

The Commonwealth had rallied to the motherland from the beginning. Canada lost 42,666 killed and 53,145 wounded; Australia 37,637 killed, 25,856 wounded; New Zealand 10,764 killed, 19,345 wounded; South Africa 9000 killed, 15,000 wounded. India, where the Vice-Roy aroused political agitation by thoughtlessly declaring India at war without consulting Indian leaders, lost 48,674 killed, 65,184 wounded, mostly in Burma. Another 10,000 men from smaller territories also gave their lives for Britain's victory.

The Japanese lost 1,555,308 killed in battle (twenty for every one wounded) and 658,595 as a result of conventional and atomic air raids. Most of these casualties came in the last year of the war when defeat was already known by Japanese leaders to be inevitable. Of this total 208,026 Japanese were killed fighting the British in South-East Asia, more than the 202,958 Japanese killed in seven years fighting in China. Another 199,511 Japanese died fighting Australians. By far the heaviest losses were inflicted by the Americans in the Pacific War, a total of 485,717 killed.

Index

INDEX